LET THE ROCKS CRY OUT

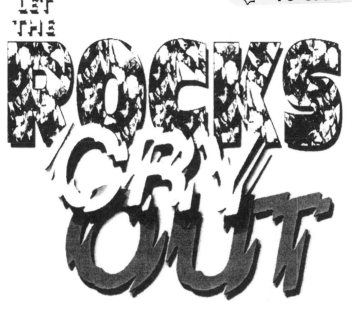

A 50-year history of missionary Radio Station 4VEH and the associated ministries of OMS International (formerly The Oriental Missionary Society)

1950 – 2000

Compiled by
Rachael Overstreet Picazo

International

Dedicated to the memory of Bill Gillam, whose visit to 4VEH in 1954 influenced OMS to later become involved. As he himself ministered among us in Haiti, his dynamic, Spirit-filled life left an indelible impact. In Haiti he was stricken with illness that proved fatal in 1971.

Picazo, Rachel
THE ROCKS CRY OUT

ISBN 1-880338-28-9

Printed in the United States of America

ACKNOWLEDGMENTS

Dr. Vernon Hall asked me if I would consider writing a history of 4VEH. My immediate reply was definite: "No!"

But Mardy and I were visiting in Haiti some months later when that same question popped up. Sensing it was God this time doing the asking, I answered, "Yes." So I was ready a few minutes later when 4VEH Manager Marilyn Shaferly approached me about it. 4VEH's 50th anniversary was three years away: June 2, 2000.

I brought about 50 pounds of files and pictures back to Kentucky. Now, how to go about it? Where to find time?

I have to admit it was the hardest thing I had ever attempted. For two years I struggled, and the loving advice of experienced writers didn't seem to fit my situation.

At last with only a little more than a year to go, I found a path that seemed the way for me. Going back in the *OMS Outreach, Missionary Standard*, and *Action* files, I got information from articles that had been written about things in the past. I was awed at the way it came together. I wanted so much for three things to happen:

1. God would receive the glory due for His miracles;
2. It would be as accurate as possible;
3. It would be interesting and easy to read.

I acknowledge God's help first of all, giving me strength, waking me often at 5 a.m., furnishing fresh ideas.

I thank Mardy, my husband, for his unwavering support, his very practical help on his computer in scanning materials, etc., and helping with housework.

If I listed all who have been essential to this book, I could fill pages. But I must note some of them, including my daughter, Rachel, who critiqued the first stories; Marilyn Shaferly, who reassured, "Don't worry about a deadline"; for Miriam Stockton Mason, who freely gave her professional services as editor; for Vicki Lake and Valetta Steel Crumley, who arranged for its printing: for Gwen Pinkerton who worked long hours on the computer lending her expertise; to Codo Ciméus at 4VEH for the program he started in 1996, from which this book takes its title.

I am grateful for those who have written about incidents, who gave me personal interviews, for everyone in the OMS and MFMI offices who went out of his way to accommodate Mardy and me as we researched.

"The LORD is great, and greatly to be praised!"
(Ps. 96:4)
- Rachael O. Picazo
Missionary to Haiti, 1952-1992 (Retired)

FOREWORD

The history of many nations is replete with stories that identify certain "critical turning points" in their national life. Some of these turning points have resulted in making that people a greater nation. The nation known as "La Republique d'Haiti" is now at one such point. This is the nation whose people were once a French colony until they won their freedom from Napoleon's France in 1804. Many evils came to the new world from Africa by way of the slave traders. But now, in these days, the forces of evil are in retreat. From event to event, victory to victory, the story unfolds herein, clearly outlining a "critical turning point" for Haiti.

In reading these essays, you will understand the origin of the title of this book, *LET THE ROCKS CRY OUT*. The name has its roots in Luke 19:40. By way of this compendium, the author, Rachael Picazo, clearly depicts, by treatise after treatise, the nature of Haiti's "critical turning point."

The writer is qualified in many ways to catalogue these basic events, happenings that are bringing to pass the arrival of this turning. Her missionary career, with roots in Kentucky, flowered beautifully in the land of Haiti. Her love for the lost is preeminent throughout this collection of her own renditions of previously printed articles and stories, plus many word-of-mouth reports.

Supported and assisted by her husband, Mardy, and their family, plus many missionaries and visitors, the writer has created a work that is a milestone marker in God's march to victory in Haiti. This work will stir your soul with the impossible made possible by God's grace and power. You, the reader, will excitingly experience the highs and the lows, the victories and the disappointments, as the harvest is gathered in. These are days when darkness is being dispelled, days when the light of the Gospel is turning back some of the forces of evil. This is a book of "God-happenings" and should stir us all to greater prayer, giving, and going!

A word of congratulation must go to Rev. G. T. Bustin (now deceased) and his family, whose vision and obedience to God's call started this unusual missionary work in the 1940s and capped that achievement by starting Radio 4VEH in 1950. One also can but marvel at, and thank God for, the efforts of the past and present missionary staff at Radio 4VEH and all the supporting ministries of clinic, Bible school, and also the Every Creature Crusade with its church-planting victories. Indeed, much credit also goes to Men For Missions International and to OMS International, as well as to other cooperating missions and agencies.

The most compelling reason for the existence of Radio 4VEH is the overwhelming spiritual need of the people, both the elite and the common folk. It is well known that the witch doctors control the religious aspect of the life of the average Haitian. It is also well known that only the power of God's Word and His Holy Spirit can deliver from this bondage. In these days, such deliverance is taking place. The forces of evil are in retreat.

The recent conversion of several witch doctors has stunned the local populace. Testimonials aired over 4VEH by some of these witch doctors have created new enthusiasm for the gospel. A report from the Shaferlys in 1998 states: "There is an increasingly vocal cry throughout the Christian community in Haiti that it is time to break Satan's stronghold, time for Haiti to be delivered."

Yes, the forces of evil truly are in retreat, and Haiti is at a "critical turning point." This is a turning point that could make the Haitian people and their country a greater nation. To God be the glory! And the call to every believer is: "Forward to the Battle!"

- Eldon Turnidge
Past President, Men For Missions International
Haiti Field Director, 1959-1968
Former Member Board of Trustees,
Oriental Missionary Society (OMS International)

Radio 4VEH sign in 1950

Rev. G. T. Bustin in 1950

Mardy Picazo at radio controls about 1952

New studios in 1953

Studios in 1990 with annexes on both sides and back

The Bustin tabernacle housed radio 4VEH's first
transmitter in the back rooms in 1958

June 2, 1950

4VEH STARTS BROADCASTING
By Rachael Picazo

Not many people have the audacity to obey God as did Rev. G. T. Bustin. For example, when God told him to go to Andros Island, he didn't even know where it was. He found it in the long chain of islands known as the Bahamas, southeast of Florida. Since he was an evangelist, Rev. Bustin began preaching as soon as he arrived. A revival broke out. From all over the island people rushed to the services where they fell on their knees begging God to forgive their sins. Soon they were praying also in their homes at all hours of the day and night.

An old lady was the key to all this. She had been saved 40 years earlier and had been praying for revival on her island all that time. In one of the meetings she stood with tears running down her ebony cheeks and pointed at Bro. Bustin.

"This is the man!" she declared. "The man the Lord showed me in a vision! This here white man coming thousands and thousands of miles across the hungry ocean to preach the Gospel to these folks in Sodom!"

On Andros Island Bro. Bustin himself experienced a vision while asleep one night. He was walking along a countryside he recognized as Haiti, which he had just recently visited when he accompanied the Neal Bonner family going there as missionaries. However, he hadn't seen this particular place. Someone walking beside him called his attention to the grounds on their left where there were several buildings, fruit trees, and spacious lawns...and pointed out, "This is property that can be bought for a Bible training school."

The dream was so vivid that he sat straight up in bed and woke his wife to share what he had seen. He wrote Mr. Bonner in Haiti telling about the dream and the estate he had seen.

1

His friend answered, "There is such a place as you described, and I believe it can be bought. It would be ideal for a Bible training school."

This was during World War II, with travel hazardous in the Caribbean, so two years went by before Bro. Bustin could investigate. He went first to Mr. Bonner, and together they traveled 200 miles across Haiti to Cap-Haitien on the northern coast. From there they took a taxi out five miles to the site Mr. Bonner thought fit the description given him. When they drove onto the property, Bro. Bustin exclaimed, "This is the place I saw in my dream! We must find out if it is for sale."

It had been for sale two years before, but since nobody bought it, the Seventh Day Adventists had just about decided to reopen their school there.

However, Bro. Bustin felt certain that God wanted to give him this piece of land. So the two of them climbed partway up the mountain overlooking it and knelt on the rocks. Bro. Bustin said to Bonner, "My brother, Jesus said, (Matthew 18:19), '...if two of you shall agree on earth as touching anything that they shall ask, it shall be done for them of my Father which is in heaven.'" So there the two of them agreed to ask the Lord for three things: first, that the owners would be willing to sell the property; second, that they would sell it for a reasonable sum; and, third, that the Lord would provide the money for it.

Bro. Bustin ended with this prayer: "Oh heavenly Father, we don't know where one dollar will come from, but we thank Thee, God. The property is ours!"

As they walked back the five miles to Cap-Haitien, they kept saying, "Thank God for the property!"

When Bro. Bustin returned to the States, he published in his missionary magazine that they were going to buy a compound in Haiti and even showed pictures of it.

Soon they received word from the management that they would sell the grounds for a certain amount of cash.

"It was wonderful beyond words," Bro. Bustin declared later, "how God worked and provided us with the needed funds." In fact, when the donations were all counted, Bro. Bustin's mission had $500 more than the amount named to buy the property. As it turned out, they needed that too. Bro. Bustin had to travel to Haiti himself to complete the transaction, and his plane fare cost him $150. Then he discovered that the government tax was $348. So with that extra $500 he had all he needed with two dollars to spare.

In January 1946 Bro. Bustin finally arrived at the Haiti mission compound with his wife and six children, as well as other missionaries to staff a Bible training school. At last he was there—nearly four years after the night of his startling vision.

But he was in for another shock. As he walked across the new campus, he heard a message unmistakably from God, "I want you to build a radio station to evangelize Haiti. It is to be called Radio 4VEH, 'La Voix Evangelique d'Haiti' (Evangelistic Voice of Haiti)."

His wife was enthusiastic and encouraged him to undertake the project. Bolstered by his wife's approval, Bro. Bustin mentioned the broadcasting station to one of his friends. That friend protested, "But you haven't had any experience or training in radio. How could you expect to carry on even if you did get a radio transmitter and equipment installed? You have no staff nor budget. And besides, most of the people of Haiti are too poor to buy radios. And Haiti is a thousand miles away from the United States. How could you ever hope to reach those friends you were talking about in Pennsylvania?"

Those were serious objections, so Bro. Bustin did not proceed. Time passed.

Finally the conviction was so clear that he declared, "I know nothing about radio, and I do not know how we will carry on, but I know that God is leading, and He will surely provide. When God wants us to do a thing, it can be done."

He remarked later, "In those days the declaration of Jesus stood out like letters of gold; 'All things are possible to him that believeth!' Thus we were assured that God would see us through."

In 1948 Bro. Bustin boldly announced that he was going to build a missionary radio station in Haiti. He traveled that year to Australia, where he told about it in a meeting just before his exploratory trip into New Guinea.

A radio technician happened to be in that meeting in Australia, and he wrote to his friend Paul Shirk, a fellow engineer in California, telling him about Bro. Bustin's plans.

Paul Shirk felt the Lord wanted him to go to Haiti to do this work. Loading an old model white truck with thousands of pounds of radio equipment, he drove all the way to Florida.

When Mr. Shirk arrived in Haiti and saw the location of the grounds, he was dismayed. Though picturesque, at the base of a 2500 foot mountain, it was certainly not a good transmitting site. He declared that no radio engineer in the world would choose such a place to establish a broadcasting station.

"Just look at that mountain! It will dissipate 90% of the radio power. Further, a station located there cannot be expected to be heard directly north over that peak into the eastern part of the United States."

Bro. Bustin was disappointed because he had hoped to reach into Pennsylvania where he had many supporters and friends. Yet he knew this was the exact location where God had led him to build the station. After considering a moment, he declared, "Well, Mr. Shirk, our Lord can, if need be, cast that mountain into the sea so far as its power to hinder the broadcasts!"

Paul Shirk was a capable engineer, expertly assembling the 700 watt transmitter which would be broadcasting on the 31 meter shortwave band, the frequency Bro. Bustin was able to obtain from the Haitian government. Paul designed the studio,

4

control booth, and transmitter room which were housed in the back of the new tabernacle under construction. He also set up the antenna towers.

After hundreds of hours of work, Mr. Shirk projected a day when they could test the new transmitter. He wrote to some of his technical friends at the pioneer missionary radio station HCJB in Quito, Ecuador, asking them to be listening at a certain time on a given frequency to see if they could hear Radio 4VEH in Haiti. Bro. Bustin also wrote a friend who had a good radio in Pennsylvania, asking him to be listening as well.

At the appointed hour, Bro. Bustin and all his family, along with a gathering of the missionaries, Bible School students, and friends from the community, clustered at the door of the radio studio and watched the proceedings. Charles Bustin, who was present, described the moment:

Long will we remember that night in 1950 when the transmitter was first tested on the air. Anxiously we waited as Paul Shirk, engineer, gave our call letters, 4VEH, then invited HCJB to come in. The suspense was terrific, but only for a moment. Then we heard, "HCJB, Quito, Ecuador, calling 4VEH. You are coming in clear and strong."

You can imagine the cheers that went up from the audience gathered at the studio door. The dream of a radio station had become a reality.

A few days later on June 2, 1950, Radio 4VEH transmitted its first public program, then launched into a regular broadcasting schedule.

And oh, yes...one more thing. In a few days Bro. Bustin got a letter from that friend in Pennsylvania, who declared that "4VEH is coming in like a local station!"

At once Radio Station 4VEH became Bro. Bustin's pulpit. He was a fiery preacher; some of his listeners declared that cold chills ran up their spines when he pronounced warnings about coming judgment.

5

RADIO 4VEH LISTENERS
By Rev. G. T. Bustin
(From his book, *My First 75 Years*)

Letters soon began to pour in from many parts of the world, even both sides of the world, thanking God for 4VEH and the message of hope it was bringing.

Letters were showered upon us from many islands in the West Indies. Sometimes we would laugh, weep, and praise God aloud while reading these soul-lifting letters. The testimonies of those who were being helped and blessed were ample pay for all the effort.

Within a few months it was my privilege to visit the islands of Curacao and Aruba where thousands listened to us daily. What a joy to meet with these precious listeners. They treated me like a prince, and many of them turned to the Lord. It has been my pleasure to make three visits to these islands and minister the Gospel in person. Some of these people I consider my dearest friends.

I was told there were hardly any radios in Haiti, but then a prominent Haitian told me that there are forty thousand sets in the country. While it is true that many thousands of poor people have none, it is also true that many thousands do have radios in the cities and towns, especially where they have electricity. It is a common matter for a Christian owning a radio to invite others into his house to listen to the Gospel.

Friends in Aruba have told me that when they have had to leave their homes en route to their work a few minutes before my program ended, they were able to pick it up all along the street, and by the time they arrived at their place of activity, they had heard the whole program.

Perhaps our greatest accomplishment with the radio station is among the Spanish-speaking people. In certain sections of South America the way is blocked to missionaries, and many church buildings and mission stations are closed, so the Gospel cannot be heard except by radio. Some who have receivers crowd their houses with friends who are hungry for Bible teaching. We have hundreds of listeners in these areas.

Here at Radio 4VEH, our Lord has raised up faithful friends who have made it possible for the station to broadcast daily, with the exception of Thursday, which is the rest day. All who have thus stood by us will share in the rewards on that day when the work is all done.

1950   **RADIO 4VEH**
                          By Rachael Picazo

Bro. Bustin continued to broadcast daily devotionals on the new radio station. The rest of the approximately two hour daily schedule (18 hours a week) consisted of programs received by mail on tapes and long-play records, including one in Spanish, from American broadcasters. Another favorite feature was a half-hour of organ music. An organist, Mrs. DeMille, had visited the 4VEH studios and dedicated several days to recording familiar hymns on reel-to-reel tapes.

Each Sunday the Creole services held in the newly-constructed tabernacle were broadcast over 4VEH. This was convenient since those first studios were constructed in the back rooms of the church.

Bro. Bustin's oldest child, Claudine, now Mrs. Victor Chamberlin, was an important member of the inexperienced staff prayerfully feeling its way along. One of their programs broadcast replies to letters from friends who heard 4VEH in the northeastern United States, especially Pennsylvania, as well as other parts of the world.

4VEH was broadcasting with 700 watts in the 31 meter shortwave band, but nobody knew for sure how far the programs would reach. Soon, however, listeners from Cap-Haitien five miles away began coming to the church services to check out what they were hearing on their radios. Letters arrived from the Caribbean islands and South America.

Late in 1951, only 18 months after it began, suddenly tragedy struck. Radio 4VEH was silenced by a bolt of lightning which burned out the transmitter.

The engineer, Paul Shirk, a radio genius, set about designing a more powerful transmitter of 3,000 watts. It was very efficient but unique, quite different from conventional ones being manufactured in the United States. The parts were ordered to be shipped to Haiti, and Paul began the demanding task of assembling them. It would take him six months to complete the project, while he himself was plagued by malaria and dysentery. He asked Bro. Bustin to find a replacement for him so he could return to the United States to recover.

Bro. Bustin prayed earnestly for the engineer that should come. Actually, for the past several years God had been preparing that man, Mardy Picazo.

1952   A NEW RADIO ENGINEER
By Mardy Picazo
Mardy's full name: Mardoqueo Evaristo Picazo

DATE: July 15, 1952 Here we were at last...the island of Haiti! We could make out the city of Port-au-Prince crowded around the harbor.

Our Pan Am DC6 thundering over the bay seemed to be on a crash course with a jumble of one-story buildings.

8

Actually, the runway was there, just a couple of blocks off the main street which went up to the heights of Petionville. This was their only airport and served also as headquarters for their military planes.

Our family of four—Rachael and I with our five-year-old Esteban and eight-month-old Daniel—were starting the adventure of our lives. We had enjoyed a relaxed flight after leaving Miami four hours before. Now, what was awaiting us at the terminal?

Stepping off the plane we were engulfed in the warm damp air of the tropics. People were everywhere, waiting. All of them were black...no, we saw a few lighter faces here and there. A long black Buick was parked nearby with distinguished looking men standing around, watching the arriving passengers.

Then one of the men approached me and introduced himself as Armand Malbranche. He was the one I had talked to by ham radio when we were in Miami a couple of days before. He cordially helped us with the officials, the papers we needed to sign, and the baggage we had to claim. When we were properly entered into the country, Mr. Malbranche led us to the Buick.

We had instructions how to find the Mission's rented house where we were to stay until we could travel north to our destination at Cap-Haitien. Our friend Armand took us right to Fort National and the very house. Before he left us, he made me promise that I would join him in the Amateur Radio Club meeting that night at his home. He offered to take me and bring me back. We really were in Haiti, at last.

We marveled as we considered all the steps that had guided our lives... I had been in the U.S. Navy training as an engineering officer when the Lord showed me that I was to allow Him to direct my life.

I was busy with 18 to 24 semester hours of studies required by the Navy and courses toward my university degree. I was also part of a group of Christian sailors who held a daily prayer meeting after the noon meal before we returned to classes. We had subsequently formed a gospel quartet and were singing in churches, public parks, prisons, and wherever we found the opportunity. We also had weekly Bible studies, inviting pastors or teachers to speak to our group of sailors and a few coeds from the university.

At one of these Bible studies the speaker held up a blank sheet of paper and said, "Let's say this represents your life's plan." Then he wrote on the top in big letters "MY LIFE." Below it he wrote:

#1. My Education
#2. My Career
#3. My Marriage Plans
#4. My Retirement

At the bottom of the page was a blank line for a signature.

"Young people," he said, "many of you have done this. You've carefully laid out plans for your life and handed it to God for His signature. That is fine, for many young people never give God a thought in preparing for the future."

I was pleased with myself, for this is exactly what I had done. My plan included getting my engineering degree and credentials, and after the war, when I would be making good money, I would give my tithe and offerings to the Lord in large measure. But then the speaker declared, "However, that is not what God wants."

Then he took a clean sheet of paper and wrote across the top "MY LIFE." He put the numbers down the side of the page with nothing written after them and at the bottom he again put the signature line. Then he said, "God wants that sheet blank, and He wants your signature on the bottom line. He wants you to hand Him that empty sheet and let Him fill in the plans for your future."

That hit me hard. I wanted to reject it. In fact, it troubled me so much that for several days I couldn't deal with it at all. But finally, one night by the side of my bunk, while the others were on weekend leave, I determined to pray until God returned my peace. After several hours of tearful confession and submission, I suddenly felt the load lift, and I found myself telling the Lord that if He wanted me to become a street sweeper for Him, I would gladly do it. I didn't say I would become a preacher, nor did He press me at that time. But I rose from my knees with a heart full of joy, knowing God was in control.

For the next few weeks I was on an emotional high. Our Bible studies and the services we held were my greatest pleasure, my engineering courses less important. However, this was my last semester and I knew I had a responsibility to maintain the strict Navy standard.

Then one night we were singing for a tent meeting on the outskirts of Albuquerque where the university was located. Suddenly I found myself in tears as I realized God was asking me to work for Him full-time. My heart responded, "YES, YES!"

My immediate thought was that I would become a pastor like my father, going to seminary as soon as I got out of the Navy. Then came that day in Norfolk, Virginia...

When I proposed to Rachael, my life was set towards an electrical engineer's career. But six months before my graduation I told her that I now had God's call to work full-time for Him. This did not disturb Rachael, however. She consented to become my wife, whatever I chose to do.

I still had a few months to serve in the Navy, though the war was over. My assigned ship sailed from San Francisco to Norfolk, Virginia, to be decommissioned. After crossing the Panama Canal I got my first glimpse of Haiti, though of course I did not know what that land held for me.

Rachael took the bus across the country to join me in Norfolk, and Sunday evening we went looking for a place to worship. Several churches we passed were either dark or deserted. Finally we found one where people were singing. There were several other Navy men and everyone was friendly.

I don't remember the preacher's message, but as soon as the service was over he made a beeline for us. In a matter of minutes I told my story. I was a graduate electrical engineer but also called into full-time service for the Lord.

His face lit up as he exclaimed, "You are just the kind of person needed at Missionary Radio Station HCJB!"

I said, "Missionary radio? What is that?"

Then he told about the powerful shortwave station that was broadcasting the Gospel from Quito, Ecuador. The engineers there, like myself, had been trained for professional careers, but God had called them to go there to make this ministry possible. He said that the mission organization couldn't afford to hire professionals. Their engineers had to be on missionary status.

When Rachael and I heard this, the Holy Spirit witnessed to both of us that this was the work He had in mind for us. Rev. John Dunlap, pastor of the Norfolk Tabernacle Church, gave us some names and advice on how to contact these people. We went back to our rooms marveling at how our lives were directed that night.

The people of HCJB told me I must get a radio operator's license from the Federal Communications Commission and needed experience working at some station as engineer. They asked us to keep in touch with them.

Through a friend we learned about John Brown University in Arkansas, where I got a year's intensive course in broadcasting, including working as engineer at their radio station. I also got both the official FCC and my amateur radio licenses and, as a ham, started learning how to build my own transmitters. It was there our first son, Esteban, was born.

My first job as a radio engineer was helping build station WVLK in Lexington, Kentucky, from the ground up. After it was on the air I worked for a few months as their control-central operator.

Then I heard about a lucrative opportunity in TV at WLW with the starting salary twice what I was earning there. The increase in pay was attractive. Also, the constant worldly input through my headphones as I controlled the mikes, music, etc., of the station, was dimming my vision of a missionary call.

Just then a friend rushed in from the mountains of eastern Kentucky, declaring there was an urgent need for me in a Christian station being built at Vancleve, KY. The FCC would not allow them to proceed unless they found a licensed engineer to be on their staff. Naturally I asked, "How much do they pay?"

"Oh, they don't pay anything," he explained. "They furnish you a place to stay and food. You trust the Lord for all the rest you need. It is a work of faith."

I had never heard of such a thing. I said, "Listen, friend, my father has been in the ministry 30 years, and he always has some kind of salary, even if it isn't very much. I know he is certainly a man of faith!"

My friend smiled. "You just pray about it, will you?"

Surprisingly, Rachael was intrigued. We did pray about it and decided we would at least go visit the place and talk to the people. So we took a Greyhound bus for Vancleve, KY, about 100 miles from Lexington, where I was working.

We decided to stay a year to help build and start the radio station. But we told them that we planned to go to HCJB in Ecuador after that.

This was the beginning of our "boot" training for the mission field. Radio Station WMTC was truly a project of faith in the work started by Dr. Lela G. McConnell. We were amazed at what the Lord was doing through these people in Breathitt County. It was called "Bloody Breathitt" because at least one

13

murder was committed every week in this area of the feuding Hatfields and McCoys.

I helped them design and wire their studios and oversaw the laying of the ground wires for the tower. The 270' tower was erected professionally; then they constructed the little transmitter building near its base. I installed their transmitter and tested and operated the equipment. At last the station was ready to broadcast.

As their only licensed engineer, I was required by the FCC to be with the transmitter every hour of operation. Rachael began to learn some of the programming procedures, helped with script writing and music scheduling in the eight-to-ten-hour day of broadcasting, and experimented with Bible dramatizations.

After a time, the Lord started me on the "living by faith" curriculum. First, our finances were touched. We had not received a penny from anyone during that year, and every week or so I had been writing checks to buy canned milk for our one-year-old Esteban. Finally, one day I wrote a check for the last five dollars in our account. I told Rachael, "That's it, Sweetheart. From here on we'll have to trust the Lord."

I had never had that experience before. As I walked across the Bible School campus on my way to the transmitter building, a student from infamous Harlan, KY, stopped me and said, "Brother Picazo, as I was praying this morning, the Lord told me to give you this," and he handed me a five-dollar bill.

I was shocked speechless. God was getting my attention to what faith is. I felt immensely rich all of a sudden, as if someone had handed me a blank check from the Ford Foundation, or something. The rest of the day I was on "Cloud 9," for I realized God knew exactly what I needed and would supply it. On the mission field, this lesson was invaluable as we relied on Him to provide necessary funds in that far-off place.

Then came another type of faith training. One day the transmitter wouldn't go on. I checked to see if everything was normal. It looked all right, but it just wouldn't start.

I opened the back doors and carefully inspected everything for evidence of burning or a faulty part, but it seemed all right. I rechecked and even called some engineer friends by ham radio to ask their advice. Nothing.

Finally I decided, "I will call on the Lord." So I got on my knees behind the transmitter cabinet and asked the Lord to show me how to correct this problem. The broadcasts were vital to the community and I knew the Lord cared.

I thanked Him, then opened the transmitter cabinet doors again for the umpteenth time to look at the maze of wires and components before me. The equipment was turned off as I leaned my hand on the frame of the transmitter cabinet, my thumb resting on a stiff wire being held by an insulator. The wire moved under my thumb. It wasn't supposed to move! It was supposed to be soldered solid. Ah! I jiggled it again and saw that the solder joint had crystallized and was no longer making contact. In a matter of five minutes I had resoldered the wire, and we were back on the air.

The number of lessons the Lord taught us as we worked at WMTC are numerous, and each one had its parallel when we were in Haiti. He was also showing us that His plans for us were good and would be revealed in their time.

When our first year was completed, there was no one to take our place, though I had trained two or three different ones. But they had either gone into the army, got married, or something else. We even got a call from HCJB, waiving some of their requirements if we could come immediately to help in their move to a new location. But we did not feel released from this work yet. And it was there our second son, Daniel, was born.

Finally, in 1951, it seemed we were on the way. The World Gospel Mission was starting a radio station in Bolivia. We were accepted as missionaries and were to report to them as soon as we were released in Kentucky. An engineer in Oregon agreed to come to WMTC at the end of the year to replace me. So I put in our resignation, effective May 1, 1952. We were on our way to the mission field.

Then it happened. WGM informed us they were not able to go on with their project in Bolivia due to a revolution. Would we accept a position as teachers in Honduras? We prayed. We felt the Lord direct us not to accept, but rather to be still and wait.

We were all ready to go and no place to go. In fact, only a couple of months more and we would have to leave WMTC because we had resigned. Another mission asked if we would go to Costa Rica to help with a school and do some radio work. Again, we felt checked.

One day I had "by chance" left the transmitter to go to the office for a quick errand. While I was there, a long distance call for me came in. It was from a man named Rev. G. T. Bustin. He told me that someone from his staff in Haiti had been in correspondence with a friend in Kentucky and had heard of our availability to serve as missionaries. He said he needed a radio engineer immediately, as the one who was there was ill and was preparing to leave the field permanently. He asked me a few questions and promised to write more details.

In his letter Rev. Bustin said his organization was called the East and West Indies Bible Mission and that it was a faith work. He said that if we could get $25 support a month, they would supply the rest as the Lord provided. We had just experienced four years of faith living, so this did not stagger us. As we prayed, we knew God was telling us to go.

We were on our way by late May, driving a car we had just bought, pulling a small trailer with drums of our personal effects. We traveled south by way of Texas, where I saw my mother for the last time, and my father, brothers, and sister. From New Orleans we shipped our baggage and drove on to Florida.

The mission's headquarters were near Orlando where we were invited to speak at the local church. The pastor wanted to help with our expenses but apologized that the only ones in his congregation now were those who couldn't afford to go north for the summer. He asked me to tell about the work we were going to do, but I knew nothing about the radio station and very little about Haiti. Mostly I gave my testimony. The pastor invited the congregation to put gifts to help us in my hand as they left.

In order to keep the church records straight, the pastor asked how much his people had given. He speculated, "I imagine you got around $20, though I could hope it might be up to $30 or $40." When I told him we had received $158, he was astounded. That supply lasted more than six weeks until the day we arrived in Haiti.

We sold the car, sending back all we received to pay those who had loaned us the money for it, and then took a bus for Miami. It was hot that early June. The people we stayed with were supporters of the East and West Indies Bible Mission, and they provided us with a room and breakfast, sometimes a main meal. We expected to be there only a day or two before going on to Haiti. It was not to be that way.

The home where we stayed was not far from the center of town and only one block from the beach. We spent many afternoons on the sandy shore with our children. We often ate our hot dogs and crackers there.

But just getting permission to go into Haiti took six long weeks in Miami. Confusion had been generated by an official in the Immigration Department who wanted to keep Protestant missionaries from entering.

When we had arrived in Miami on our way to Haiti, I had gone to the Haitian consul, applied for an entrance visa, and paid the necessary fees. The consul said that the visa had to be sent from the immigration office in Port-au-Prince, with our representative there paying the cost of the telegram. He told us to come back the next day to see if an answer had been returned. So I had gone back every office day for six weeks.

In the meantime, our missionary in Haiti was being told that I was the one who had to pay in Miami for the telegram.

After some weeks I met a Christian radio amateur who, on hearing of our plight, put me in radio contact with a friend he had in Port-au-Prince, Haiti, named Armand Malbranche. After learning about our situation, he said, "Mardy, you go over to the consul's office tomorrow and your visa will be there. I'll wait for you at the airport the next day."

Armand was an important personage. He strode confidently into the immigration office, asked if my visa permit was ready, demanded they give it to him, and he himself paid for the telegram to the consul in Miami.

Now, there I was, waiting for my new friend Armand to take me to his home for that Ham Club meeting. Soon the Buick glided in front of the little house where we were staying.

The group I met that night was comprised of distinguished businessmen, engineers, merchants, and officials in elite society. They were the only ones then who could get radio licenses or afford the equipment needed. One of the men was the director of Haiti's Federal Communications, who told me to stop by his office the next day, when he would furnish me with my Haitian licenses, giving me authority to operate Radio 4VEH as well as my ham equipment.

Another man was the technician for the RCA Global Communications. He offered to drive Rachael and the children to the airport for her flight to Cap-Haitien and to take me to the bus/truck terminal for my transportation overland.

In the years to follow, many of these men helped us get materials or services for Radio 4VEH that would have been nearly impossible to obtain otherwise.

After seeing Rachael and the children off on a plane for Cap-Haitien, I climbed on a truck/bus to travel overland. I was fortunate to be one of the four people riding with the driver on the front seat. It took 13 hours to negotiate the 170 miles, most of the time crawling over the roughest road I had ever seen. At one o'clock in the morning, the driver dropped me off at the compound gate, five miles south of Cap-Haitien. The watchman, and later some of the missionaries, helped me carry our baggage to the house where Rachael and the children were, which was to be our home for the next 11 years.

In the morning I met Paul Shirk, who already had his bags packed to leave, but he promised to stay long enough (four days) to help me get acquainted with the equipment and my responsibilities. He showed me the control console and various other pieces he had built, how they were connected in the transmitter/control room and adjoining studio in the back part of the church tabernacle. The cable for the antennas was fed through the wall to two 50' towers in the yard that held the antenna wire in place.

He taught me how to start the diesel and gasoline generators, as well as how to hook and work them together. Later I had to learn how to overhaul the Witte engine.

In the studio was the library of tapes and records that were to be used for the daily three-to-four-hour broadcasts. I was put in charge of all the Spanish programs and some of the English.

For the previous six months, Paul had been building a new 3,000 watt transmitter. That very night he was ready to test it for the first time. He explained what it should do, then he fired it up and put it on the air. It sat there performing just as Paul had planned.

I was almost overwhelmed with the enormity of the task ahead. I praised God for giving me "boot camp" at WMTC in the mountains of eastern Kentucky. And I thanked the Lord that He was the One who would be handling the brunt of my ignorance.

1952 **WE MEET REV. BUSTIN**
By Rachael Picazo

Rev. G. T. Bustin was nearly 50 years old when we first met him—a trim, energetic, and enthusiastic pioneer missionary. We had come to Haiti as a result of his telephone calls and follow-up letters, but he was not there when we finally arrived in mid 1952. His tall, capable teenage son Charles met us and showed us around.

When Rev. Bustin did arrive at 4VEH some weeks later, he was on his way back to New Guinea. He was founder of the East and West Indies Bible Mission and Radio 4VEH, where we had come to work. Nevertheless, he insisted that we address him with the simple title of "Brother."

While he was in Haiti, he spoke at the Vaudreuil church. The Haitians sat spellbound as Bro. Bustin told of how God had led him in 1948 to contact one of the unreached tribes in New Guinea on the other side of the world. All of those primitive people, many of whom were cannibals, had warriors with bows and spears, and it was considered unsafe for anyone to venture into their territory. However, that is what Bro. Bustin felt God wanted him to do.

It was hard to find guides to take him, and even if he actually met some of the savages, how could he communicate that he had come in peace? God showed him that he was to walk right up to them and hug them! So that is what he did. The savages smiled and accepted him. It opened the way to start missionary work among them.

So he was on his way back to New Guinea to oversee the progress of the church, school, and clinic he had started there. When we arrived at 4VEH, he was already looking for some mission group that could take over this work he had pioneered in Haiti.

I don't know how he found time to write his memoirs, "My First Fifty Years," when 1953 came, but I am glad he did, for much of the information about how God led him in starting 4VEH was recorded in that book.

1952   THE EARLY YEARS AT 4VEH
By Mardy and Rachael Picazo

When Radio 4VEH returned to the air with 3,000 watts, the response was immediate. Former listeners wrote from the islands of the West Indies, Central and South America, the United States, and from all over the world, including Europe, Australia, and New Zealand. During this period letters began to pour in for the Spanish programs.

One of the questions Bro. Bustin had asked Mardy when he was interviewing him as a missionary candidate was if he could speak Spanish. That seemed strange since the dialect of the Haitian people is Creole and the official language is French. But once he was there, Mardy saw the letters written in Spanish, coming from Colombia, Venezuela, Cuba, the Dominican Republic in the Caribbean, Mexico, and Central America.

One of the first rules established was that those who spoke on the programs, whatever the language, had to use their "mother tongue." In this way there would be no strange accent to hinder the clear understanding of the listener.

Mardy's first language is Spanish, which was spoken in his home. His minister father was strict in his use of correct Spanish, and he did not allow his children to slip into the "Tex-Mex" slang used all around them. At the Lydia Patterson Institute where Mardy attended high school, Spanish was spoken more freely than English, and Spanish grammar and literature were studied in depth.

The Spanish-speaking listeners, especially those in Colombia, caught Mardy's attention because of a revival God had sent in the central part of that country. Then, early in 1953, letters began arriving with shocking news of persecution. Churches were being closed, some burned. The evangelicals were being thrown into prison, their lives threatened, and there were even some martyrs in the uprisings.

4VEH was coming in loud and clear, and hundreds were looking to it for spiritual encouragement. Mardy started daily Bible studies in Spanish, along with prayer for the stricken ones in Colombia. Christians from countries surrounding the Caribbean joined in these prayer times via radio. Mardy read their letters on the air telling of their prayer intercession, being careful not to divulge information that could cause repercussions for those who wrote.

In one village in central Colombia, a listener told how the church had been closed and members threatened. This particular man was arrested and accused of being an evangelical. He asked to bring his radio along to prison. The surprised officers said that they had not been instructed otherwise, so the man turned on his radio full blast every day there in jail. The other prisoners listened eagerly to the programs over 4VEH, and it came to the attention of the authorities. Finally after six weeks, to get rid of the radio, the man was allowed to go home.

A lady wrote that one of her mother's last wishes had been that her daughter write to 4VEH and tell them that she had become a Christian through listening to the messages.

1952   **LIFE ON THE 4VEH COMPOUND**
By Rachael Picazo

Haiti is so poor that living things seem stunted and gaunt. Visitors remark about the scrawny chickens ..."More like athletic bantams"... and the bony little horses... "Why, that horse isn't big enough to properly be called a pony back where I come from." The corn growing in the fields is only shoulder high, with miniature-sized ears, and even the dogs are often so malnourished one can count their ribs.

Pastor Napo used to tell about a Haitian who got tired of hearing some American visitors brag about how much bigger and better their animals were, so he decided to show one of them that Haiti had big things too. That night he put a turtle in the visitor's bed. When the American's foot touched it, he jumped out of bed and threw back the sheet. "What is this in my bed?" he demanded. His Haitian host mildly explained, "Oh, that is just a Haitian bedbug."

Actually, Haiti does have some things that are quite large, among which are the cockroaches. They are the kind that grow in the trees and fly —yes, actually fly—into the houses, where they multiply like...roaches. They are a rich reddish-brown and grow to be about two and one-half inches long. The first house we lived in was so riddled with termites that their tunnels in the walls provided excellent nesting places for the roaches. One of my daughters reminisced recently about taking her pet chickens into the kitchen at night and then suddenly turning on the light so they could feed on the roaches that were scurrying for cover.

Eventually, a certain kind of pesticide came on the market that could kill them. So, armed with my spray gun, night after night I went into the kitchen, turned on the light, and did battle with them. I swept the dead roaches up into piles and picked them up by the dustpan load to burn. However, since the new spray had no residual properties, it never seemed to diminish the population. Then came "Powder D," which I am sure was more poisonous than DDT. It killed them, and it kept on killing them for years. But it was also deadly to people, so we had to be careful how we used it. I would dissolve it in water, then carefully paint the bottoms of the kitchen drawers, the backs of the cabinets behind the drawers, the undersides of cupboard shelves—everywhere no one's fingers or food would ever touch. It only had to be done once every three or four years. After that the only cockroaches we saw in our kitchen were dead ones.

When we first arrived in Haiti in 1952, the missionary staff ate together in a dining hall, a separate building that had a long room with dining tables and chairs. In one corner was a kerosene refrigerator. Attached to the back of the building was a similar long room that served as pantry and kitchen, containing an iron wood-burning cook stove.

Groceries were bought in the city once a week. In that tropical land where there is no freezing weather to deter the cockroaches and ants, and where rats thrive by the thousands, one has to be ingenious to keep the food protected.

Such things as flour, corn meal, sugar, rice, and beans were kept in large, tightly-sealed metal cans. Such food as bread, vegetables, and fruit were kept in guard-mange's (pronounced "MAHN-jay's"), which were open cabinets with tight screening all around to keep out the cockroaches. They stood on long feet which were set into tin cans kept full of water to thwart the ants. The cook went to a neighbor down the road each week on butchering day and bought a dishpan full of meat for the week, almost always beef, though now and then it was goat. We only bought a few canned things a month—tomato paste, mostly. Fresh fruit and vegetables were available the year around.

A Haitian cook was employed to prepare the meals. Every person who ate in the dining hall contributed a certain amount a month towards the cost of food. Each missionary lady

24

took a two-month turn planning the menus, overseeing the purchase of supplies, and preparing the meals on the cook's day off. Water was piped into the kitchen.

In fact, each home had running cold water into a kitchen area and a shower room. But there were, as yet, no septic tanks dug on the compound, so each home had its own outhouse. These were substantial structures made of brick, plastered over and kept spotless with regular whitewashing.

We had only been in Haiti a few days when Hilda came to pay me an evening visit. Since she had grown up in the Bahamas, we could chat in English, which was nice, because the Haitian Creole was still just a confusion of sounds to me.

In fact, we were so busy talking that we were caught by surprise when the lights went out. We had no idea it was already ten o'clock. but the lamp was ready, and it took only a moment to put the match to the wick. The crickets and other bugs sounded louder in the subdued lamplight.

But then I noticed Hilda staring at something beyond me. I turned to see —and there on the floor, ambling in our direction, was the largest spider I had ever seen. It was huge and hairy, and it seemed infinitely more so in the lamplight with its shadow thrown out behind it. Later, I learned that Haiti has some of the largest tarantulas in the world. With its legs spread out, one of them could fill a dinner plate.

I had not been one to be squeamish—mice, snakes, bugs did not upset me. And I had seen tarantulas before. Once while we were driving in the Ozark Mountains, one had walked across the road in front of us. But in that case, it was on the road and I was in the car. Now this one was in the same room with me, only a few feet away. An icy fear seized me.

Hilda's calm remark pierced my mesmerism, "Oh, a tarantula..."

As she stood, she began surveying the room for something she could use to kill it. Mardy was building a playpen for our baby Daniel, and he had the sanded sides and posts stacked ready for assembly. Picking up one of the short posts no more than two feet long, Hilda stepped close and tapped the tarantula on the back. It crumpled. The thing was dead.

But it was only a couple of nights later that another tarantula came picking its way across our living room floor. This time there was no Haitian friend nearby to rescue me. I was alone in the house with our two little boys asleep. But Mardy was at the radio studio just across the field from us, so I made a dash for it in the darkness, probably more reckless than prudent, considering my extra bulk at the time. (It was only two months before Baby Rachel would be born.)

Mardy was not experienced in dealing with those large hairy spiders, and I noticed that he chose the six-foot side post as his weapon. Now a tarantula is sizable, but when you are standing that far away it is hard to hit, and especially if it is moving. Mardy crashed the floor instead of the spider in his first attempt, alarming the creature. As the stick went bang, bang, bang, the tarantula scrambled to flee. I could hear the dry scratching of its long legs on the bare wooden floor. But Mardy finally succeeded in killing it. In fact he took care of several more in like manner over the next few weeks.

Then one night after Mardy had gone to take a shower, there was a loud commotion in the bathroom. It sounded as if the walls were being knocked out.

"What's wrong?" I yelled, not that I wanted to help kill whatever it was.

"A convention of scorpions," came the shout between thumps. "I think I got most of them." Mardy was wielding a shoe in his hand as he poked his head out the door and grinned.

But it was no laughing matter with me. By this time I had learned to vigorously shake out each shoe before I put it on and carefully scan the floor before kneeling to pray. Even the kneeling was abandoned the night I saw a centipede on our bedroom floor as it disappeared under the bed. It was almost a foot long, or at least ten inches. As big around as my thumb, it slithered like a snake.

Armed with a broom and sturdy stick, I lifted the bedspread to see how to corner my prey. Nothing. The centipede wasn't there—only a hole in the floor. After making sure it could have gone nowhere else, I put a big heavy board across the hole.

Terror struck me. Unreasonable fear such as I had never experienced consumed my daylight moments and dreams at night. I would awaken with a start in the darkness and rush in to make sure there were no tarantulas in bed with nine-month-old Daniel, nor any scorpions skulking around five-year-old Esteban. It wasn't a healthy, normal fear. I was ashamed to tell my husband.

Realizing I had to have help, I studied the Scriptures carefully. They had to have an answer. They did.

I found it in the second epistle to Timothy, first chapter, when verse 7 came up at me out of the page (KJV):

For God hath not given us the spirit of fear; but of power, and of love, and of a sound mind.

It was as clear as if an audible voice had said, "God has not given you, Rachael, that spirit of fear." Well, I certainly had a spirit of fear, and if God hadn't given it to me, then I knew where it had come from. In that moment of revelation, the fear left me. It had been like a tangible thing, and I knew it was gone. I reveled in the rest of the verse. *God gives us His Spirit of power, love, a sound mind.*

How wonderful to be free from unreasoning fear! And, of course, I told my husband once the problem was resolved.

I had forgotten all about that incident when Mardy brought it up some years later. Then he pointed out something I had not noticed before. Even though the same termite holes were in the floor and walls where the big spiders had entered the house, and it was still tarantula season, we did not see another one in our home after that day. In fact, we lived there another ten years, yet no tarantula came inside again. Nor did we have any more scorpions.

And in all the rest of our 40 years there in Haiti, I saw only one other centipede like the one that had slithered across our bedroom floor. It was a dead one brought in some years later by a little boy from a remote village, who was showing it around as a rare and dreadful curiosity.

1953   THE ENGINE THAT WENT HUNTING
By Mardy Picazo

Everything at the 4VEH studio was running smoothly that quiet morning, with nice music playing. Then all of a sudden it turned weird. The music developed an up-and-down change in pitch, and the lights went from bright to dim in sequence with the music. I was working in the shop area when this happened, so I quickly shut down the transmitters and rushed out the back door toward the motor house.

My first concern was to turn the power off since the varying voltages would damage our equipment. I was completely ignorant about what was going on, but I looked carefully anyway at the Cummins engine. It was sitting there changing speed, going faster and slower in deliberate but very definite cycles.

I turned off the engine and checked the fuel supply, which I knew was all right, but I checked anyway. The lube oil was also in order. So I started the engine again. Again it started to change in speed as it had done before. I was stumped.

At this time we had no diesel mechanic on our staff. I knew there was an engineer at the sugar refinery in Port-au-

Prince who maintained the Cummins diesel locomotives. But that was 12 hours' travel away, and he probably would not be available for several days, if he would consent to come at all. The expense would be enormous, and we had no funds.

I stared at the engine for a long time, checked, and rechecked everything I knew to do. I had not known much more than how to maintain the engine in changing the oil and filters, checking the fuel supply, and keeping the unit clean. I had worked with our one-cylinder Witte engine and knew it pretty well, but this 6-cylinder, 1200 rpm engine that ran our 25-kilowatt generator was a maze of gadgets, tubes, and protuberances that made me dizzy looking at it.

I had used the thin operator's manual that came with the engine, but there was also one I had not had occasion to look into—a thick "Engine Rebuilding" book which had instructions and pictures of every part of the engine. It told how to dismantle every major component and how to check it for wear. A few paragraphs here and there gave clues on how to adjust certain parts if the engine was not running right. All this I discovered much, much later.

At this point I was becoming frantic about what to do. I got down on my knees and said, "Lord, you know my limitations in this situation. Please help me with this mysterious problem and show me how to correct it. Thank you, Lord. Amen."

Then at random I opened that heavy book, which was about 1½ inches thick. The pages before me displayed pictures of parts of the fuel system. I skimmed the pictures and the explanations, but nothing clicked until I turned the page. There in bold print I read, "If the engine starts to hunt (the technical term for cyclically changing speed), look at the illustration on the previous page, locate the small plate on the pump that you see...." Then it went on to explain how to take a small screwdriver and carefully adjust the screw under the cover until the engine speed stabilized.

Praising God for so quickly leading me to the answer, I went to work. Sure enough, in about 15 minutes everything was running smoothly again. I flipped the power switch, hurried back to the studios, and turned on the equipment. We didn't have much time left to broadcast that morning, but it was enough for our listeners to know that we were back on the air.

1954   **MIRACLE TUBE**
By Mardy Picazo

For two years the 3,000 watt transmitter that Paul Shirk designed and built ran without a moment's problem. And then one morning it happened. When I went to start the transmitter, there was a bang!—a spark!—and it wouldn't go on.

Puzzled, I nevertheless suspected the problem to be serious. After a bit of checking, I pulled out the big tube and took it to the workbench. We were operating on such a minimal budget that we didn't have any spare tubes. These cost from $300 to $400 each and had been in operation these two years.

At my workbench I attached leads from my meter to the suspected elements in the tube through two of the pins. Sure enough, there was a short circuit. It was not repairable. Those tubes were bigger than gallon milk jugs and sealed under vacuum. The wires inside the tube were high-precision installations with tolerances in the thousandths of an inch, spaced to withstand thousands of volts of potential between them. The only solution was a new tube.

As I pondered prayerfully about this and wondered what I was going to do, I absentmindedly tapped the bench with the tube. Suddenly I noticed that the meter no longer registered a short! I checked to see if the leads had come loose or were not making good contact with the pins, but found everything was in order. So, not daring yet to believe it, I went back, plugged the tube into the transmitter, and fired it up. It started working normally! It had to be a miracle tube. So we went on with the regular broadcast.

That incident happened on a Saturday morning. Feeling that I had to do something to avoid a future situation, I got on my amateur (ham) radio and called Atlanta. Rev. Louis Latham lived there, and he had told us that if ever we had a serious problem at 4VEH to call on him, and he would ask the Lord to show him how he could help. He was not a person of means but one of great faith, an evangelist who spoke in different churches where he was invited.

I was able to contact a ham operator in Atlanta who got Rev. Latham on the phone. I told him my situation with the transmitter. He asked for all the technical details and promised to see what he could do. However, before I could confirm that he had received my message accurately, our small generator ran out of fuel and I was suddenly off the air. I rushed to the motor house, fixed the fuel matter, and returned to see if the ham operator was still there, but he was gone and I never contacted him again.

If we could have ordered the tubes from a company in the States, it would normally take three weeks to two months for them to reach us. Just the transshipping across the island from Port-au-Prince to Cap-Haitien takes a week. So, naturally, I did not expect to have any reply about the tubes for at least a month. We went on broadcasting daily with no further interruptions.

Exactly one week later on a Saturday morning the same thing happened all over again. There was a bang!—and a flash!—and the transmitter would not operate. Again, I pulled the offending tube and attached my meter leads to it. Sure enough, it had the same problem as before.

"Well," I thought, "if I was able to cure it last week, why not today?"

So, I started tapping the tube on the bench lightly as I had done before. Nothing happened. I tapped a little harder and looked hard at the meter. It was still shorted. No matter how hard or how long I tapped, the problem persisted. I raised my eyes, "Lord, help us."

That day had been cloudy and stormy. The rain pelting down made everything look dismal and discouraging. Just then I saw the headlights of a vehicle coming up our driveway. It was an open military-type jeep with no top, and a very wet individual stopped in front and jumped out. He carried two large cardboard boxes as he pounded on the door. Then I recognized him—a friend from the Customs Department. I had told him earlier in the week about our predicament and asked him to be on the lookout for some parts we desperately needed that should be coming soon.

His greeting to me was, "Pastor Picazo, I thought you said you were in urgent need of these things. They've been here since yesterday but you did not come in!"

I was overjoyed and overwhelmed! The tubes had come in exactly when we needed them. Further, the customs official had brought them to us himself, without formal preliminaries, inspection, and other regular procedures.

I immediately unboxed the tubes and plugged them in. After their warm-up, Radio 4VEH was back on the air. We had lost only four hours and were now able to resume normal broadcasting. The miracle tube had lasted just long enough to allow the replacements to get there.

Later I learned about the marvels involving their arrival. After my phone call, Rev. Latham wasn't sure what he could do since it was already late Saturday afternoon. He was scheduled to speak at a Nazarene church Sunday morning. He preached his message and at the conclusion, almost as a by-the-way, he said that he had a call from Haiti needing help for Radio 4VEH. In a minute he gave the request and then sat down.

The pastor told his congregation that if they wanted to help, they could give Bro. Latham their offering as they left the sanctuary. The evangelist usually got an honorarium of $75 from the church. To Rev. Latham's amazement, when he later counted the gifts, they amounted to almost $1000!

The next day he went to a wholesale supply for broadcast stations and asked if they had the particular tube.

"No," the salesman replied, "we don't keep it in stock, but we can order it for you. It will take three weeks to a month to get it here."

Bro. Latham didn't know what to do next since this was the only establishment in Atlanta that handled such special items. About that time the clerk said, "Say, I just remembered that there was a radio station that ordered two of those tubes some weeks ago but have never picked them up. I'll sell them to you since you seem to have an emergency need." So Bro. Latham bought them and also four smaller tubes I had mentioned that we needed, and he went on his way to send them to us.

There he encountered the next barricade. At the air express he was told they would have to have a notarized permit from the Haitian embassy before they could ship to Port-au-Prince. The problem came when he couldn't find a Haitian embassy in the city. The airport official told him to just get a paper from any embassy and he would ship it. So Bro. Latham got one from the embassy of Costa Rica and sent the packages.

When the boxes got to Port-au-Prince, they had to be transshipped to Cap-Haitien on another plane, a procedure which normally took a week for paperwork. This time they were processed almost immediately. So the tubes, which were purchased on Monday in Atlanta, arrived in Cap-Haitien on Friday of the same week, an event of very high improbability!

When God does something great like this, we can but marvel that we are allowed to witness and be a part of such an awesome thing.

1955   **NEW SHOES**
By Rachael Picazo

My shoes fell off again, first the right, and then a few steps later the left one. It was so annoying. And worse than that, there was absolutely no money to buy new ones.

We had food to eat, a home in which to stay, so we were not suffering. But this matter of my shoes...

I had a conversation with God right there in the middle of that grassy field I was crossing to reach the radio studios. It went something like this.

"Lord, look how my loafers are all worn out. After these three years here in Haiti, they have become so floppy I just walk right out of them." I was feeling very sorry for myself.

Then a voice spoke in my mind, as clearly as if I had heard it with my physical ears. "Have you ever asked me for a pair of shoes?" I thought I detected a note of sadness in the question.

Had I?...No, I hadn't. Not once. It came to me in a rush how God had become angry with the Israelites in the desert when they complained instead of asking God to supply what they needed. "Oh, Lord!" I cried, "I have been just like them. Please forgive me."

God did forgive me. I knew it in my heart. Then my conversation continued on this line, "Thank you, Lord, for forgiving me. And now I am asking you for a pair of shoes....Thank you, Lord. I know you have heard me."

About two weeks later a letter arrived in the mail. In it was a check with a brief note, "This is for a new pair of shoes for Mrs. Picazo..." The check was more than enough for a nice pair of sturdy shoes.

A couple of years later when we returned to the States for furlough, we learned "the rest of the story." Rev. Louis Latham of Atlanta, Georgia, was excited about the things God was doing through Radio 4VEH in Haiti and wanted to help however he could. He believed that if more Christians in the States knew about the station, they would support it. So he decided to publish a brochure. He made a special trip to the 4VEH studios with his camera, taking pictures of the staff, equipment and listeners.

He wanted a photograph of Engineer Mardy Picazo and decided to include the whole family. That caused quite a stir in the household, dressing the children in their Sunday best, and Rev. Latham patiently waited even for "the Mrs." to trim Mardy's hair. At last they trouped out into the yard to arrange themselves for the picture. Everyone was sparkling.

Then Rev. Latham noticed that "the Mrs." had forgotten to change her shoes...Well, they wouldn't show much anyway, and he didn't want to embarrass her.

It was some months later that Rev. Latham was busy at his desk in Atlanta when suddenly the idea invaded his thoughts, *The reason Mrs. Picazo didn't change her shoes is because she didn't have any more to change to.*

"Is that true, Lord?" He was shocked. Right then and there he reached for his checkbook, wrote out a check, and along with the brief note sent it to Haiti.

But that is not all. Some weeks after I had bought my shoes, a box came for me through customs from the Post Office. In it was a stylish pair of dress pumps from Mama--my exact size.

1952   4VEH STUDIOS IN THE CHURCH
By Rachael Picazo

Engineer Paul Shirk had carefully designed the radio rooms at the back of the new tabernacle. I was astonished to see that the walls in the main studio were in undulating curves of sound-absorbent Celotex, expertly fastened to frames of differing diameters. It gave the effect of vertical corrugated roofing, but with much larger, flatter humps. A thick carpet covered the floor, and the ceiling slanted so there were no parallel surfaces to cause echo. The acoustics were excellent.

The main studio boasted a baby grand piano and a spinet organ. High-quality microphones rested on stands, one on a boom. It was more sophisticated than any studio I had seen in the States.

But even while these facilities were in use, a whole new building across the compound was taking shape. By the time our family arrived in mid 1952, the new structure was under roof and the inside was being finished. After Paul Shirk returned to the States, Mardy continued the work. In deep ditches he buried the heavy insulated cables that carried the power from the motor house to the new facilities. Antenna towers were erected close by, and, of course, all the equipment had to be moved as well. By December 1953, the transmitter and radio instruments were in place at the new location.

THE NEW 4VEH STUDIOS
By Aldean Saufley

I had helped an evangelist friend in the USA with some radio, but never had broadcast experience beyond that. In 1957 when I looked at a photograph of the 4VEH studio building in Haiti, I tried to imagine what was inside. I failed completely. The long front wall with a couple of windows and doors disguised a complicated inside layout. Mr. Shirk, as a true engineer, designed the studio to have good acoustics without echo. As a result, the inside rooms fit together at peculiar angles.

36

Later, when we decided to do some remodeling, Edwin Moore (who worked with us two years during the '60s) attempted to draw a floor plan of the building. I think he almost tore his hair out trying to measure all the angles Mr. Shirk had put into its construction. For a starter, Edwin found that the main studio had five sides — not four — and went on from there to figure out the rest of the complicated pattern.

Slashing diagonally across the center of the building ran a "strip" in which were designated three spaces: the active control room, an adjacent area for a future second control room, and the tape library.

On one side of the "strip" was a spacious studio lined with Celotex wallboard. The baby grand piano had been moved into it, as well as the Hammond spinet organ donated to the station by John and Romaine Woodhouse. Using that organ, Mrs. DeMille had recorded several reels of sacred organ music that moved from one selection to another without a break.

The control room console was built by Engineer Shirk, and the tape machines were of the home variety, not professional units. A cardinal rule for radio operators was that one always had standby music ready in case of technical problems, so one player was always cued with a DeMille organ tape. I am sure our listeners often said (as well as staff members at home) when organ music suddenly came on, "Uh-oh! Problems again!" In my own mind I called those tapes "trouble music."

A record case in the control room held the entire station music library: about a hundred 78 rpm discs which were used for daily song request programs and a literal "handful" (since I could put my hand around the pile) of 33 rpm records, and some classical and a few sacred pieces.

On the other side of the diagonal "strip" was the transmitter room, and at one end a smaller section was closed off to form a radio shop with work bench and spare parts cabinet. Since there were no offices in the original building, secretarial work was done in missionary homes.

The transmitter room was filled with fieldbuilt equipment that reached audiences as far away as Australia, New Zealand, Finland, Norway, Denmark, Sweden, and Germany, as well as the United States.

Stewart West, who was on the field when I arrived, knew which frequencies could reach certain audiences at different hours of the day. We had one frequency on the 31 meter band for our largest transmitter, a frequency on 49 meters for our 50 watt "peanut whistle," which the Lord used to reach audiences in so many parts of the world, a fixed frequency on the broadcast band, and a transmitter that changed frequencies at different times of the day to target specific audiences.

There were several small towers around the compound, but these were not antennas in themselves; they supported the ends of overhead wires which were positioned to send radio signals in various directions. Since these antennas—even the one for the broadcast band frequency—produced more sky waves than ground waves, Radio 4VEH was largely "without honor in its own country," reaching around the world but skipping over Haiti except for parts of the country where our 49 meter band frequency could be received.

In 1968 4VEH added a long overdue addition to the crowded studios of Radio 4VEH. A 10x40 foot annex, built on the side of the studio, will accommodate a tape library for approximately 16,000 tapes, which come to the station at the rate of over 100 per month. The new wing also houses the news department. The entire annex was paid for by missionaries on the Haiti field.

In 1976 another annex was constructed on the back of the building to house a new French control room, studio, and newsroom.

1980 saw the construction of a new reception/shop annex on the other side of the original building and remodeling of the offices.

1957   **WESTWARD HO!!**
                              By Mardy Picazo

When 4VEH started broadcasting, it was on the 31 meter shortwave band. Soon we were receiving letters from listeners all over the world. Though we were not a powerful radio station, the fact that we were broadcasting from Haiti—and in English—was enough to attract numerous shortwave listener hobbyists.

These are people who like to tune around on their shortwave radio receivers picking up rare or faraway stations. They carefully note the time and frequency, the conditions under which they heard the station, the details they were able to hear, i.e., music or speaking, content of speech, the clarity and strength of the signal, and other information that might be useful to a broadcaster, and send it to the station. In turn, the radio station is asked to send them a verification card acknowledging that it was indeed their station that was heard. This was called a QSL Card, and people collected them, sometimes by the hundreds. It was a strong motivation for them to write to 4VEH—and we benefited from the information they gave.

We soon saw the necessity of designing our own 4VEH QSL card and, before long, were sending them out by the dozens. Sometimes the reports proved that it was not our station they had heard. We kept accurate logs of our broadcast days so we could identify the day and hour anyone reported having heard us. Several publications for these hobbyists told of 4VEH.

Among the first who wrote us in 1952 was Stewart West, a U.S. Navy sailor at the Fleet Weather Central, NAS, located at Norfolk, Virginia. He started suggesting that we might try using other frequencies to escape interference that was too overwhelming for our meager signal.

In 1954 he wrote to us from the USS Wright (CVL49) in the far Pacific, on the other side of the world from us. He was involved in getting weather for his ship so he had access to powerful shortwave radio equipment, and he gave us reports from wherever his ship went.

The Haitian government allowed us to request any frequency we desired to test on, but we could not officially use it until it had been approved by world authorities in radio broadcasting. However, because of this young man's faithful monitoring of our broadcasts, we were able to find good locations on a very crowded shortwave band.

Stewart West continued this interest in 4VEH even after he had finished his stint in the Navy. In fact, he spent a month at 4VEH after he got out of the Navy in early May 1955.

A couple of years later, 1957, our Picazo family needed to return to the States on furlough since we had been in Haiti five years. During that time God had blessed us with three little daughters—Rachel, Paula, and Suzanna—besides our two sons, Esteban and Daniel, who had come to Haiti with us. We knew we needed to touch base with our family and friends in the States, but our staff was still so small.

Charles Bustin was acting field director in the absence of his father. He was knowledgeable in the running of the diesels, and I gave him instruction in the operation of the transmitters. But he often had pressing duties that took him away from the compound. I began to pray for God to send someone who could take over my engineering duties full time for the year while I was gone.

Suddenly Stewart West came to mind. He had had adequate training to be able to operate the transmitters we were using, and I felt confident that he could manage the rest quite well. I contacted him about this possibility.

So Stewart came and I was able to walk him through the normal operation of the station with no difficulty. This fine Christian man, who began his friendship with us while serving in the U.S. Navy, proved to be God's provision at Radio 4VEH until I returned.

Many years later, Stewart and his wife Edith, a competent registered nurse, came back to Haiti with their two daughters and ministered for some time. They have continued their vital interest in the work of OMS in Haiti and, especially, Radio 4VEH.

1958   THE COMING OF OMS AND MFMI
By Rachael Picazo

From the time Bro. Bustin first contacted that savage tribe in New Guinea in 1948, he knew that he must minister to those people. In fact, it was at that time he began to establish a church for them, a clinic, and a school where they could be taught the Gospel of the Lord Jesus Christ.

But Bro. Bustin also knew God had given him the concept of Radio 4VEH, so he came back to Haiti to see it become a reality. But with his thoughts more and more focused on New Guinea, he began to pray for some other missionary society to take over the work he had started in Haiti.

There were a couple of criteria he set for such an organization:

41

1. They must be of the Arminian-Wesleyan doctrine.

2. They must continue the ministry of Radio 4VEH.

Several organizations approached him, but, though some of them fulfilled the first requirement of doctrine, none of them wanted the responsibility of the radio station...but 4VEH was the "apple of his eye."

In 1954 Dr. William Gillam, a young missionary with OMS (The Oriental Missionary Society) in Colombia, South America, visited Haiti. His travels brought him to spend the night at Bro. Bustin's compound. As he entered the big French-colonial gates beside the tabernacle, he sensed that OMS was going to have something to do with this place.

Radio 4VEH was having a tremendous impact among the Christians of Colombia at that time, and Dr. Gillam was impressed. When he learned that the station and property were available, he began to ask the Lord to open the way for it to be transferred to OMS.

In January 1958, a delegation from OMS visited Bro. Bustin and his work in Haiti, especially Radio 4VEH: William (Bill) Gillam, Eldon Turnidge, Byron Crouse, and also, as radio engineer consultant, Clarence Moore. Dave Graffenberger, then a high school student on his way to Colombia with Eldon Turnidge, came along. Harry Burr and his wife, Eleanor, also came by Haiti at that moment on their way back from visiting Colombia.

The delegation began initial negotiations with Bro. Bustin for the Oriental Missionary Society to assume responsibility for the radio station, the compound church, and the La Rue outstation five miles away. Bro. Bustin's numerous other churches scattered across the country were taken under the umbrellas of the Nazarenes and Wesleyans.

The delegation reported favorably to the Executive Board of the Oriental Missionary Society, which voted that summer to take Haiti as another field, buying the properties from the East and West Indies Bible Mission. OMS's Men For Missions organization pledged to underwrite the expenses for the expansion of Radio 4VEH.

In September 1958, Mr. Eldon Turnidge, president of Men For Missions, flew to Haiti in his own plane with Bill Gillam, director appointed for this new field, where the transaction was officially completed. The president of Haiti, Dr. Francois Duvalier, welcomed OMS in a 25-minute interview with Dr. William Gillam, Eldon Turnidge, and missionaries Mardy Picazo and Charles Bustin. The meeting had been arranged by Haitian Senator Arthur Bonhomme. President Duvalier said, "I believe in God, I believe in Jesus Christ, and I know you are the right people for my country."

Larry Burr, Executive Secretary of MFM, wrote in The Missionary Standard, December 1958:

"Everything that you read concerning 4VEH shows the miracle work of our Lord, and we praise Him for His seal upon this ministry."

1958   BRO. BUSTIN'S FAREWELL GIFT
By Rachael Picazo

Bro. Bustin's heart was at ease that the radio station God had told him to build would prosper under the leadership of the Oriental Missionary Society. He could set his face toward the thriving work in New Guinea. Yet, he had forged strong friendships with the Haitians, and he wanted to leave them with a gift. He asked God to send a revival.

Thus, shortly before he left, Bro. Bustin, with Pastor Napo at his side as translator, began a series of meetings in the big Vaudreuil tabernacle. People came as always when there was a service at the church. But these services were different even from the first night. The second night as the invitation was given, such a spirit of repentance swept over the congregation that almost half the people rushed forward to pray around the altar at the front.

During the week a man who worked in the Mission garden brought back a grubbing hoe he had taken. A woman who helped in one of the homes returned a blouse she had confiscated off the line. A man walked several miles into the country to apologize to his brother and heal the estrangement that had kept them apart for several years. It is very hard for anyone to say, "I am sorry. I have done wrong." That had to be the work of God's Spirit.

By the third night the church was packed. Again, the power of the Lord was present as people came forward eagerly to repent and then stayed to tell of the deliverance God had given them from their burdens of sin. Songs and testimonies rang out in the church until two o'clock in the morning.

The following night, there was standing room only in the tabernacle. The windows were crammed, and crowds stood outside the doors. The song service began, but before Bro. Bustin could begin his message, people began rushing to the altar. The seekers prayed so loudly and earnestly that there was no thought of trying to proceed with a structured service. People were pleading without shame for God's forgiveness. Christians knelt beside them, helping them pray, rejoicing with them as they found the salvation they sought. The mass cries of prayer continued on and on.

I needed to tuck my children into bed, so I left the service before the lights went out at ten o'clock. But when everything was quiet at home, I made my way by flashlight back to the service. It was about one o'clock in the morning. The church was still half full, and a kerosene lamp burned on the platform.

The tabernacle was 40-feet wide, and the wooden bench altar ran the width of the sanctuary at the front. There I saw a sight I shall never forget— people dancing in the Spirit of the Lord. On one side of the altar about a dozen men were pacing in stately ecstasy, lifting their hands heavenward, praising God quietly with tears streaming down their cheeks. On the other side were women, old and young, looking upward, arms raised in adoration, gracefully marching back and forth. I especially remember Carmen, who was only about 13 years old, with such joy on her face it actually glowed. I was mesmerized. I don't know how long I sat there, wonder and delight washing over me as I watched. The worship continued all night long and into the next day.

During the last few nights of the revival, one service continued until time for the next to begin. Victories won through prayer there will ring through eternity.

NOTE: Rev. Green Tolbert Bustin died in Florida in July, 1995 at the age of 92. Mr. Paul Shirk, engineer, died in Oregon on November 12, 1996 at the age of 89.

1959   **SUZANE**
                        By Miriam Stockton

Suzane Georges trudged along the road that Sunday evening in March with a heavy heart. For three weeks her 18-month-old son, Serge, had been very sick, fever and convulsions wracking his thin frame. In his delirium he would throw everything away within reach. Neither Suzane nor the child had a full night's sleep all that time.

Following the custom of her people, Suzane had taken the baby to the witch doctor. He concocted a foul-smelling potion for Suzanne to use in bathing the child. But the liquid burned the baby's skin, making him writhe in agony. Then the witch doctor told her to put leaves of a sweet orange tree on the boy's head. These and other "remedies" were tried, all to no avail. Serge grew steadily worse.

Meanwhile, Suzane used all her possessions to pay the witch doctor. After she had given him all her money, he demanded her goats, her furniture, and even her clothes. Finally nothing was left.

At last the witch doctor told her that a demon was tormenting the child, and he demanded that she buy a piece of paper on which he could write a letter to the demon. This would cost two cents, but by this time Suzane had no money at all, and it was several days before she was able to borrow the coins.

Now she was walking to the city five miles away to buy the paper for the letter. This was her last hope, as little Serge was very near death. Suddenly Suzane heard music. She noticed that she was walking past a large building. It was time for the regular Sunday evening service in our 4VEH church, and the congregation had just started singing so she stopped to listen to the words:

"Afflictions are everywhere,
And we cannot understand
How God leads us to arrive
In the blessed promised land;
But He guides us with His eye,
And we'll follow 'til we die;
Yes, we'll understand it better bye and bye."

Suzane was touched by the joy she sensed in the singing of these people. "Oh, if only I had my baby with me," she thought, "I would take him into the church right now. Perhaps they could help me."

But her baby was not there so she trudged on down the road consoling herself, "Surely the witch doctor can heal him tonight."

When she arrived at the house of the witch doctor later that night, she begged him to promise that the baby would get better. He assured her Serge would be well as soon as she put the letter he had written on his head.

But that night Suzane saw that the paper didn't help. In anguish she watched little Serge grow worse, the convulsions increase. It seemed now that he would certainly die. She kept vigil by his pallet through the long night and toward morning made a decision that whether the baby lived or died, she was through with the witch doctor. She exclaimed aloud, "This is the end!"

The neighbor women heard this and passed the word from house to house, "She said, 'This is the end.' The baby must be dead."

But to Suzane it was the turning point. She had decided to transfer her confidence from the witch doctor to the Christians. In the little settlement where Suzane lived, surrounded by witchcraft, was one Christian man. So, early the next morning Suzane went looking for him. He told her, "We will send for Pastor Napoleon. He will come to pray with you."

Napoleon was our Haitian radio pastor. That day he was unable to go, so he sent Joseph, one of our radio control operators at 4VEH. Joseph explained to Suzane how to become a Christian, and she gave her heart to Jesus.

Then Joseph prayed for the little boy. Instantly his convulsions stopped and he dropped into a peaceful sleep for the first time in three weeks. He slept all day and through the night. On the following morning the child woke up well, asking for food.

It was apparent immediately that Suzane was a changed person. She had been one to stand on the hillside where the paths crossed and argue with the women who walked past carrying their baskets of vegetables to market. Now she took her stance at the same place, telling everyone about the peace God had given her, the forgiveness from her sins. Little Serge who had been so ill scampered about her well and lively, proof of God's powerful grace.

Needless to say, that kind of salvation got people's attention. It was not long before Suzane's neighbors also wanted such a transformation. Within a few days 15 others had come to know Jesus Christ as their Savior and Lord.

AFTER SUZANE'S CONVERSION
By Rachael Picazo

A spirit of revival has been electrifying our Haitian church here at Radio 4VEH for the past five months since Suzane Georges was dramatically saved.

Last Sunday Pastor Napoleon didn't have a chance to preach because of the spontaneous testimonies of excited new Christians, among them the very witch doctor to whom Suzane had taken her sick baby.

He himself had become very ill. In his desperation he remembered that great God who had healed Suzane's son when his own remedies failed, so he sent word for the Christians to come pray for him. He, too, accepted Jesus as his Savior, and he also recovered.

There he stood in the church, a wizened little man with bald head, wreathed in smiles. Everyone was eager to see him, myself included. Pastor Napo asked him his name. He replied, "My real name is Durant, but everyone knows me as 'Fatra.'"

At that the whole church burst out laughing, for that is the word for "trash."

"No, no!" Pastor Napo objected, "that is not your name any more. You are a new man in Christ. Now we're going to call you 'Frère Prop' (cleaned up)."

48

Why is this spirit of revival continuing month after month? I believe part of it is because of faithful prayers. At four o'clock every morning the Vaudreuil church bell rings to remind the Christians that prayer meeting starts in half an hour. At 4:30 they gather in the sanctuary for an hour of singing praises and praying.

Perhaps another reason for the revival is the active witnessing of the church. In the evenings believers meet at different homes for services, and almost every night another person accepts Christ. Once, while a service was being held at Pastor Napoleon's house, someone told him that a man wanted to be saved but that he didn't have clothes to come to the gathering.

Starting the group on a song, Pastor Napo slipped away and searched in the box of used clothing sent by Christians from the United States and Canada, which by this time was seriously depleted. However, he did find a pair of women's slacks and a shirt. Tucking these under his arm, he went out to the brush where the man was listening from afar.

He was indeed almost naked, with only a little ragged cloth around his loins. He was overcome with gratefulness for the clothing. Now he could attend the service. Later he came forward and was saved.

1959   **THE LAND IS IN POSSESSION**
By Mardy Picazo

With the coming of OMS and their enthusiastic Men For Missions arm came plans to expand the Radio 4VEH ministry.

1. 4VEH needed a new location for the transmitter site.

2. 4VEH needed new and larger transmitters.

3. 4VEH needed a new transmitter building and steel towers for the antennas.

After much work at Port-au-Prince with the government officials, we were granted a plot of government land where we could put the 4VEH antennas and transmitters near the ocean. Moving to a site close to salt water would increase the effectiveness of our outreach on the standard broadcast band because of the increased conductivity of the ground. Also, it would take us away from the foot of the mountain where we were partly barred from our shortwave broadcasts, giving us a wide and low horizon.

The plot of ground granted us was half a mile outside Cap-Haitien, a strip about 300 feet wide and half a mile long, flanked by the ocean on one side and a salt marsh on the other. There would be power from the electric company and even city water available. Accessibility was excellent since we would be on the main road to the airport. It seemed to be perfect for our operation, except perhaps we would be a little tight on having enough width for our ground wires around the towers. But, all in all, it was far better than what we had back at the mission compound.

A few days later, our presence was requested for a conference concerning the new property. We met at the Hotel Christophe where this person was staying, and he informed us that we would not be able to continue with our plans on the use of that section. He, himself, had been granted a large parcel of land, including our piece, to develop into an expanded airport project. However, he said that his allowance included a quantity of land that he would not be using, and we could have our plot anywhere in that area. He showed us where to go, so we went to see what this new move would do to our plans.

The area was near the little town of Petite Anse, on the opposite side of the main road from the airport, about three miles across the bay from Cap-Haitien. We drove as far as our vehicle could go. Then when the road ended at the cemetery, we got out and walked. The narrow path was along a very old colonial road that had become overgrown with brush and thorny plants.

As we were looking around, a tall, very muscular Haitian man came up and offered to help us find what we were looking for. He said his name was Edner Hilaire, and he lived in that village we had just come through. With his machete he widened the path so the thorns wouldn't make the passage so uncomfortable. Soon we came to the edge of the salt marsh. We could see some places that were above the water level, suitable for building. The tide marks showed how far the ocean would be likely to come.

A very wide area stretched before us to the ocean bay, which was covered with sea mango and mesquite-like plants that thrived in salty ground. It was perfect for our antenna ground wires. I had checked the statistics in my engineering books and found that a salt marsh was rated at 5000 in conductivity, where we only had 12 for the soil on the mission compound. The only place the conductivity could be better would be in the middle of the ocean. Here was all the ground area we needed in a very desirable location for the transmitter and towers. The Lord had again given us more than we had asked for, or even known how to ask. And...we had found Edner.

We contracted Edner as our foreman to clear off the brush growing there. In the course of a week, this very capable young man, respected in this community, had not only directed his crew in clearing the nine acres where our building would be located, but also had opened a wide road leading from the center of the adjoining village. Although Edner was not yet a Christian, he won for us the goodwill of the neighbors and property holders, making it possible for us to obtain additional private land comparatively easily as needed. The work we gave to 48 local men was deeply appreciated by these destitute people. It is hard for us to imagine their poverty.

One of the divisions of the American Point Four program working around Cap-Haitien cooperated with us in allowing us to use their heavy bulldozer when it was not busy in their program. In half a day the bulldozer took out almost all the stumps in two acres, leveled it, and completed the preparation for the new building. Then it did a considerable amount of work besides, clearing the stumps and leveling the 1000-foot driveway to the property.

The mayor of Petite Anse voluntarily came to the location and made a speech urging the people to cooperate with us and to give us a road through. So the property holders on either side set their lines back to give us about 40 feet of clearance. The mayor also told the police to handle anyone who might offer any trouble.

So the new transmitter property was cleared, and we felt it would be proper to have a ceremony dedicating it to the Lord. A Men For Missions group was to come to Haiti at that time, as well as the founder of MFM, Dr. Dwight Ferguson. Edner, our foreman, went around the community at Petite Anse telling all the people about the meeting.

There was an air of expectancy and curiosity among the black-skinned inhabitants as they came in from all directions. They listened with respect to the Zionaires and Jimmy Willis, the black American tenor, as they sang about the Lord Jesus Christ. Some of the Christian businessmen from the States told of how Christ had changed their lives. Now they wanted to help others find Jesus by coming here and testifying to them and by helping to put up a radio station that would tell the world Jesus saves.

To close the service, Dr. Dwight Ferguson gave a talk and prayer of dedication. Under the leadership of the Holy Spirit, he gave an invitation to those who had never received Jesus as their Savior to step forward so that he might pray with them.

While the Christians bowed their heads, one stepped out. It was Edner, our foreman. He was quickly followed by another young man, and then seven others came forward to surrender their lives to Jesus. And it did not stop there, for several others came from the audience and said that they, too, had accepted Christ as Savior where they were standing.

Three days later another walked six miles to our compound to find Jesus as a result of that service. Truly God set His seal on this move of Radio 4VEH at the dedication of our new transmitter site, February 20, 1959.

1959   THE NEW TRANSMITTER BUILDING
By Mardy Picazo

For more than a year, definite plans had been made for the construction of the new transmitter building for Radio 4VEH. At the 1958 OMS Convention at Winona Lake, IN, Men For Missions voted to back the project with the finances necessary. An architect drew up detailed plans for the design, others of the MFM sent a load of building materials, and many gave substantial gifts. Yet there were other obstacles to overcome.

The first difficulty was in obtaining possession of the plot of ground the Haitian government had earlier granted us for the house and radio towers. But at last another suitable location was found and secured. The building materials coming from the States were next. They sat in customs several months. Then after much prayer, we were given a special franchise allowing them to enter duty-free.

The structure was to be of cement block with steel-reinforced concrete roof, metal doors and window frames—as termite-proof and saltwater-resistant as possible. Now our next big hurdle was a construction engineer to put up the building. Who knew where to find such a man?

Mr. Frank Allen (affectionately called "Uncle Frank" at our OMS Headquarters in Winona Lake), though retired, was enthusiastic for OMS's outreach in Haiti. He firmly believed that Jack Endicott was God's man for this job.

Jack was an expert in concrete work and he knew construction from A to Z. His business was booming at Winona Lake. But when Uncle Frank approached him about the Haiti project, Jack replied, "It is impossible for me to go, especially now!"

But Frank challenged him, "Will you think it over and pray about it?"

Immediately Uncle Frank gathered a few friends and they prayed earnestly for God to show Jack what he should do. From that moment, Jack reported later, the task in Haiti kept intruding into his thoughts. While sitting in church the following Sunday, he decided to borrow a large sum of money to donate for the transmitter building project. But this did not give him peace.

In the meantime, Uncle Frank had left for Haiti, willing to go see what he could do to help erect the building. But though he had had some experience himself, he soon recognized that this project called for the skill of a master builder.

Back at Winona Lake, Jack Endicott began to see that he could not reason this matter away, but for real peace of mind he must go to Haiti. He sent a cable that he was coming, and we met him at the airport. The building project was on its way again.

Jack was in Haiti. He had left his business, his tools, his partners, his loved ones—but not his God! When the enemy came upon him like a flood and threatened to defeat him with the overwhelming problems that confronted him, the Holy Spirit gently reminded him that He had called and would help him accomplish the task.

The necessary local construction materials were hard to find, if not impossible, and many substitutions had to be improvised. First of all, the only concrete blocks available were "green" or still uncured. Every time we picked one up we didn't know if it would come apart in our hands. But we went ahead to start the construction.

Jack Endicott and Frank Allen, missionaries Mardy Picazo and Kent Ragsdale, along with six Haitian laborers, made up the crew. We got up each morning at four o'clock to start work at daybreak and kept at it, with quick sandwiches for lunch, until it was too dark to see. God marvelously protected us and gave us strength.

Since the concrete roof would be so heavy, it was essential that the walls be strong...but with green blocks? Jack put steel rods with quick-hardening grout every few feet inside the wall. The sloppy concrete ran down through the holes of the block and around the rods, strengthening the whole thing firm as it cured. Actually those walls were stronger than the specifications called for. (Many years later, when we needed access windows for our new antenna cables, we had a terrible time cutting through that hard, strong wall.)

At every turn, new decisions had to be made and, to top it all, there were breakdowns in the equipment. But God always worked things around so that the substitutions came out better than the original plans.

We had been able to buy iron rails in Haiti from a company taking out an old railroad bed. Those rails were the basis of our roof trusses, with rebar welded to them. Jack formed them on our missionary compound, then transported them on a long trailer by back roads to the construction site eight miles away. They spanned the 24-foot width of the building and extended to make a 4-foot overhang on each side.

It was an enormous undertaking to form up the underside for the concrete roof to be poured, enclosing the trusses. Jack used intricate scaffolding and galvanized corrugated roofing, designing everything so that when the 2½ inch-thick concrete roof cured, it would compress into a strong waterproof slab. Jack kept finding ways of doing things or substituting so the whole project was successful.

When the concrete had cured and we went to remove the scaffolding and forms that held it, there were termite trails already going up those ten-foot walls to some little wooden wedges that had been used in leveling the forms.

After thirty days, when Jack and Frank had to return to the States, the new transmitter building stood with all walls up, the cement roof and canopy finished, and the windows and doors installed. Some have remarked that it would be hard to find a better-built building in this entire area. We feel that it is a monument to God's mighty grace, a remarkable answer to prayer.

It was not completed, for our new, powerful transmitters had to go in first, before the floor and partitions were put in place and the building was finished. But we were encouraged to believe that God would complete the work that had begun for the new Radio 4VEH expanded outreach to the multiplied thousands.

1959   **FLASH! PRAISE THE LORD!**
                The Missionary Standard

Again God had provided for the needs of Radio 4VEH. Through the Charitable Contributions Committee of The Cummins Diesel Engine Company of Columbus, Indiana, $936 worth of new diesel parts had been given to the station for a complete overhaul of our engines at the transmitter site in Haiti. We wished to state publicly our deep appreciation to the

Cummins Company for their magnificent cooperation in making 4VEH a great Christian voice.

In addition, we were happily surprised by the gift of a 15 kilowatt diesel generator by Mr. Clarence Moore of International Radio and Electronics Corp. of Elkhart, Indiana. This was another gift from Mr. Moore who has stood with us in the rehabilitation program of the station.

1959   **HOME ALONE**
                 By Rachael Picazo

Our five children were well aware that their father was not at home those five months. Esteban, the oldest, was twelve, and Suzanna, the youngest was four. They all remember and sometimes speak of it. The children and I didn't actually put hands on to help build the new transmitters for 4VEH, but by being home alone without Mardy, we were involved in the radio station receiving new transmitters.

Actually, when Mardy left Haiti in mid-September, 1959, he expected to be gone only six weeks. There was a Latin American "Congress" of Gospel Communications in Colombia, South America, which included the Christian printing presses and missionary radio stations of all Latin America. Our radio station is a member of the Pan-American Christian Network of missionary radio stations, and since Bill Gillam, our director, could not go to the meeting, they appointed Mardy to go as the OMS representative from Radio 4VEH.

According to Mardy's letters, the Congress was inspirational, as well as providing a storehouse of important information he could use at 4VEH. It was all in Spanish, and he heard Dr. Montano, "The Monk Who Lived Again," preach several times.

Since he was so close to missionary radio station HCJB at Quito, Ecuador, when the "Congress" was over, he went to visit there. He gained valuable information about distributing transistor radios and even about how we could assemble some of them.

Mardy was shown every courtesy, and when his hosts learned he was from 4VEH, they showed him their wiring, took him to the site of their transmitters and towers, which is quite some distance from their studios, and interviewed him on their program, "Caribbean Call." They gave him seven minutes to tell about Radio 4VEH and then made more comments after he was through. I missed it all. I didn't even know he was going to Quito until after he was already back.

One of the missionaries in Haiti heard part of that program and told me about it. He had just tuned in HCJB by chance, and they were talking about Mardy and Radio 4VEH!

When Mardy returned to Colombia, he visited OMS churches in Medellín and Cristalina and some of the villages. He traveled by boat through dangerous rapids and rode airplanes across the mountains. One incident in Mardy's own words follows:

I had the privilege of visiting an evangelical church in Medellín, Colombia, and was presented to the congregation as being from Radio 4VEH. I noticed a bright-faced couple sitting on the front seat. After the service they greeted me as an old friend, and the lady said she wanted to tell me a story. Her husband stood beside her but said nothing.

She told how she had been a Christian for many years but her husband had been against her, being part of a group of militant fanatics in her area.

On one occasion he and his cronies had surrounded a little evangelical church where there was a service going on. They barricaded its doors and windows, piled dry wood against it all around, then set fire to the building. They stood around watching to make sure no one escaped. As the church was enveloped in flames, they heard the Christians inside singing, "Shall We Gather at the River." The singing continued until the burning roof crushed them to death.

When the man returned home, he was deeply troubled. For many days he was silent and morose, but finally one day, as his wife was listening to 4VEH, he told her what he had done and asked her to pray for him. She was shocked, yet happy to know he wanted to repent.

His wife persuaded him to listen to the broadcasts from Radio 4VEH, and he was converted. One of the programs they heard daily was my Spanish "La Hora de Devocion" (Devotional Hour). She said he then became a very active Christian and had already led many to the Lord.

The lady had been doing the talking, but now her husband stepped forward and asserted that everything she had said was true. He said that the most important thing he wanted to accomplish was to win as many people for Jesus as he was responsible for killing in that fire.

As for the plans under way for Radio 4VEH, the new transmitters for the seashore location had been in the process of being built for some months, but the work was slow. Our directors felt it would speed things if Mardy went back to the

United States to help complete them. So Mardy flew directly from Colombia, South America, to Louisville, Kentucky, where Clarence Henson was building one of the transmitters. However, Mr. Henson became seriously ill and had to be hospitalized.

The project was transferred to Elkhart, Indiana, where Mr. Clarence Moore of International Radio Electronics Corporation, provided materials and a place to construct the two new 2500-watt transmitters for 4VEH.

At Christmas I wrote home:

The only thing missing about Christmas was Mardy. We did have a thrill the day after Christmas when we were able to talk to him by ham radio, and he told of the many kind friends who had gone out of their way to make his day a happy one. The family that had invited him to dinner asked him to show his slides of Haiti, so he had a little missionary service with the family gathering.

In Haiti we focused our attention on God's gift of His Son. After what He has done for us, it was a privilege to bear loneliness so His work can be accomplished.

FEBRUARY 22, 1960--Mardy arrived back in Haiti, having completed the electrical part of the two new 2500-watt transmitters. The cabinets were still being finished in Elkhart, Indiana.

The engineers had much work to do in Haiti, preparing the new location at Petite Anse for the arrival of the new transmitters. As each hurdle loomed into view, we prayed and God provided what was needed.

The new transmitters arrived in May, all dismantled. Then began the long hours of reassembling and testing. In the final weeks, engineer Kent Ragsdale became the proud father of a second son, so he was necessarily diverted to work closer to home. But just at that time, Clyde Moore arrived and provided the collaboration Mardy needed.

Mardy and Clyde pushed themselves night and day, racing against the deadline they had set for themselves of October 1. Some nights didn't end until 5:30 the next morning. But along with the talent God gave these men, He also gave them genuine love for radio work. Their enthusiasm never dampened, and their vision never dimmed. The last night they didn't get home until two o'clock, but Mardy was up again at 4:30 to be there when the transmitters were turned on with their first regularly scheduled broadcast at 5:30 in the morning.

How beautiful—how powerfully beautiful it sounded when it came in on the radios! We were on the air with the new transmitters. It was October 2, 1960.

Since that day, our listener letters from all over the United States, Canada, the West Indies Islands, Europe, and other places, have more than tripled.

Newly-installed shortwave directional antennas further increased our effective power more than eight times, boosting it up to an effective 15,000 watts.

May 1960   4VEH TOWER--170 FEET
By Rachael Picazo

At an OMS convention in Florida in March 1960, Major Kermit F. Stanfil of Orlando, Florida, was challenged in a Men For Missions meeting by the need for our antenna erection. He is a retired army engineer and had had such experience in Germany.

He planned to come to Haiti, and bring a helper at his own expense, to see the tower go up. But later when he was not able to come, he paid the expenses for two professional tower men to make the trip to Haiti to get the job done.

They arrived Thursday evening, May 5, and by the evening of the next day the 170-foot steel tower stood completely erected! The last section was pulled up at dusk and bolted into place in the dark.

Only those of us who knew the problems and dangers involved in improvising where materials were lacking can fully appreciate the supernatural providences of God that the job was done so quickly, with not one worker suffering so much as a scratch.

1960   JEEP GOES TO HAITI
OMS Outreach Praise

Response to the need of Haiti for clothing and shoes was very gratifying. Twelve barrels were put on the Jeep truck that appeared on TV and was advertised over the radio. This truck met a vital need at Radio Station 4VEH. (Amen!)

January 1961   ON THE AIR
By Kent Ragsdale

For the past few weeks Radio 4VEH has been "ON THE AIR" with our two new transmitters. We have been broadcasting with a power of 2500 watts in the standard broadcast band with a frequency of 1035 kc and with a power of 2500 watts in the 49-meter band with a frequency of 6000 kc.

Not only is the Gospel being heard more effectively in Haiti, but we have been receiving many good reports from other parts of the world as well. One excerpt from Turks Island: "I listen to your service every Sunday afternoon in my home, and when I go out for a drive, I pick up the same service. Your transmission is loud and clear in our locality, very clear. I enjoy it greatly...Brothers and friends, pray for me. I'll pray for you and your services likewise."

There has been a great amount of prayer and work in the past months bringing our endeavor here to the beginning of new and greater service for the Lord. Mardy Picazo and I began installing the transmitters when they arrived here in May of 1960.

Antennas were erected and feed wires were installed between the transmitters and antennas. It was necessary to make many adaptations in the equipment to meet the existing conditions here in Haiti.

For a while the work was held up by a breakdown of our power generating equipment, which is not reliable. We are praying for the Lord's guidance and help in this matter.

Mr. Clyde Moore's arrival in July was a very great help in getting the transmitters on the air. Clyde will be working with us here in Haiti for the next two years.

With the realization of increased facilities, we are challenged to increase our programming time. Pray with us that the Lord will provide the necessary programs and personnel.

1961   **DIESEL GENERATOR**
By Rachael Picazo

We praise God for the brand new 75 kw diesel generator that has arrived here at Cap-Haitien for us! A very generous donation on the part of the Cummins Company itself for part of the cost, plus gifts by faithful friends, have made possible this very valuable and necessary unit. It is four and a half tons of machinery that will supply electricity for our transmitters.

Much prayer has gone up for this engine over the months and even years, for the electrical plants we have already in Haiti are old and constantly needing repair. This new engine didn't come one day too soon, for it had no sooner been deposited in the motor house than the old diesel broke down and we are unable to get parts immediately. So the new diesel was promptly put into operation, meeting the emergency that would have meant several days off the air with the radio broadcasts.

February 23, 1961
DEDICATION OF TRANSMITTER BUILDING
By Rachael Picazo

Two new 2500-watt transmitters in a new building at a more favorable radio site—this was the project taken on by Men For Missions when OMS assumed responsibility for Radio Station 4VEH in Haiti. It was fitting that 21 members of MFM should be present to help us celebrate its completion at the special dedication service February 23, 1961.

Of course, a lot of finishing touches were made on the building so it would be as attractive as possible: painting, putting down ceramic tile on the floor and sound tile on the ceiling, erecting partition walls, etc. The place sparkled as much as we could make it when the great day of February 23 dawned bright and clear. That was important, because rain would have been damaging on our dirt road, not to mention the people gathered outside in the yard for the celebration.

At two o'clock the service began with a stirring rendition of the Haitian National Anthem by the Cap-Haitien army band, followed by the singing of the United States National Anthem by all our American friends present. There were several fine speeches and excellent music, one number being sung by the

64

choir from our compound national church under the direction of 4VEH Program Director Miriam Stockton.

Mardy Picazo, as radio manager, gave a welcoming speech in behalf of all the staff. The dedicatory address was delivered by the father of the Men For Missions movement, Rev. Dwight Ferguson, with our able translator Pastor Napoleon Etienne interpreting into the Creole language for the radio audience as well as those present.

Representatives from missions in the north of Haiti and government officials were in attendance, as well as listeners and friends. Many complimentary notes in behalf of this event were received at the station. The crowning benediction to the service came when one lady stepped forward to give her heart to Jesus Christ.

With its antenna roots now buried in the salt marsh at the edge of the ocean, Radio 4VEH can be heard over most of Haiti and the West Indies Islands. Response since the inauguration of the two new 2500-watt transmitters at this site has increased more than eightfold in the Caribbean, and more than threefold in our secondary listening area of the USA and Canada.

1961   **HAITIAN STAFF**
                      By Mardy and Rachael Picazo

Until the new transmitters began broadcasting, 4VEH was heard mainly on the 31-meter shortwave band. Now people can hear us on the regular broadcast band throughout Haiti and reaching into the West Indies. The transmitters have made a big difference, as has our new broadcasting location about three miles from Cap-Haitien.

This site is becoming a popular visiting point on Sundays for listeners in the city. They come by the dozens to visit the transmitter building, receive tracts at the hands of our missionaries, and ask about 4VEH. Sometimes fifteen or twenty are there at once, and one group has not gone before another comes. They show a feeling of pride that such a powerful radio station is in their city. However, we are constantly confronted with the question: "Why don't you put on more French and Creole programs?"

Only two hours of the ten that we broadcast each day are in French and Creole for our Haitian audience. The rest are in English and Spanish, with one program a week in Russian and Chinese. Yet Radio 4VEH was established to evangelize Haiti, so this need for more Haitian programming has been much in our thoughts, plans, and prayers. Quite obviously, we need qualified Haitian staff to originate the programs, since only a few are available in French from such places as Canada and Belgium.

Mardy didn't have this need on his mind that day some months ago when he stopped at the filling station on his way to the transmitter site. The attendant there introduced him to a young man named Claude Bazile, who spoke good English and was interested in radio, having had a six-month training course in radio telegraphy at Norfolk, Virginia, while he was in the Haitian Coast Guard. Mardy invited him to accompany him to the transmitter site where he showed him the 4VEH installation.

On the return trip Mardy told him of our purpose in spreading the Good News of Jesus Christ. The young man was interested so he gave him the whole plan of salvation, urging him to accept the Lord into his own life. When Mardy dropped him off in town, he gave him a Gospel tract and some Christian literature.

Mardy did not see the young man again until three months later, when he appeared at our transmitter site. He told how he had given his heart to the Lord shortly after Mardy had talked with him and after reading the tract. He had written Mardy a letter, but apparently it was lost.

Now he was eager to do something to help in our Christian work. In talking with him, Mardy found he was well educated, and besides the Creole that all Haitians use, he knew some Spanish as well as English. Most importantly, he was thoroughly instructed in French. He was willing to learn how to fit in at 4VEH, and as he began working, his innate ability as announcer and communicator became evident. Claude Bazile has become a valuable part of our staff, beginning to fill 4VEH's need for Haitian personnel to reach Haiti for Christ.

1959   THE STORY OF ELDON TURNIDGE
Action Magazine

In June 1959, Eldon Turnidge and his family took another big step in their dedication and have now established residence in Haiti, where Eldon has been appointed Field Director for the MFM project, Radio Station 4VEH, and all missionary activity of the OMS on that island. Eldon is the first self-supported lay missionary ever to direct an overseas missionary work. He also holds the distinction of being the first layman to serve on the Board of Directors of The Oriental Missionary Society and the first president of Men For Missions International.

Eldon and his wife, Mary, are not strangers to overseas missionary work, even though they maintain a lay capacity. Their intense interest and burden have taken them to various mission fields, including the Middle East and South America, to participate in almost every phase of missionary activity.

In 1957 Eldon volunteered his services, skills, and considerable time from his busy schedule to assist in establishing an efficient farm program at the Cristalina Bible Institute in Colombia, South America, where hundreds of young people study the Bible while supporting themselves and learning better agricultural methods.

Little did they dream, when they made their first trembling attempts to tell the story of Christ through an interpreter, that someday God would call them from their peppermint farm to go to a foreign country as missionaries, while being sustained by their own agricultural enterprises at home.

An able pilot, Eldon has commuted between Oregon and Cap-Haitien for several months, handling dual responsibilities of his farm and the Haiti work. Already tremendous advances have been made in the missionary outreach and program on the field.

The Turnidges' teenage children, Karen and Johnny, have responded wholeheartedly to this faith venture and have left the comforts and advantages of their home and school life with a definite realization of the consecration and privilege that is theirs.

Note: We Haiti missionaries gladly welcomed the Turnidge family and Eldon's capable leadership.

1960   **MFMI AND HAITI**
By Mardy Picazo

The enthusiasm of the MFMI group was contagious as they assaulted the frame house that had been occupied by termites for some 25 years before we ever entered it. This had been our home in Haiti for many years. We didn't dream anyone would come to improve it. But here was a work crusade armed with paint cans, brushes, and brown wrapping paper! They were enthusiastically attempting a repair project that seemed hopeless.

The house had been built by a plantation firm that had owned the property before the Adventists. It was pre-fab with light plywood and wood paneling that had been most attractive to termites. They had eaten so much of the building that I felt sure that the house stayed up because teams of termites held hands while others were busy eating!

One incident grabbed our attention to the need of repairs. One day when Rachael was very pregnant with Suzanna, she went into a room which we seldom used. She stepped right through the floor up to her thigh. She had to send eight-year old Esteban to the radio studio where I was working to call me to come pull her out. We were grateful that she had not suffered any serious injury.

A women's prayer circle in Columbus, Ohio, had come to do repairs on the house. The floors and some doors were repaired and they were putting on fresh paint in our dining room area. One lady dipped her brush into the paint and as she stroked the doorframe into the kitchen, the brush just went through the wood. She shook her head, got down off the ladder she was using, and secured some brown wrapping paper. She cut a piece the right size, smeared some paste on one side, and applied it to the hole her brush had left! After it dried, she went ahead and painted the whole frame without further incident. The inside of the house was sparkling with fresh color when they were through.

Then a little later, OMS sent a survey crew to evaluate the buildings to see what would be needed to accommodate the additional staff being recruited. It was decided new residences would need to be built and not to repair more than was absolutely necessary while the new homes were being constructed.

The ones who undertook this first major project of construction were the laymen of OMS, Men For Missions.

They challenged these men to go to Haiti and build what was needed. The funds were beginning to come in, and soon the crusades to Haiti were top-billing in the MFM ranks throughout the U.S.

The first groups of crusaders would come into Port-au-Prince and rent cars to drive across the island to our compound. It was a grueling 10 to 12 hour trip, and they generally arrived after dark. As a consequence of this late and uncertain time, a menu was chosen that could be prepared in advance and served almost immediately when they got there. It was a Haitian pumpkin soup, something like a stew with vegetables and meat, thickened with fresh mashed pumpkin. It was served with Haitian bread and cold limeade or hot coffee. Each home where the crusade group would be eating had the same menu.

The MFM crusades became a regular part of the mission activities. The group would work on the various projects during the day and at night would go out with the nationals and missionaries to outstations for a witnessing time. There were other crusades that came primarily to do evangelism and witnessing.

Across the years MFM has been an important factor in the development of the radio station, the Bible School, medical center, schools, church, and other projects. They have brought hundreds in contact with a "real" mission field, some of them receiving a call into missionary work when on a crusade to Haiti.

Thousands have come to the knowledge of Jesus Christ as Savior through their evangelistic tours on the fields and indirectly through the various ministries they have helped. Haiti has been blessed so much because of MFMI—and we trust that because of Haiti, MFMI has in turn been blessed.

Suzane and Serge in 1959

1959 construction of the transmitter building

Mr. Eldon Turnidge in 1959

1961 ceremony of dedication

The missionary staff of 1961 recording
"Open House" in the 4VEH studio

Haitian mother and baby in 1963

1960   HAITI ADVANCE
By Eldon Turnidge

One of the needs on our field is for staff housing. With new missionaries coming to Haiti to help in the work, there must be homes.

A businessman in Pennsylvania, Mr. Phillip Fahs and family, plus a young, enthusiastic teenager, Joe King, came to see what they could do with one of the rickety old buildings on our compound.

For six weeks the Fahs group labored on the old, unused school building. By the time they left, it had been converted into a nice place to live, complete with plumbing, inside walls and ceiling, and lights. A little finishing up was all that was needed before the Donald Hamme family could move into these new quarters.

Today, they are comfortably situated in the remodeled schoolhouse, thanks to this man who had a burden and a family that was willing to accompany him, to do an otherwise impossible piece of work.

1962   LOCAL MEN CHALLENGE OTHERS
Action Magazine

Asbury Park, New Jersey: As a result of seeing the needs and potentials for gospel witness on the island of Haiti during a Men For Missions-sponsored tour last year, local businessmen spearheaded by James Megill and Harold Harrison have initiated a plan for returning to that island. They want to construct greatly needed missionary residences and a control console for the Gospel Radio Station 4VEH. They also envision installing an intercom telephone system for the compound.

Throughout the year these men have endeavored to raise funds for building supplies. They are challenging other men to go to Haiti and give of their time and technical skills for the proposed projects. This will be at their own travel expense. These laymen desire to provide the facilities for more efficient operations on the field. They seek to relieve the missionaries from manual and time-consuming jobs for which they have not been trained, in order to free them for the task of spreading the Gospel on this voodoo-ridden island.

Already 12 men, including electricians, mason workers, and carpenters, have volunteered to make up the construction team.

1960　　　　　**PRE-TUNED RADIOS**
Donald Hamme

During the past few months we have tested several transistor radios and have found the Philips School Radio, with several channels, to be the most suitable. Each channel can be pretuned to Radio 4VEH. This receiver operates on four regular flashlight batteries, which are readily obtainable here in Haiti. The set can be heard distinctly 200 feet and more, thus making it very suitable for the villages.

Already this radio has aroused much interest, and many have heard the Gospel in their own language just through the testing program. Christians back in the States are interested in purchasing one of these radios to be their full-time voice to the people of Haiti. These sets do not have to learn a language— they speak as soon as turned on!

The first pre-tuned radio was placed about four months ago at the home of a believer in a mountain village called Port Francais. After the first week, word came that two people had accepted the Lord as a result of the broadcasts. At the end of the second week, the number had swelled to twelve.

Soon after, a party of missionaries and visitors went to the locality and were given a warm reception by the people there. The missionaries took medicines with them so they could minister to their bodies as well as their souls.

Now one of our fine Haitian personal workers has requested to go there with his family, to teach them the way more perfectly and to start a school to teach the children how to read. One little transistor radio, tuned to Radio 4VEH, has transformed a whole community.

Encouraging reports are coming from other places also where transistor radios were placed. In one location, as a result of the interest created, the people asked for a worker to come and teach them. Now a preaching point has been established and one of our national workers holds Sunday school and church services. From 50 to 80 attend the services, 7 have been saved, and 30 have given their names as desiring to start a church.

At another place a man built a high cabinet for the radio so that those who visit his store and a nearby carpenter shop might hear the Gospel.

One of these radios has been placed at the bakery in Cap-Haitien. As a result a lady across the street from the bakery stopped missionary John Raisch and inquired further about the Gospel message that she heard over 4VEH broadcasts. As he talked to her, a large crowd of people gathered and, when it was time for him to leave, they begged him to return.

A number of prominent businessmen attended the second meeting, and among them was the son of the woman who had invited John and who was opposed to the Gospel. As God's Spirit moved upon him, he invited John to place a radio in the clinic where he is the director.

1960   4VEH'S TENTH ANNIVERSARY
By Eldon Turnidge, Haiti Field Director

For ten years now the powerful Gospel message has been flung into the air by Radio 4VEH to eventually be recaptured and reach needy hearts.   And God has given a glorious harvest. Recently a listener in New Jersey wrote, saying, among other things, "I think that your programs are very, very inspiring to a person that needs Christ.   I, for one, know of at least three people saved by listening to your program. Of all the programs, I keep coming back to this one which I accidentally found on the air."

It is a privilege to have a part in such a fruitful ministry. God has led a unique set of people to serve here. And others are coming.   Yes, we give God praise for this radio ministry and all its remarkable results.

1961   INSTANT HOUSE
By Eldon Turnidge

They walked through the living room, stared at the kitchen, and gaped at the doorway of the bathroom, all 250 of them. And the majority expressed themselves best by the much used Creole expression, "Mes Amis!" (mayz-ah-mee), which has a meaning something like "Oh, Boy!" or "Isn't that something!"

It all began when God put His finger upon us individually and as a family, leading us to agree to serve Him here in the Republic of Haiti.

It sounded so easy. We would turn the 600 acres of farm responsibilities over to our partner and faithful friend, Mr. Lorin Hoven. We would ask the bank to loan, as needed, the operating monies. We would park the family car, turn our house over to our partner, load ourselves into the Piper Apache airplane, and, with the 200 pounds of allowable baggage, fly eastward from Oregon.

We would consummate the arrangements in Florida for a specially built trailer house, provided in part by some very dear friends who are dealers, and then we would fly on to Haiti to await the arrival of this new home. Into this mobile home we would move our family and baggage, plus the household items we might buy along the way.

We knew something of the situation in Haiti concerning housing and the lack of housing. We knew about the mosquitoes, the heat, the humidity, etc., and we knew a bit about trailer house living. And all this brought no little concern. Imagine the heat under Haiti's tropical sun, with an aluminum roof overhead and the low ceiling of a trailer house. Picture, also, the four of us, Mary and me with our two teenagers, Karen and Johnny, crowded together and tightly packed in a trailer house. But we had planned the work, now to work the plan!

Our wonderful partner and friend did assume all the load of carrying through on the farm, and after some frightening conferences the bank agreed to advance operating monies. However, even with the weeks of advance notice, those last days were hectic. We needed to make final arrangements concerning the farm, sell some of last year's harvest, pay bills, make decisions about what to take and what to leave, and, as always, say those last-minute good-byes. Finally, we were off, all four of us, and 200 pounds of baggage!

The trailer house arrived the other day, and, even though it was one of the most reasonably priced units available, she looked pretty nice sitting there on the dock, all gleaming white. In fact, she began to take on palatial airs. It must have been the contrast against a new and dismal background that made her look so beautiful out there. Little did we know the sensation she was about to create!

After two days of official negotiations, paperwork, and leg work, we hooked up a Ford Diesel farm tractor loaned by the local fruit company. Off we went, down from the docks, through the city, and out the five miles to our compound. What a sight we must have been! You could see it on their faces!

Through a special hole cut in the fence around our mission grounds, we towed this unusual home to what may well be her last resting place. Before parking her, we chose the most ideal location, trimmed several overhanging limbs from the brittle avocado tree just behind this spot, and then maneuvered her into place. This tree-trimming and final parking took some two hours, and by that time we had a much impressed and growing audience.

That first evening visitors started coming. An attorney and a coffee exporter, with their families, drove out from the city. It seems that one of them had seen us go through town and they couldn't wait to have a look inside. Local interest grew, too. Finally, the anxiety was nearing the bursting point, so we planned an open house and made a public invitation on Sunday morning to our local church. The hour was set for 3:00 p.m.

We placed cardboard on the floor and had missionaries stationed in each room to point out (in Creole) items of interest and to answer questions. Of course, some came directly from the morning service about 12:00 noon and waited out in front of the trailer house for the hands of the clock to reach that 3:00 p.m. position.

As the church members and local people passed through the trailer house, it seemed that the kitchen and bathroom drew the most "Ohs" and "Ahs." At the exit one of the missionaries passed out Gospel tracts, and then the visitors congregated in front of the trailer house for a Gospel service with singing, a brief welcome, and words of exhortation.

Since that day many have come to inspect, and each has received a Gospel tract or a portion of God's Word. Many of the leading citizens of this area have dropped by for a look. We trust God shall use His Word as it was passed to them, and thus He can be honored in this manner. Even while we are yet learning to speak the language, the printed portions are quietly at work.

And now we know from observations, impressions, and expressions, that our home is not just a crowded little old house trailer, extremely hot at midday—but ours is the beautiful, God provided, sparkling-bright home that is the talk of the area. And she has already proven to be a very effective missionary.

A new, well-built house could have cost much, much more, but would probably have created little or no stir. But this house! One day, nothing—and the next day, a complete home. "Mes Amis!" How could it be?

AN ANGEL IN A TRAILER?—30 years later
By Rachael Picazo (1991)

Melva Eichel was a retired school teacher. She was 72 when she first came to Haiti to help in our English Cowman School which taught the children of our missionary staff and also some Haitians of the community whose parents wanted them to have their training in English. Melva enjoyed it so much she came back the next year as well. She must have been nearing her mid 70s that spring. We had become close friends.

She was living alone in the trailer the Turnidges had brought to Haiti 30 years before, and by this time the house was needing repairs now and then. Melva noticed that the floor in the bathroom was giving a little under her weight, so Clyde Bowman started working on it while she was away teaching during the day. However, he couldn't get it all done. When he finally stopped that night, directly in front of the bathroom door was a hole that dropped more than two feet to the ground below.

Since the bathroom was unusable, our missionary hostess Marian Bowman asked Melva to stay overnight at her house.

Melva, an early riser, was up the next morning before the Bowman household was fully awake. She found that she had left something back in her trailer bathroom, so she donned a housecoat and went down to retrieve it.

The phone rang insistently at our house that morning. Missionary hostess Marian was calling. "Rachael, can you go down to the trailer and see about Melva?" (We lived closer to the trailer and I could get there quicker.) "She has left, and I'm afraid she has gone there. She might forget the hole in her bathroom floor..."

I rushed to the trailer, calling out as I ran, "Melva!"

Then I saw her sitting in the screened porch on one of the arm chairs. She saw me, but she did not answer. I opened the door and walked over to her. She looked up at me pale and shaken. After a few minutes, she began to talk.

"I knew that there was a hole in the floor," she recounted, "but when I opened the bathroom door, I forgot. I just stepped in, and my foot went right down to my hip. You know, I have a bad hip. I can't even get up off the floor by myself. But as I felt my foot going down, I yelled, 'Jesus, help me!'

"I felt myself being lifted up, Rachael. And the next thing I knew, I was sitting right here where I am now.

"Someone lifted me out of that hole...Someone set me down in this chair....Do you think it was an angel?"

WHAT GOD HATH WROUGHT
By Clyde Moore

Two years ago in July 1960, I came to Haiti, assigned to assist 4VEH as an electrical engineer.

At that time the staff was praying for the completion of more powerful transmitters. In October the weary, old transmitter was laid to rest and the new dual transmitter (2500 watts on Broadcast Band and 2500 watts on 49 meters shortwave) was put into operation.

The old diesel power plants were so badly in need of rebuilding and repair that we were off the air an average of one day every two weeks and it was getting worse. I joined the staff as they brought it before the Lord in prayer. He answered with a new 75,000-watt Cummins diesel generator...and a new missionary, our diesel engineer. In just six months Jim Wallace had the diesels and the standbys working so that the intermittent electric power was just a thing of the past.

With the new facilities, our Radio 4VEH audience expanded rapidly, so we sought the Lord's leading for a new and expanded program schedule. Three months of prayerful planning later, we felt that we had a comparable format using the four languages of the central Caribbean. Before we could put it into operation, we needed more national help and more program material.

We took the need to the Lord, and as we knocked, the door opened. Through special gifts our music library increased from 50 records and 50 tapes to over 800 records and 400 tapes.

Some talented young men were saved and filled part of the personnel need so that the new expanded service started in November 1961.

In the last one and a half years, the mail response has increased sevenfold, with each mail day bringing reports of Christians having been strengthened or some making a decision for Christ. These are just a few of the almost daily answers to prayer here at 4VEH in Haiti.

Jesus promised (Matthew 7:7), *"Ask and it will be given to you; seek and you will find; knock and the door will be opened to you."*

1962   **4VEH MUST SHUT DOWN!**
                      By Mardy Picazo

We were ready for bed about 10 o'clock that night after a long busy day. Then a knock sounded at the door. It was the campus watchman informing me that someone was there to see me. Just then an army vehicle drove up to our front porch, and an officer stepped out.

I had no idea what was going on. The country had been under high security and was tense due to especially serious political unrest. The officer, speaking to me in French, said that our station was being closed down by the government.

I was amazed and dismayed. We had tried to be very careful not to enter into any political matters. I thought we had been successful thus far. It was our policy from the beginning not to broadcast any Haitian news, just in case it might have political implications. We had strict rules that our operators be nonpolitical in even the church notices that went on the air.

The officer was the top military commander of the army in northern Haiti, and he said that, furthermore, I was to bring to him the tape recording of the news we had aired from Voice of America that evening. He said that he had just received a report that we had broadcast some serious political information and he was closing the station down indefinitely.

He told me to come to the commandant's office next day at 11 o'clock and bring the news tape with me. He would not listen to anything I wanted to say that night in defense of 4VEH. So I agreed to see him the next day.

The next morning I searched in the radio studios for the tape in question. I was dismayed to find that it had already been erased and was in place for the next recording of news from the Voice of America. Whatever was in question, I would not be able to prove otherwise.

The whole staff became aware immediately and joined in prayer for the situation. We did not broadcast that morning.

Going into town for the meeting with the commandant, I thought and prayed about what I could say or do. My French was not that good; I knew it would take some eloquent talking to help us in this crisis. Coming close to town, I spotted Mr. DesRameaux, a younger man who had helped us in our French broadcasts, a fine evangelist, well educated. I stopped and asked him if I could give him a ride. He accepted and while we were talking, I told him of our problem. Immediately he offered to help me in any way he could. I told him I would surely appreciate it if he could speak or translate for me in this important interview. He agreed and went right with me to the headquarters of the army.

At the gate the sentinel asked for my business. When I told him, he said, "Oh, yes. The commandant is expecting you and you are to go right to his office."

The commandant did not even look up as we entered, but in a very formal voice asked, "Well, where is the tape?"

When I replied that I was unable to find it because it had been erased, he was highly displeased. He began lecturing me on the seriousness of the incident and repeated the damaging news that had been reported to have come from 4VEH. During all of this, the man had not once lifted his eyes to me as I stood in front of his desk.

Just then Mr. DesRameaux spoke up. "Sir, aren't you..." and he gave the name of the commandant.

Suddenly the commandant looked up for the first time. In surprise he responded, "Yes, and I now see who you are!"

They both started talking of the days they were in the local high school together. After a while the commandant asked Mr. DesRameaux about us. He reassured him that we were not at all interested in politics and that if there had been something aired on 4VEH of that nature, it was an accident.

The commandant then turned to me and said, "Well, Mr. Picazo, you will be allowed to go back on the air, but be sure to keep all your tapes at least one week before you erase them. Goodbye and good luck."

We left him. I was overwhelmed at the miracle that God had just performed in placing Mr. DesRameaux in my path at the right moment.

1962   A DAY AT RADIO 4VEH
By Aldean Saufley

5:00 a.m.   Brrrrring.

The rude interruption of the alarm clock brings to an end another short night. Time to get going. Where to? To Radio 4VEH and another day of broadcasting.

First stop is the compound studio. Quickly we gather all of the tapes, disk recordings, log books and other materials for the broadcast, song request sheets . . . hmmmm . . . looks like we have everything.

Soon Paul Lund pulls up in the Jeep truck. All aboard for Petite Anse, location of our transmitter building. The broadcast day will begin in less than an hour.

During the eight-mile trip we pass numbers of Haitians on their way to market. Many of them have been up since 3:00 or 4:00 this morning. Their produce is loaded on lean little donkeys or stacked precariously atop their heads. The countryside around us is gradually tinted with lavish hues as the sun begins its climb from behind the ragged hills.

As we arrive at our destination, we are greeted by the dull hum of the diesel engine idling in the shed. Our watchman, Edner, has been on the job as usual this morning.

Once inside the building we set up the various turntables and recorders with prepared tapes and discs for the day.

5:50 a.m. Paul turns on the transmitters. We are ready for the interval signal and opening announcements which will begin in just five minutes. The sign-on announcement goes smoothly, and now Paul takes the controls for his "Rise and Shine" program.

We have a moment to look around. Here in the large central room are the transmitters: one dual unit which puts out 2500 watts on each of two frequencies, broadcast band and 49 meter short-wave. To the right is another transmitter which has a power of 400 watts. To our left is the large 10-kilowatt transmitter soon to be put into operation by our engineers. Still another transmitter will function on a special frequency for the village transistor radios. Stepping to the door we can see our tower (soon to be joined by a second) and our other antenna systems.

6:30 a.m. Time to head back to the controls again. We'll be here 'til 9:00, so settle down and enjoy the programs all in English for our island listeners. The French and Creole programs, as well as those in Spanish, will be broadcast this afternoon while we are busy at Vaudreuil.

9:00 a.m. Time to return to the compound. On the way back we will stop at the customs house to pick up a number of tapes for the broadcast. We can be certain that this will take some time, especially if the current shipment is a large one.

12:00 Noon. Back at the compound in time to eat dinner. We are having rice and beans today, one of my favorite dishes.

Dinner finished, we take a brief rest before returning to the studio.

1:30 p.m. Our first recording this afternoon is the Children's Radio Hour story. This is a Bible drama directed by Rachael Picazo. I will provide the organ background for the narrative.

The story is finished just in time. Here comes the rest of the staff for our Open House program. For this, Paul Lund is the director and manages to keep the entire staff busy singing in the choir, recording, or reading letter excerpts. A short practice session is followed by program lineup and last minute instructions. Then ...click! We're recording this time for broadcast.

4:30 p.m. One more program remains to be recorded before supper. Here comes our English class, a group of Haitian students and a Haitian instructor. He will be teaching in French and Creole and I in English as we prepare the radio English lesson. That completed we head for home and supper.

7:00 p.m. Back in the studio. We have some editing to do on the Open House program. A verse of a song is to be cut and several other goofs deleted. Following this tape splicing, we make another complete check before the program is finished. Now we are ready to bring the broadcast day to a close with the final preparation of tapes and disks for tomorrow's schedule.

Taking the log sheet we carefully check to be sure all recordings needed are on proper file and the tapes arranged in order. That does it. We are the last ones out tonight.

10:30 p.m. Finally it is time to head home to the luxury of a warm shower and bed.

"What is the fruit of all this?" you may wonder.

Each day the mail brings testimonies of those who have been saved as a result of the 4VEH ministry. Others send in requests for prayer and spiritual help, a service to thousands whose only contact with the Gospel is our radio station. Still others who never write are listening and gradually feeling the impact of the broadcasts.

The task remains a tremendous one, too large for us alone. That is why we take courage as you, our host of loving friends, lift us all—missionaries, nationals, listeners—in your prayers.

1963   **A WEDDING IN HAITI**
                  By Miriam Stockton

Ellen Bressler and Aldean Saufley were married in the Vaudreuil Tabernacle on the OMS compound in Haiti January 1, 1963. It was a lovely ceremony, the first American wedding that many of their Haitian friends had seen. Parents of the groom, Rev. and Mrs. Charles Saufley, attended from Chambersburg, Pennsylvania. The mother of the bride, Mrs. Bessie Bressler, and also the bride's sister, Mary, traveled from Dalmatia, Pennsylvania.

The bride wore a lovely ballet-length dress and carried a pink hibiscus on a white Bible, with white chrysanthemums and satin streamers. The maid of honor was Mary Bressler, dark-haired sister of the bride. The best man was Edwin Moore of the 4VEH staff. Carol Lund made a sweet little flower girl in blue. The ceremony was performed by Rev. Glen Barnett of the American Wesleyan Mission, assisted by Aldean's father, Rev. Charles Saufley. Beautiful organ music was provided by Miss Valeene Hayes and solos offered by Mrs. Trudy Lund and Mrs. Janice Barnett.

Unique features of the ceremony were most effective. As Ellen neared the front of the church, Aldean sang to her the traditional wedding song, "Because." Also, their vows to each other were repeated from memory.

At the close of the service they gave testimonies of how God had led their lives. It was a sacred hour and a perfect culmination of a beautiful Christian courtship.

1963   **MINISTRY TO MOTHERS**
                               By Flora Boyer

Mme. Thermidor watched in frantic concern as the strength ebbed from the thin body of her infant son. For days he had eaten nothing. She could see Odije was slowly dying. Anxiously she returned with the child to the witch doctor.

None of the old man's remedies had helped her baby. Now he demanded that a preposterous sum of money be brought before he would perform the final cure.

Mme. Thermidor had no money. Desperately the mother gathered Odije in her arms and made her way to our clinic. A few simple treatments, along with the life-restoring ministry of prayer and loving concern, were given to the wasted child. Slowly, but surely, the glow of life returned, and Mme. Thermidor rejoiced to see the baby she had all but given up become healthy and well again.

Six weeks later she appeared in church with Odije and asked the pastor to come to her house and pray. When he arrived, he found that Mme. Thermidor had not waited but had asked Jesus into her heart even before he arrived. Today she is still praising God for His magnificent salvation.

This all happened three years ago. But the case of little Odije spoke to us of two things:

1. The pitiful plight of Haitian mothers steeped in poverty and superstition, consigned to suffering at childbirth and ignorance in child care.

2. The God-given opportunity to ease the burden of Haitian mothers, thereby pointing them to Christ.

Two years ago in 1961 at Vaudreuil, we began classes for mothers in our clinic. From the small beginning with a single mother, our regular enrollment has soared to 45, with 120 names of mothers on the record book. Of 62 births reported, only two babies have been lost: one at birth, and one by miscarriage.

In the last eight months 628 pounds of powdered milk have been distributed to these mothers. I have given multiple vitamins and iron tablets sufficient for each mother's needs.

The women of the Fenton Bible Church in Michigan shared my vision and made the first 35 layettes for the project. Other churches later added to them. Each expectant mother who attends the prenatal classes faithfully receives a gift of a new layette. At this date, 52 have been given.

Each week the class meets for instruction in diet, baby care, and exercises. This is always followed by a Gospel message. One afternoon the face of one of the ladies seemed to glow with a new light, and at the close of the service she came forward to accept Jesus as her Savior.

Fifteen members of our class for mothers are Christians now. Will it not be worth all the work to see one more mother in heaven on that great day?

1963   WHY I AM A MISSIONARY
By David Graffenberger

Three major steps bring me to my present position as missionary in Haiti.

The first step was that of dedicating my life to the Lord as a freshman in high school.

This led to a complete surrender to God's will; therefore, when I had the opportunity in 1958 to work at the Vocational Bible School in Cristalina, Colombia, I knew that this was the Lord's will for me. This experience made me a missionary in mind.

The final step was taken at Missionary Internship School. There I saw myself and realized that to be a missionary in heart I must be filled with the Holy Spirit. I thank the Lord that I am now a missionary both in mind and heart.

1963   **RATS**
                         By Rachael Picazo

I am sure every missionary has a rat story. There are so many rats over the world, and some places have more than their share of them. Haiti is a point in case. Being a tropical country, Haiti provides food and warm weather the year round for the rats to multiply profusely. Our first encounter with them was a couple of nights after we arrived at Vaudreuil and were asleep in the home assigned to our family.

I felt something touch lightly and swiftly on my arm and across my chest. Mardy and I both sat straight up in bed.

"What was that?" he asked.

"Something ran across me," I asserted.

Everything was dark because the electric generator had already been turned off. We lit the lamp, but by then whatever it was had long gone.

We had a couple more incidents before we finally realized those were rat feet running across us. One of the more knowledgeable missionaries told us that rats have their own paths they frequent and suggested we move our bed. When we noted where the bed was, sure enough, there was a hole in the termite-weakened wall right over where we slept. We moved the bed.

There were no more recurrences, but I remember how I could still feel the prints of those little clawed feet on my arms and chest for a couple of days after it ran across me.

We set sturdy traps we found for sale in Cap-Haitien and caught several. But there always seemed to be just as many as before. We prayed for a cat. They were scarce in Haiti, and when a Haitian had a cat, he tied it up with a string to keep it safe so no one would steal it.

A few years later we were delighted when a missionary family gave us their cat as they left on furlough. That took care of the rat problem in our house, and she supplied many lovely kittens to other needy families.

I was startled recently in overhearing my daughter Rachel tell someone, "In Haiti my mom stomped on the rats with her feet."

Actually it only happened once, and then quite by accident. One night I needed to go to the building where I home schooled our children, but since rats were always there, I asked our eldest son Esteban, then 12, to go with me. He was unerring with his slingshot, and I felt better with him along.

Sure enough, as soon as we turned on the light, three or four rats scurried out of the room. But one ran up the wall and across the open rafters. Esteban hit him with the stone from his slingshot, but it only knocked him crazy. The rat wobbled down the wall and began stumbling in a crazy pattern across the open floor. I was standing in the middle, calling for Esteban to shoot him again, but he was afraid to try because I was standing in the way. As the rat staggered closer, I began jumping up and down in my agitation, and that rat ran right under my feet!

I sure didn't want it to get away now, so I just stood on it, yelling, while Esteban scurried for a big stick he could use to knock it in the head.

But that was nothing compared to the Haitians who lived in thatched homes, where the foot-thick marsh grass of their roofs provided soft dry breeding places for the rodents. Our nurses in the clinic often had to treat children wounded by rats chewing on them at night while they slept.

Once when I was visiting in a Haitian home, my friend remarked that they had not had rats in their grass roof for the past three years, since Pastor Wallace had collected all the rat tails in Vaudreuil. I had heard various versions of Jim Wallace's battle with the rats, which happened while we were in the States on furlough. So I asked him to give us the accurate story and, incidentally, tell us what he did with all those tails!

1963   WAR AGAINST RATS
By Rev. James L. Wallace

One serious problem at Vaudreuil was an overpopulation of rats. It seemed that every time I opened the door of a depot, several rats confronted me. One thing for sure, I don't like rats.

In 1963 Eldon Turnidge, our field director, encouraged me to think about putting five acres of our mission property under cultivation, experimenting with hybrid corn he had secured from Mexico.

I expressed my concern: "But what about the rats? If they don't destroy the corn on the stalk they will surely get to it in storage."

"I've heard about a new poison they have developed," Eldon encouraged. "I'll bring some in from the States to use on the rats."

He was as good as his word—he brought several pounds, paying around $35 dollars for it. I set the poison baits out where the rats could get them, but dogs or children could not. In just a few days the baits were all gone... but I never saw a dead rat nor any sign of decrease in their numbers.

I knew if we didn't take care of this menace, we were going to have a problem. Then I remembered the pest drives we used to have in the rural high school where I attended. Every year there was a contest among the fellows who were in the FFA (Future Farmers of America) in which points were given to the students who destroyed the most pests. Of course, we didn't get paid, but those pest drives were quite successful.

I was thinking about this when several boys approached me where I was repairing the mission truck at our mechanics workshop.

"Pastor Wallace, do you have any jobs we can do?"

"No work for you today," I replied. And then **the idea** came to me.

"Go kill some rats and I will pay you for it," I promised.

"Rats? Really? How much will you pay us for a dead rat?"

At that moment I must have been pretty discouraged because the poison hadn't done the job. "I will give you five cents for every dead rat you bring me," I pledged.

"You are joking!" exclaimed one.

"What do you want with dead rats?" another asked. "Are you going to eat them?"

"No, I do **not** eat rats," I assured them, "but I will pay you for every rat you kill."

At that time the daily wages for an adult in Haiti was about sixty cents, so five cents for a dead rat may have been too high. Anyway, the boys left and I thought that was the last I would see of them.

Not more than an hour later, here came the boys with two dead rats. "Very good!" I complimented them. "Here is the ten cents I promised."

"Wow!" They got excited, "Do you want any more?"

"I will buy every dead rat you bring me," I reassured them. They were yelling enthusiastically as they rushed out the gate of the mission compound.

My Haitian helper, Frank, had been observing all this. "What do you want me to do with those dead rats?" he queried.

"Throw them in the garbage pit," I said. It was a deep hole that had been dug specifically for trash from our numerous homes on the mission grounds.

"You know, Pastor Wallace," Frank reminded me, "when it gets dark, someone could go get those rats and sell them to you again."

"Well," I replied, "take that hatchet and cut off their tails. There is no way I am about to buy a rat without a tail!"

It wasn't long until here came the boys again. This time they had a pole they were carrying on their shoulders. Tied neatly to the pole were 15 dead rats.

"Fifteen! So soon?!" I was amazed, as I counted out the 75 cents.

"Can just anyone bring in rats and get paid?" they wanted to know.

"Yes," I assured them, "the price is good for anyone."

I think at that moment the pest drive was started. The whole community went rat hunting and, needless to say, Frank was kept busy cutting off rat tails. The corn was growing great and I wasn't so worried anymore.

The rat project reached its peak in about three weeks, and then it began to taper off.

"We can't find any more rats," the boys complained.

A few people came to me from neighboring communities.

"Will you buy our rats from Limbé?" they wanted to know.

It probably would have been a good idea, but by this time I had bought 700 rats, so I declined their offer.

When we stored our harvest of corn that fall, we had no problem with rat infestation—and neither did our neighbors. Several people told me it was one of the best things that had ever happened in the community.

1963   GOD USED A TRACT
By Paul Lund

Roger Samson had heard the Gospel at street meetings near his home in Cap-Haitien and also over his neighbor's radio tuned to Station 4VEH. When I met him, he told me that he especially listened to the messages on Sunday. But he had not yet found the Lord, and he did not attend church anywhere.

The Lord was speaking to him, however, and he felt conviction. Several times he had walked the five miles to our mission compound to find someone to pray with him, but each time he was too timid to come through our gate.

On Wednesday morning he came again but stopped outside the gate, lacking the courage to come in. He walked on a little farther to buy a cup of coffee and some bread at the roadside, telling himself that he would go in when he passed by our gate again. But he did not.

The next afternoon something lying on the street attracted his attention. It was a tract with the words "Christ is the Answer." These tracts had been distributed house to house in the Every Creature Crusade, but someone had discarded this one.

Roger read the tract's illustration of a boy who asked a man how he could be saved. The man told him that he would show him how. He put a basin of water before the boy and had the boy kneel in front of it. Then he forced the boy's head under the water and held it there for a moment. When the man let loose, the boy gasped to breathe in the air.

Then he told the boy that when he desperately desired to be saved the same way that he desperately wanted air to breathe, **he would be saved.**

This was what it took to encourage Roger. The next morning he came, entered the gate, and asked for someone to explain the way of salvation and pray with him. He was directed to me and we talked. I could see the corners of his mouth trembling. But as soon as we had finished praying, a smile spread across his face and joy shone in his eyes. God had done a work in his heart!

This is but one incident of how God is using tracts to bring souls to Him in Haiti. The effective and historic method of Every Creature evangelism, which has been a distinctive feature of the OMS since its inception, is producing gratifying results. Already 1400 homes have been visited and 32 conversions reported. Many Haitians have enrolled in the follow-up Bible Correspondence Course.

With the help of World Gospel Crusades, gospels and tracts have been obtained in both the French and Creole languages. The distribution is being done entirely by Haitian Christians. Haiti's 90% illiteracy rate presents the greatest barrier to the effectiveness of the Crusade. Nevertheless, in many homes at least one member of the family is able to read to the others.

1964   **TO TOP IT OFF**
By Marilyn Murphy

It was early one morning when the Haitian radio quartet, pastor, and several of us missionaries piled into the back of a pickup. After two hours of bouncing over roads, trails, and paths, even fording one mud hole on foot to avoid getting stuck, we arrived at our destination.

I wish you could have seen the church—a rather large, concrete-block building, the inside decorated with beautiful red flowers, and packed with people. But the roof! Just a few palm branches lightly laid over the top.

We soon understood, however. The people had built their own church, and this was the final step—a roof. After the special music—including nine quartet numbers and my accordion—the pastor brought the message. Then came the highlight of the day—the offering for the new roof.

As the money was received (five or six offerings), the sheets of aluminum roofing were purchased from the vendor outside, brought down the center aisle, and laid in front of the podium. The steady stream of shiny metal with the sun glinting on it through the palm leaves above was indeed a thrilling sight.

Then I saw an old peasant lady come up to the treasurer. As I watched her unfold and hand him bills and coins, I realized how many pounds of vegetables or charcoal she must have carried to market and how very long it must have taken her to save that offering. Yet she was giving it all with a radiant smile of joy!

I wondered if I had that kind of love?

1964   **COOL CLEAN WATER**
                 By Rev. James Wallace

Word came to our mission that a banana plantation near Cap-Haitien was going out of business and that they were going to sell much of their equipment. I was delegated to investigate in case they had anything we might want that was within our budget.

Most of the equipment they had was much larger than we could ever use. They were preparing to ship everything back to the States that they did not sell. One item that caught my attention was a well-drilling rig. It was a huge thing that they used to drill ten-inch wells but the price tag on it was $20,000. That was much more than we could afford, but definitely a good buy.

While looking at it, I noticed that they had a complete set of tools for drilling a four-inch well. I asked the manager, "What do you have that for?" He said, "We use that to drill test wells."

"Would you consider selling just that without the big drilling rig?" I heard myself asking. That had to be the Lord prompting that question, as I had no idea how it could be used without the drilling rig.

"Sure, we will sell you that if you can use it," the man responded. The price he quoted was $400. It was certainly a bargain, as he was throwing in several hundred feet of four-inch pipe. That had to be several thousand dollars' worth of equipment!

I told him I would be back the next day with an answer. Our treasurer assured me he could spare that much, so the next day I took our farm wagon and purchased what I hoped would be a valuable asset to the mission.

I had no idea how to go about drilling a well. But we did need drinking water at our transmitter site near Petite Anse. No city water was available, even if it had been dependable, so the fellows who worked their shifts there had to bring drinking water along with any food they would need. We had drums positioned under the eaves of the buildings to catch rain water for cooling the diesel engines that provided our electricity.

Petite Anse was located on the bay across from Cap-Haitien, and the 4VEH towers had their roots in the salt flats by the ocean. According to the radio engineers this made an ideal spot for the towers, but it was a poor spot to even hope to find anything except salty water. However, shouldn't we try?

Shortly after this we received word that Mr. and Mrs. Lynn Schellack were coming to work a couple of weeks in Haiti with the missionaries. Mrs. Schellack, Deane, would be helping Nurse Flo in the clinic, and her husband, Lynn, was familiar with drilling oil wells in Oklahoma. He had visited Haiti two years before and had wanted to come back ever since to drill a well for water.

I had a multitude of questions all prepared to ask Lynn. I was hoping he would be able to show us how we could use this equipment in drilling the well.

When Lynn arrived, I showed him what we had purchased. He was impressed and said we had made a good deal.

"Now, he asserted, "All you need is a drilling rig."

"Could we build a tower out of wood?" I suggested.

"No, he replied, "You need something that is portable."

We began exploring some of the things among some junk that had long been abandoned. Lynn felt that an old truck frame had some real possibilities, but it lacked wheels.

Our field director had purchased a new mobile home and placed it on blocks at the mission. The wheels were just hanging underneath. But our field director was not there, and we had to make a decision fast since Lynn's stay was only two weeks. With not enough time to contact him, we decided to just borrow them and hope he would approve.

It took hours of hard work and welding at our compound shop to convert that old truck frame into something that could work like a drilling rig. It had to be made so that the derrick would fold down in order to transport it to Petite Anse seven miles away. By the time we finished its construction and all the transporting, the first week of Lynn's vacation had been spent.

97

We drove the equipment onto the transmitter site near Petite Anse and looked around for a place to start drilling. Lynn swept the environs with his gaze, his attention coming to rest on a familiar-looking plant among all that strange tropical vegetation. It was a peanut bush! He walked over to it and pulled it up. As he held it aloft, there hung clusters of peanuts among its roots. Somehow that seemed just the right place to drill the well. So the work began.

The mission had a long rope that was heavy enough to lift the drilling equipment but the big question was how we were going to do it. We had plenty of manpower, so first we tied one end of the rope on the drilling bit, which weighed close to 500 pounds. We then passed the rope over the pulley on top of the drilling rig, and I had about ten men on the other end of the rope to lift the bit.

Well, they could lift it all right and then let it drop to start drilling a hole, but it was hard work, and in just a short while they had to stop and rest. We saw right away that this was not going to work. We needed some way to raise the bit just a foot or so and then drop it just enough to hit in the bottom of the hole.

Suddenly I remembered something that happened when I was in the U.S. Navy years ago. We had a round winch on board our ship. They could turn it on and it moved constantly. Rope was then wrapped around the winch and one or two men could pull the whole ship up to the dock. To stop pulling all they had to do was release the pressure on the rope and let it slip.

We jacked up the rear of our jeep and put on a rim without a tire. I then started the engine and let it idle in reverse gear. Sure enough, the rim was turning, not too fast. I loosely passed the rope around the rim a couple of times and was able to lift the drilling bit by myself. I could just release the rope and the bit would drop. We were in business.

However, it had taken almost all of Lynn's two weeks for us to arrive at this point. During the last day he showed me many things that I would need to know in order to continue drilling after he left. When we stopped, we were at a depth of 20 feet.

The next day as Lynn and Deane were ready to leave, word came that Haiti's president had proclaimed a holiday, and there was to be no travel on the roads either that day or the next.

Two more days! Lynn and I spent every daylight hour drilling that well. The first of the two days of grace, we began to hit into something very hard, and we only made it down to 45 feet.

The last day of Lynn's visit, we were really getting tired, but we were at it bright and early. We drilled hard all day, and finally at 65 feet we hit something extremely hard. We pounded on it for more than half an hour and it hadn't moved an inch. Finally we decided to stop for the day.

Usually after we had drilled several feet, well casing would be added on to the existing casing in the well. Weights would be clamped on the bit, and then the casing driven down to the depth that the bit had reached. We decided to do this before we quit.

When the casing reached the point where we had stopped drilling, we gave it a couple of extra hits just to be sure. Suddenly it dropped about three feet farther than we had drilled. We couldn't figure out what happened. Even Lynn with all his knowledge had never seen anything like that before.

We shut everything off and were standing beside the well trying to figure out what to do next, when suddenly we were standing in water that was coming out of the ground around our well casing. We dug a trench so it could flow away from the well—and it was then that we realized we had hit an artesian spring. Water was flowing at several gallons a minute. I dipped my finger in and tasted it. It was fresh water, not salty! Oh how we praised the Lord! We could hardly wait to get back to the compound and tell the good news. As we drove in the gate, Lynn's wife came running to meet us.

"You hit water, didn't you?" she called out. Lynn and I were both surprised at this statement as she had no way of knowing.

"What made you say that?" Lynn asked.

Deane was beaming. "I was praying about an hour ago," she said, "and the Lord told me you had water."

Yes! We now had water at Petite Anse, thanks to the Lord! The well had to be bailed out and cement poured around the casing. We installed a pump with a 20-foot pipe down into the well to provide water under pressure into the transmitter and generator buildings and also to an outside fountain where the people of the community could come to fill their buckets and jars. For many years it was the main source of good drinking water for the whole community of Petite Anse.

And after 36 years, that artesian well is still providing clear sweet water at our transmitter site.

1964   OUR FACILITATORS
By Eldon Turnidge

"Through the help of your broadcasts our son, Dean, who was a reckless sinner, was saved a few months ago," wrote a listener of 4VEH.

We understand the plight of a lost sinner, desperately needing such a miracle. On the other hand, patiently waiting is our wonderful Savior who has made provision for the miracle. Here at Radio 4VEH, missionaries and nationals regularly participate in these glorious experiences. But how difficult our task would be without those people who facilitate our work.

Are you the busy builder, laborer, or farmer, who took time to visit Haiti with a hammer and saw? Because you came we have a new transmitter building, a better water reservoir, completely renovated housing, two new missionary homes, and a host of other memorials. These assist us in the job.

Are you the businessman who could not come to Haiti to work with your hands but sent a Jeep truck? Or are you the musical evangelist who sent your personal Hammond organ for our program studio? These have been very effectively used by God in the overall ministry of making Christ known.

Perhaps you are the broadcaster who asked your radio audience to help you send a 10 kw transmitter to Radio 4VEH. Or are you the manufacturing corporation that extended to us that tremendous discount on your new 75 kw diesel generator? Or are you the widow who set aside a large part of your late husband's estate to provide that Cummins diesel generator?

Maybe you are the awning manufacturer who shades our windows from this tropical sun? Or are you those who sent us this telephone system? Could yours be the family that provided this 170-foot broadcast tower to direct our signal? Did you or your company freely donate these machine-shop tools: lathe, press, saws, or welders? Was it you or your family that provided us with these several excellent Crown tape recorders or this fine new FM link?

You are our facilitators, coming alongside again and again in making the Gospel known in Haiti. You, our valued coworkers, plus a host of others who pray and send cash offerings, have a very real share in all the victories. We know you rejoice with us when listeners write, "I cannot explain my thanksgiving for this station to which I have listened almost every day...for one day it led me to repentance."

1965   BETHESDA MEDICAL CENTER

By Ben and Helen Hoover from Linwood, Pennsylvania
Action Magazine for February 1965

It started with a burden to do something about the sick of Haiti. We had watched, during our MFM Crusade in 1964, while Miss Janet Elam, the only nurse, tirelessly and lovingly labored at the crude little clinic. We; had observed the hundreds of patients come in the early morning hours to be treated and receive medicine and food. We had seen the 100-150 patients per clinic day received in a little building only 10x12 feet. We had been shocked at the lack of equipment, the one small microscope.

We knew we had to do something about the situation. God loved these people no less than He did all of us who had come on the MFM tour. We began to ask questions:

How much would be needed to erect a new clinic?

What type building should it be?

Could we have a rough sketch of the architectural layout to take back to the States to show other concerned people?

We could not stay as missionaries, but perhaps we could raise the necessary $10,000. On the plane returning to the States, we discussed the possibilities.

Where could we start? It seemed like an impossible amount, but perhaps if we showed the slides we had taken and gave a report of the need, the Lord would multiply our efforts.

And He did! Not only were people interested in giving money but also, as the word spread, many volunteered their labor.

Today, just a little over a year later, the clinic is well under way. Francis Gibbs of Indiana, Jack Hanney and Lester Hyatt of New York, Bill Pugh and Thomas Moore from Florida, and Harold Megill of New Jersey have joined with us on the field to put up the building.

The first wing is almost ready for use and the second well along. Never could so few have accomplished so much except for God's help. Our faith is strong that the balance needed to complete the project will be given and that other workers will find it possible to go and finish the job.

1965   **MIRACULOUS**
                     By Miriam Stockton

"Miraculous" is a word we hear almost every day here in Haiti. We are convinced that our God delights in surprising us with miracles.

In June 1964, we drilled for water at our transmitter building located in the salt flats by the sea and struck an artesian well which keeps us more than adequately supplied with fresh, sweet drinking water—a miracle!

Then there was the day a $250 part burned out in our 10,000-watt transmitter, and we knew of nowhere in the country to find a replacement. It seemed our broadcasts for Haiti would be silenced for days and even weeks while we sent to the States for a replacement. Then God prompted the engineer to look in an out-of-the-way place in our own installation, where he found exactly the part he needed!

There was the time a new missionary arrived in Port-au-Prince unannounced. No one was there to meet her, and she could not understand a word spoken. There were no telephones to contact us, and she did not know where to go! But again in God's providence an American from another mission was able to direct her to our OMS home in Port-au-Prince.

Another miracle—our new clinic is well under way. Eleven months ago we had only a small amount in the project fund, and it was predicted that the new facility would be at least

103

three or four years away. But God has worked another marvel for us.

But the greatest miracle is taking place in the hearts of listeners to Radio 4VEH. Both locally and in our far-flung audiences through Haiti and the Caribbean, they have written: "I listened...Christ spoke to my heart...I received Him as my Savior." Thank God for the miracle of lives transformed through His redeeming love!

1965   **MUSIC IN MAHOGANY**
                   By Marilyn Murphy

It seemed incredible that here in the heart of a primitive island, emerging from mud huts and jungle trails, and with little or no education, a group of bright-eyed young people could so skillfully transform simple gospel choruses into spine-tingling experiences. Natural musical ability had responded to disciplined training. Built-in rhythm had combined with heartfelt reality. Heads, hands, hearts, and feet had endorsed each beat and radiant faces had given meaning to every word.

Captivated crusaders exchanged enthusiastic comments as they filed from the crude, termite-eaten church which moments before had seemingly swayed with rhythm.

"Sensational! Absolutely terrific!" they declared. Then a moment later, "They must come to the States!"

This was 1964. On the OMS compound near Cap-Haitien, Haiti, businessmen and ladies of the Men For Missions Crusade had just "discovered" the 32-voice Haitian Radio Choir. Their enthusiasm soon developed into pointed questions.

"Could the choir tour the States to show American Christians the positive proof of missions? What better way to

104

The 4VEH choir and quartet that toured the USA in 1965 with Valeene Hayes, their director, on the left

The 4VEH choir sang on the steps of the U.S. Capitol

L-R Miss Valeene Hayes, "Aunt Rachael" and "Uncle Mardy" Picazo, and Eldon Turnidge pilot, boarding for a visit to 4VEH island listeners in 1966

Aldean Saufley playing the Rogers organ in 1966

say 'Thank you' to those who have invested through prayer and purse?"

Elated missionaries weighed the prospects against mountainous obstacles. "Humanly impossible," they deducted, "but you could pray."

And pray they did, until one year later, during the next MFM crusade, the exciting announcement was made: a selected group of 16 voices, plus a male quartet, would give a concert tour in the eastern United States for approximately six weeks.

Haitians love to sing, and the choir of the Vaudreuil church, trained under Claudine Bustin (later Mrs. Victor Chamberlin), had performed on a Cap-Haitien radio station even before 4VEH was built. Their prodigious ability to memorize both words and music had captivated every music-loving missionary since.

When Valeene Hayes visited the OMS work at Cap-Haitien in 1962, she taught the church young people some of her hymn arrangements. Soon her choir and quartet were performing for Radio 4VEH and many nearby churches.

Although Valeene had been forced to spend much of her 32 years in bed, the rheumatic fever that had damaged her heart had not daunted her spirit nor hindered her musical talents. It had, however, seemed an impossible barrier to serving on a mission field. She had hoped for God's special healing so she could join her fiance as a missionary in South America. But when her condition did not improve, the engagement was broken. At this heartbreaking crisis her good friend, OMS Field Director Eldon Turnidge, invited her to Haiti.

The doctor gave permission for a six-week visit. In Haiti Valeene was convinced this was the place for her. Her health improved so greatly the doctor allowed a longer stay next time. It was then Valeene began to systematically train the choir that visiting MFM crusaders enthusiastically insisted must tour the States.

Not specially chosen voices, but volunteers from the local church youth group practiced Negro spirituals and gospel songs taken from available translations. As soon as a number was learned, it was recorded and used for radio broadcast. Public performances were limited to the local church until April 1963, when the choir sang in the Methodist Church of Cap-Haitien. Then an ever-increasing number of invitations in the nearby area enlarged their ministry.

And ministry was the constant goal. One day after rehearsal, a member of the choir informed the director he would be unable to sing the following Sunday. When questioned, he revealed he had no shoes to wear and, although he was willing to attend the service barefooted, he felt he should not appear with the choir. Carefully, Valeene reminded the young man that singing in the choir was not to impress men but to render service to Christ. So Sunday morning found him on the risers with the choir— barefooted, but willing to suffer embarrassment to give glory to God.

Even rehearsals represented a certain sacrifice for each young person. One boy lived five miles away and walked home after each session. For several of the girls who worked as cooks, it meant preparing the evening meal early enough to be at 4:30 rehearsals.

Although the story of the male quartet is somewhat different, it is equally thrilling. In 1959 three young Haitians who were control-board operators in the radio station, on their own initiative, began singing together. Listening to radio tapes in English, they imitated harmony and arrangements, then translated the words from English to French or Creole. After a year, a new member replaced one of the original three, and another was added to form the present quartet.

In addition to singing to our local congregation, the four pedaled many miles on their bicycles to Cap-Haitien, Acul-du Nord, and other churches. With the arrival and assistance of

Valeene Hayes, the quartet began recording for 4VEH broadcasts. Through this radio ministry they became well known throughout the island and were invited to take part in many special celebrations and weekend meetings.

With the big venture of a U.S. tour many obstacles had to be faced. Replacements must be trained for those who were to go. The quartet members filled important posts: radio operator, day school principal, transistor radio distributor, and pastor. Many of the fellows in the choir helped on the compound, in the machine shop, or at the radio station, while some of the girls worked as domestics. Their jobs must go on.

Then, ascertaining the correct legal name of each choir member for passports and other legal data was an unforeseen problem of some consequence. Bound by superstition and fear of evil spirits, Haitian non-Christian parents give their children two names—one for the birth certificate and another for common use.

Mandatory physical examinations, x-rays, vaccinations, and tests were other hurdles. With the high ratio of TB on the island, x-rays were taken with apprehension. There were no active cases.

Now all Valeene's strength was geared to preparing for the trip, only a few weeks away. Rehearsals, stepped up to twice a day for the choir (four hours of practice), in addition to the quartet rehearsals, individual voice lessons for soloists, and guitar work, took some doing in an already tight schedule. Many other long hours were spent writing original arrangements and planning the program. In addition, they decided to offer at their concerts a souvenir long-play record, which they titled, "Music in Mahogany."

Since the choir spoke only Creole, the English songs must be learned by rote, sometimes taking more than an hour to perfect one phrase. To help with learning English words to several of the new songs, as well as teach a few useful phrases of the language, a class was started. They were also briefed on the history and geography of the United States. And they spent time praying together.

There were also practical things, such as teaching the Haitians how to use doorknobs and eat strange American foods such as cereal and Jell-O. When the word "hamburger" was introduced and explanation given of this very American diet staple, a grimace crossed the face of one singer as he announced, "I surely wouldn't like to eat that!"

Toast, too, seemed to be a problem, but all agreed that with cheese it would be tolerable. The choir listened eagerly to the exhortations of Rev. Napoleon Etienne (Pastor Napo) who had visited the States several times.

The task of outfitting the group was another matter to be considered. Every item of clothing, shoes, and personal effects had to be supplied—both for traveling and everyday wear, as well as costumes for the concert. The program was divided into three sections, each member requiring three changes of clothes. Some lovely dress suits and frocks were donated for their appearances, but also many seamstresses were kept busy.

How did the young people react to the idea of traveling to the United States? For many there was fear—first time away from home, first airplane ride, ignorance of language and customs. For others it was the realization of a longstanding desire. But for all, there was a growing awareness of the responsibility placed upon them, not only to represent Radio 4VEH and the Republic of Haiti but also, and most important, to be ambassadors of Jesus Christ to America.

One miracle after another opened the doors before them. Passports were obtained in a matter of days instead of years. All the costumes were finally ready. Even a bus was provided. At last on May 5, 1965, the 16 choir members, the men's quartet, Rev. and Mrs. Etienne, and Valeene Hayes boarded the chartered plane for the USA.

Only a divine daily strengthening could have kept the frail director from collapsing under the strenuous schedule. She began the tour with only four hours' sleep in the previous 48. Often there were several concerts a day and long trips between, plus the routine chores and responsibilities of mothering 20 young people in a strange country.

In rapid and miraculous succession, plans and preparations dovetailed. And what began as a six weeks' tour in a few eastern states telescoped into 110 concerts in 28 states from coast to coast and into Canada for over three months. Yet Valeene returned to Haiti in better health than when she left.

The program was given by divine inspiration to the director, Valeene Hayes, and delighted audiences everywhere. First, it depicted actual Haitian market scenes, work bees on the mountainsides, and humble gospel services of the peasant people. Then, in pleasing contrast to their patchwork skirts and tattered trousers, the singers donned snappy suits and crisp blue dresses to praise their Savior with the majestic "Down From His Glory," "A Balm in Gilead," and "Oh, for a Thousand Tongues." Many listeners wept when the fitting song "Soon I Will Be Done with the Troubles of the World" was climaxed with a very dramatic "I'm going to live with God!" And none could forget the final whispered petition, "When You Pray, Will You Pray for Me?"

The presentation gave not only an unforgettable glimpse of Haiti and what the Gospel is accomplishing there, but it also had a ministry. In all but four concerts, which included eight TV appearances, one or more individuals claimed spiritual victories. In their final service, a man for whom many had prayed for 12 years found Christ as his Savior. The general opinion of pastors was that it was the best presentation of missions that had ever been given in their churches.

Nor was their ministry limited to Christian circles. In New York the singers captivated crowds at three pavilions of the World's Fair. Their appearance at Disneyland in Southern

California also included a salvation impact and was well received. Then in Washington, D.C., the group was officially welcomed by Assistant to the President, T. A. Wilson. A private tour of the White House included an invitation to sing (the first performance permitted there in three years).

After a lunch at which the choir were guests in the Speaker's Dining Hall, they were requested to perform on the steps of the Capitol. There, for two and a half hours the United States Information Service filmed and recorded their unique presentation, along with welcoming speeches from Senators Gibbons and Hungate of Florida and Missouri, respectively. This film, sent to the Haitian government as well as other Latin American embassies, extended the witness of these Haitian peasants to social levels and areas otherwise untouched with the salvation message—another success wrought by prayer.

1965   4VEH CHOIR RETURNS
Compiled by Rachael Picazo

The choir had received a warm welcome by the people of the United States, and now they were ready to return to Haiti. Then they received a cable from Port-au-Prince, sent by order of President Francois Duvalier himself: "Choir expected in Haiti for President's celebration." When this news was shared with the 20 Haitian singers, it was like throwing the switch on a string of Christmas lights. Each face beamed with joy and excitement.

The president's reception for the 4VEH Haitian choir was a momentous occasion—one of the most impressive ever held in Haiti. By printed invitation from the president, over 2,000 government officials and dignitaries gathered at the palace to witness the full choir program. At the close of the concert, which was broadcast live over all 15 Haitian stations, Mardy

Picazo, on behalf of OMS and 4VEH, presented to the president a beautifully bound Bible. Radio stations carried the palace performance for days.

Graciously accepting the gift, President Duvalier complimented the OMS, 4VEH, and, of course, the choir and Miss Valeene Hayes for their splendid work. After personally greeting each of the performers, he invited them to the palace gardens for a royal reception with 750 select guests. It was an occasion to relate to future generations.

Though the choir was back in Haiti, they had not actually arrived "home" yet. They still had to make the eight-hour bus trip over the mountains to Vaudreuil. Here at 4VEH, preparations began early in the morning of August 19, 1965, to welcome the 20 young people and their three attendants, who in 90 days had made a name for Haiti and Radio 4VEH across the U.S. and into Canada.

Piles of bright blossoms were knocked from the trees. Armloads of hibiscus were gathered and woven into the palm fronds forming a double archway over the compound drive. Paper streamers lined the sides of the roadway, and the large schoolroom blackboard was set out announcing "Bienvenue" (Welcome home) in colored chalk.

By 3:00 p.m., some 50 bicycles, along with innumerable people, horses, and donkeys, formed a two-mile brigade down the road. Meanwhile, the choir bus was delayed for repairs and church services en route. However, everyone was still eagerly waiting three hours later when the big yellow bus finally came into view! A mutual shout arose. Then all the friends and relatives that had lined the highway followed the bus into the grounds to the joyful peal of the church bell.

When at last the doors opened and the choir stepped off, such a time of rejoicing followed, as one would never expect to see this side of heaven. For several hours, hundreds of friends and relatives celebrated with the choir in the yard beside the

Vaudreuil church, embracing one another, laughing, and raising their hands in thanksgiving to God for their safe return.

Later that night, the choir members tried to tell about their experiences. But how could they describe it to those who had never been in an airplane, to those who had never traveled more than a few miles from home?

They had suddenly been thrust thousands of miles away into the modern cities of the United States! They had gaped at the skyscrapers in New York and marveled at mighty Niagara Falls. They had whisked up and down elevators, gingerly mounted escalators, talked on telephones, whizzed along superhighways at 70 miles an hour, plunged into tunnels through mountains, and dashed along roads balanced on stilts above the ground!

They had stared at the hundreds of cars in parking lots and wondered if there were enough people to drive them. They walked through doors that opened by themselves. How could they ever explain it all? Who could believe them?

Back with their families in little two-room huts, many of them stayed up all night trying to describe their experiences. And in the weeks ahead they repeated their descriptions of the trip, to the delight of continual audiences.

But one of them summed it up this way: "All these are not nearly so wonderful as what the Lord did for me on this tour. He broke my proud heart and gave me His Spirit. I have come back a different person."

1965   MUSIC ALONG THE WAY
By "Aunt Rachael" Picazo

They say that anyone who comes to the mission field should be willing to do anything. But one assignment that really flabbergasted me was given in December 1964, when our main English radio announcer, Dale Sloat, returned to the States. He had dozens of programs every week, but the most popular by far was the daily half-hour song request program, "Music Along the Way." During the eight months he had hosted it, he had made it into a master production, and the mail response had more than quadrupled.

Then they asked me to take the program five days a week, with Nurse Janet Elam being hostess on the weekends. Now, it's possible to scrub floors or plan meals for visitors—anyone can try. But to take "Music Along the Way" was so stupendous, I told the Lord that surely the committee had made a mistake. But I couldn't find real peace until I was willing to accept this job.

After my first program, with all its stumbling and mistakes, I was convinced that I was not the one for it. But I could only find calm in my heart when I became willing to go try again the next day. Gradually, the stark fear began to be replaced by joy in being able to talk to our listeners each day and give a Scripture passage or word of encouragement along with the songs they requested.

I expected the mail response to drop off to a dribbling after Dale left, and it did slump—but not for long. When "letter month" came in March, nearly 600 letters came to "Music Along the Way," nearly twice as many as many as any cord high.

The response of the listeners was heartening, such as the letter from a lady in Turks Islands: "I really love 'Music Along the Way.'"

Another wrote: "I listen every morning to the requests...I now seek the Lord Jesus to be my personal Savior through listening to the broadcast every morning."

About 1973 a broadcasting station which carried religious programs was established on South Caicos in the Turks and Caicos Islands. It broadcast all day and late into the night so it provided more for the English-speaking audience than 4VEH could with their three hours of English in the morning and two hours again in the evening. Also, being that much closer, it had a stronger signal.

At that time, also, the fuel prices in Haiti escalated to the point that we had to cut back our broadcast time. The "Music Along the Way" program was eventually discontinued. However, the song request programs in French and Creole have continued to be among our Haitian audience's favorite times of the day.

1966   **RADIO PARISH**
                      By Rachael Picazo

There had been trips made to visit our 4VEH English-speaking listeners on some of the Caribbean islands. Aldean Saufley had been to Grand Turk, North and South Caicos, and Providenciales with Cleve and Dorothy Irvine, and a couple of times he had visited with Rev. Elry Pontious in the Turks and Caicos Islands. Dale Sloat had also spoken in several churches in the islands on his return to the States in December 1964. There they told him that more people came to greet him than came to greet the Queen of England on her visit there.

But now we were about to take the first official trip with a team from the staff of 4VEH.

Our field director, Eldon Turnidge, spearheaded the plan and piloted his two-engine Piper Apache to carry two planeloads. On the team, besides Eldon and his wife Mary, were the White Sisters Trio and accompanist Valeene Hayes (our Haiti Choir director), my husband Mardy Picazo and I (known as "Aunt Rachael" to our listeners), and missionary nurse Margaret Bonnette.

I hardly knew what to expect on this, my first trip to the islands. We arrived on South Caicos, of the Turks and Caicos Islands in the West Indies, about 120 miles across the water north of 4VEH. Almost immediately I heard a soft voice call at the door of the house where we were staying, "Aunt Rachael?"

When I opened the door, half a dozen shyly smiling faces were lifted to mine from as many little dark-skinned children. These were my personal friends.

No, I had never met them before, but we were well acquainted—through radio. As they gave their names, I recognized them at once. How often I had read their letters, dedicated songs to them, and sent them on their way to school with a melody fresh in their hearts from our 4VEH daily request program, "Music Along the Way."

A steady stream of smiling friends soon assured us of friendliness as genuine as their letters had implied. It seemed a dream that I could be on South Caicos greeting those on the other end of the powerful radio waves from 4VEH in Haiti.

With us were the well-known "White Sisters," whose recordings were often requested by our radio audience. They had come to visit Haiti with the Men For Missions Crusade and gladly joined us on our trip to some of the small islands of the Caribbean.

At our first service in Cockburn Harbour, the local church bulged with people, and some 200 stood outside straining to hear and see. At least half of the island's population of 840 were there that night. The White Sisters held them spellbound, and when "Uncle Mardy" (as he is known on the children's radio programs) gave the message, one could sense the presence of God's Spirit. Many indicated a desire to become Christians.

The next day our itinerary took us to the island of Grand Turk, 20 miles away, where some 2,550 people live. The welcome was equally as warm, and our hosts—the Jack Harveys—opened their church to us.

115

When the services, which were announced over 4VEH and from the local communications system, started that afternoon it was soon evident that the room was inadequate. Children filled the benches, windows, and doorways; stood in the aisles; and crowded onto the street in front of the church. There was no disorder, however, so all could hear the thrilling songs by the White Sisters, testimonies from the team, and then the message, which it was my singular privilege to bear. I say "bear" because it was a very real burden that God had placed on my heart for these hundreds of beautiful children in our daily meetings.

When the simple message had been delivered, God made His claim on their tender hearts. Over a hundred children tarried after the service was dismissed! Each one opened his heart to receive the Lord Jesus Christ as his personal Savior.

No sooner had we finished praying with the children, when the older ones began assembling for the evening service. There was no time to eat, and when we returned in just a few minutes, the church was already filled, with hundreds standing in the street. Our team stood in the doorway for the service so that all inside and out could see and hear.

As Mardy Picazo brought the evening message, a hush fell over the audience. With no room to kneel in the tightly-packed throng, the many who raised their hands for prayer simply yielded to Christ where they stood as Mardy led them in the penitent's prayer.

The second day on Grand Turk, services were held in the open air with the aid of loudspeakers. Crowds increased and at the close of the children's meeting, about 30 teenage girls knelt on the tennis court and gave their hearts to God. At the same time, Valeene prayed with some 75 smaller children who came forward. Eldon led seven teenage boys to the Savior. Mardy worked with the town drunkard, who was weeping with conviction, while the trio and the rest of the team spread out to help other young people and children.

In the evening service, an estimated 1,000 people gathered to hear the songs, testimonies, and message. Five stepped forward at the close to openly declare their faith in the Lord Jesus, and dozens of others raised their hands revealing hungry hearts.

Between services we visited shut-ins, shops, and offices, and talked with people on the street. Programs from 4VEH could be heard coming from homes and stores. Everyone greeted us by name for we had long been their friends through 4VEH.

Back to South Caicos the last day of the tour, God blessed again in the children's meeting as nine little girls found the Savior. But the evening service was one of the most unusual in my experience. The message over, some had responded and it was time to dismiss. Yet such a sense of God's presence hovered over the church that no one wanted to leave. Emcee Eldon Turnidge was constrained by the Holy Spirit to keep the service open.

Testimonies were given; yet no release came. More than an hour the Spirit held the audience steady. Even little children on the floor in the aisles sat alert and did not stir. When 10 o'clock came, Eldon felt that he must pronounce a benediction.

But then the break came! Five lovely girls, leaders on their island, at last yielded to the Master's wooing. One was the schoolteacher, another a dispenser at the clinic, and a third a clerk in the main store. While these five wept their way to victory, three other teenage girls followed their example.

What rejoicing followed as these young people, the cream of the island's youth, surrendered their all to God. It was a thrilling climax to our four days in radio rallies, mingling among the people of our "radio parish." We felt we had been in the middle of a miracle. These old friends, whom we had just met, came in a steady file to say goodbye, give us gifts, and leave letters they had written to the station. One of those letters read:

117

"We pray that you all will come to our islands again and visit us—not for two days but for two years, or even stay with us forever. We are also praying that whenever you all will come again, not only nine of you, but the whole Radio 4VEH staff will be here."

Upon returning to her island home after many years, one listener wrote:

"It was like finding a long-lost love, a spiritual love. I never really knew how much I missed hearing that familiar sound. From childhood I grew up with Radio 4VEH. Though I traveled to Nassau to attend high school and college, I now live in Inagua and work for the salt company as a secretary. I'm married and have a daughter that is four years old. It's so good that in raising my own family, I can have Radio 4VEH to help us spiritually."

THE NEW ROGERS ORGAN
By Rachael Picazo

Dr. Vernon Hall not only ministers to the sick, he loves to play organ. When his family visited in Haiti, he went to our 4VEH studio and relaxed by playing the organ, a little spinet donated by song evangelists John and Romaine Woodhouse.

"Is this the organ you use to make all the mood music and sound effects for your dramatizations?" he inquired incredulously of Aldean Saufley, "Why, what you need is an instrument with the capabilities of a theater organ."

That is when he decided to do something about it. He found that the Rogers Organ Company in Portland, Oregon, would accept S&H Green stamp books to pay for such an instrument as he envisioned, if there were enough thousands of books.

So for two years, Dr. Hall through Men For Missions International inspired faithful housewives across the nation to donate their treasured books. It took a wheelbarrow to hold them all.

But now the magnificent organ is installed in the studio at 4VEH, thanks to the ingenuity of Dr. Hall, the hearty cooperation of Men For Missions International, and the thousands of generous housewives who lovingly surrendered their S&H Green Stamp books.

1966   **THE POTHOLE WOULDN'T MOVE**
By Mardy Picazo

It had all started one afternoon on my shift at the radio transmitter site when I heard a peculiar grinding noise coming from the motor house. Our six-cylinder Cummins diesel was generally purring smoothly under the background of a mix of Spanish programs on one channel and the French/Creole programs on the other. So when I heard this abnormal sound, I immediately went to see what it was.

But the motor was outside my expertise, so I placed a call for our diesel mechanic, Jim Wallace, back at the missionary compound. By radiotelephone I described the noise to him. He immediately jumped on his motorcycle and came to Petite Anse. It could normally take 45 minutes to negotiate the ten miles, but he made it in about 20. He listened to the engine, checked the gauges, and asked when we would be off the air. I told him that we were scheduled to sign off at 10:00 p.m. but that the last hour was mostly music, so we could go off earlier.

Jim said, "Well, Mardy, the engine has a serious problem and must be stopped as soon as possible. The bearings are gone on one piston arm, and we don't want to ruin the crankshaft by allowing it to run too much. I'll go back to get the necessary parts and tools. If we work through the night, we may be able to get the engine overhauled before we have to go back on the air at 5:00 tomorrow morning."

So off he went, and I called the studio to prepare them for the early signoff. He came back ready to work through the night, and I stayed with him for whatever help or moral support I could give. We started up our auxiliary engine generator when the station signed off so we could have electricity while we worked, and we shut down the big diesel. We had to drain the oil from the crankcase and do some other preparatory work before Jim was able to disassemble the engine. Besides that, the motor was still hot and the night was also hot. For long hours, Jim worked diligently taking that Cummins diesel apart and putting in the replacement bearing shells. Since the engine was already torn down, he went ahead and replaced the other cylinders' bearings and the oil rings.

About 4:00 a.m., it was ready to be tested. The oil and water had been replaced and everything had been tightened down to specifications. He primed it, and then while both Jim and I prayed, he pushed the starter button. The huge engine started right up. The speed was gradually increased until it was running at full velocity. Jim slowed it down again and then brought it back up to let it idle for a while. Everything was looking great, a good 30 minutes before we would have to be back on the air for our regular broadcasts. Jim was satisfied that all was well; there were no leaks, oil pressure was normal, and the temperature had risen to its proper reading.

It would now have to be tested under load, so after another ten minutes he brought the engine up to operating speed and we transferred the power from the small generator to the big one. The transmitters were turned on to heat up and the adjustments made as needed on all the equipment. When everything was ready, we threw on the full load. The generator hardly made a quiver, and the readings on the engine did not change.

It was then that we were confident our broadcasts would be able to resume, with the Spanish and French/Creole programs starting the day. At this point Jim broke down in tears of joy.

"Praise God!" he cried out. "I can't preach a word of Spanish nor of Creole, but because I was able to repair this engine, those that can preach will be able to do so now!"

In my own spirit I was likewise rejoicing for being a part of the team that worked together at this station. Now we could go home.

We loaded the tools and old parts, back into the truck Jim had used. I got into my own vehicle, and we headed for the compound. It was about 5:45 that morning, and I was so tired I could hardly see straight. It was all I could do to steer the car down the road.

I got through town all right, the streets already full of vendors and others, most of them on foot or riding bicycles. When I got near the gate of the city on the road that led home, I found half a dozen trucks and buses loudly sounding their horns to make their way through the milling crowd. Others were taking on their loads of people and cargo preparing to go to all points south. I added to the confusion by leaning on my own horn and inching my way toward the gate.

The road leading out of the city was especially bad in this area due to the heavy truck traffic. There were potholes several inches deep and stretching three feet wide. Normally we tried to dodge these bone-jarring "devices" that could even crack an axle. But this particular morning as I wearily approached a very large pothole, I honked at it.

The pothole didn't move, of course, and I hit it square on. Not until then did I realize what I had done! The laugh I had at myself helped wake me up enough to get on home without further incident.

1967   **BABY BRENDA**
                                    By Lucy Hess

Brenda had been a healthy, chubby baby. But now her skin folded in wrinkles where fat had once filled out her form. Bones were protruding. For seven months her stomach had been expanding, until now, after meals, she could hardly walk for the weight of it. Unable to sit up, she chose to lie on the floor with her blanket. Her pained expression and continual whining were constant reminders of her distress. We knew she was approaching a physical crisis that might take her from us.

Although tests and specimens revealed nothing, doctors felt she had roundworms. All kinds of medicines were tried, but none was effective. Just before Christmas our field director felt I should take her to the States. Friends offered to care for us while there. But how does a mother of five make such a decision?

At the same time, several of our Haitian Christians encouraged me to trust God for a divine touch. "I know God will heal her," Jackson, our faithful Haitian worker, spoke with conviction. I recalled his testimony of how God had relieved him of a terrible asthma malady when a child. Now his declaration infused faith and courage into my aching heart. Simply but earnestly I asked the Lord for a sign that He would heal her.

The next morning Brenda began to eat properly. She seemed much happier. Unmistakably this was the sign; God would heal her in Haiti.

Miracle processes became evident immediately. Almost overnight Brenda's weight was redistributed and her stomach returned to more normal size. The next week she began gaining weight. Everyone noticed the new life in her expression and eyes.

Then the letters started coming "How is Brenda? We have been praying daily for her."

Relatives wrote, "We are still holding on in prayer for Brenda. Believe God is working."

From close friends, "When we got your letter about Brenda, we shared it with our prayer group and had special prayer."

Other letters arrived from OMS Prayer Fellowships saying, "How is the Hess baby? We are praying for her."

The January Intercessogram had listed the prayer request for Brenda, and thousands in the OMS prayer family knew the need. What prayer power had been set in motion!

As our Brenda gains weight, looks normal, plays outdoors, laughs, and smiles, I know that faith can touch God and that He performs miracles. I had known this in theory, but now I know by experience, for God healed our Brenda.

1967   EMMAUS VOCATIONAL BIBLE SCHOOL
By Marilyn Murphy

"Lord, help me find a place to study the Bible," prayed Tony. Only 16 years of age, he had found Christ as his Savior through the ministry of our little compound church. Though his family was Catholic, he had attended our services for many years. And the day he told his mother of his desire to follow Christ, she decided to take the step with him. A few weeks later Tony's father became a Christian, and within a year all in his family were saved.

From the moment of his conversion, Tony began praying for a way to learn more about God's Word. There seemed no place to go, however. So Tony joined with others of the church in house-to-house evangelism and open-air services.

Then one day it was announced that a Vocational Bible School would begin in January 1967 on the OMS compound at Vaudreuil. "I will be one of the students unless I die first," Tony determined, "for there's only one thing in this world I want to do, and that's evangelism."

For Petiel, God seemed to make things happen faster than he could imagine. Raised in a Christian family, he had always dreamed of someday having Bible school training, but he supposed that day was far away. When work began on construction of the church at Hostin in the spring of 1966, Petiel was there to help make blocks and serve as watchman of the property.

Having never mentioned his desire to attend Bible school, he was amazed one afternoon when missionary Dave Graffenberger told him of Emmaus Vocational Bible School, which would open at Vaudreuil in January 1967. Would he like to attend?

Would he like to attend! Petiel had gone to public school five years. But when he realized he was being taught to serve Satan, he left, preferring to stay "with the little knowledge I had rather than risk losing faith in God."

Now, here was the opportunity for the training he wanted! Following entrance examinations, Petiel was tested severely. He returned home to find a good job waiting for him, arranged by his non-Christian godfather. Should he take it? He needed money for Bible School.

As he calculated what he could earn, he realized that when it was time for Bible School to begin, the temptation to continue working might be too great. So Petiel refused the job, saying: "Money is something which is just for a moment. While I'm young, I'll serve the Lord."

It is for young people like these that the Vocational Bible School in Haiti was established. On January 9, 1967, Tony,

Petiel, and 18 other Haitian young people began a four-year Vocational Bible School training program at Vaudreuil.

But the story begins long before that—as early, in fact, as 1952, when Eldon Turnidge, now Haiti field director, visited the OMS work in Colombia. Thrilled with the newly-begun vocational school there, he provided their first tractor. In 1957 Eldon returned to Colombia with a group of five men—the first Men For Missions Crusade. On that first Crusade Eldon wanted to take Dave Graffenberger, a young Oregon farm lad, but Dave was in Wheaton College at the time and couldn't go. However, the next year, 1958, both Dave and Eldon returned to Colombia, where they spent several months working in the farm program of the Vocational Bible School in Cristalina.

Dave left Colombia a changed person. Now his one desire was to return to Colombia as a missionary, to work in the Vocational Bible School program.

But God had other plans. Five years later Dave and his wife, Marilyn, with their little boy, Brian, were in Haiti, appointed to establish a Vocational Bible School there.

That same year, 1963, God was at work in other lives. Two Oregon farmers agreed to pay $1.00 per pound instead of the usual $.85 for distilling their mint crop. Use of the still was given free and the distillery workers donated their time. As a result, $2000 was applied to the Vocational Bible School in Haiti.

In 1965 some of these same farmers wanted to go to Haiti and build the school, but a clinic was then under construction. It was not yet God's time. In the fall, however, at an MFM banquet in Portland, Oregon, the Lord spoke to several builders concerning the project. They approached Don Turnidge, Eldon's cousin, who said that he personally would see that the project was a success.

So, in January 1966, Don chartered a plane and took 16 men to Haiti. In two weeks they erected two dormitory/classroom buildings and a large dining/study hall.

But what kind of training are Tony, Petiel, and other young people receiving?

The number one aim of the Emmaus Vocational Bible School at Vaudreuil is to train dedicated Christian young people, first in biblical truths and, secondly, in vocational skills. Many of them will become pastors or evangelists; others will fill important posts as laymen in Haitian churches.

Classes in Bible, Christian doctrine, personal evangelism, language, music, and mathematics provide a well-rounded foundation for each young person. In addition, each student chooses from a series of vocational classes: radio electronics, home economics, secretarial practice, and agriculture. Classroom instruction is supplemented with actual practice in one of the departments of the OMS work in Haiti. There the student learns by experience, while contributing to the ministry of OMS in Haiti. One of the unique features of the Emmaus Vocational Bible School is that everyone works. Regardless of the pupil's financial status, the work program is an integral part of his training. Because Haitian economy is based primarily on agriculture, a major emphasis is placed on agriculture. Every student learns better methods of farming, animal husbandry, and related subjects to equip him for making a living and improving the economic level of the country.

Tony... Petiel... Jacques... Daniel—in four years, by God's grace, will graduate as well-trained, enthusiastic, dedicated Christian pastors and laymen.

Bible School students assembling the radio kits and making their boxes in 1967

Children listening to one of the pre-tuned radios in 1967

Nurse Flora Boyer in the lovely new
clinic courtyard in 1968

In 1968 Transmitters inside the Pettie Anse building, the
new Baurer is behind the operator at the desk

1967   PRE-TUNED RADIOS FOR HAITI
               By Rachael Picazo

We all recognized that not very many of the Haitians living in the countryside had radios. They were barely able to stretch their garden produce to feed their families, and the cash in their pockets for a month, even if they spent every penny, would not be enough to buy a radio. Besides, most of them had never heard one, so there was no desire.

But we had seen how God used the transistor pre-tuned radios we had distributed. We needed a plan to get them into the hands of more people. Men For Missions stepped in, and helped us buy 2,000 kits from Japan. Those arrived in January of 1967, the year the Emmaus Vocational Bible School opened.

The kits had to be assembled, which fit in with the work assignments of the Electronics Department. Then boxes needed to be made to house them, and the woodworking students in the Bible School's vocational training did a fine job.

With the pre-tuned radios ready to distribute, missionary Hudson Hess was assigned the next aspect of researching the villages and homes where the receivers would be placed. He had a fine, Haitian young man, Joseph Thermidor, work right along with him.

After the sets were distributed, Joseph visited each radio regularly to replace the batteries and make any necessary repairs. He also took that occasion to find out how many were listening and to encourage the new believers.

During the next three years, the price of transistor radios became drastically lower, so more of the people of Haiti were able to afford them. In 1970 we stopped our program of distribution, but listeners continued to increase as the people bought their own radios.

A BIT OF FAITH

By Harold Brown, (as told to Rachael Picazo)

I had barely arrived in Haiti for my first term as a missionary when I started helping Dave Shaferly drill our first well on the mission grounds near the Bible School buildings. The students helped us. We just pounded it in crudely, and we got the bit stuck.

We tried all we knew to do to get it loose. At last darkness overtook us so we put on the wench and left the old jeep's front end swung up in the air so its weight would keep tugging on the bit all night.

We had missionary prayer meetings on Friday nights in those days, and we had special prayer that night for the Lord to cause the bit to be released. But the next morning, it was still stuck.

Dave borrowed two 20-ton jacks and jacked up the casing. It still didn't come loose. Dave had two or three other ideas, which we tried, and which also brought no success.

"What are you going to do now?" one of the students asked as we stood around shaking our heads.

"I don't know anything else to do," Dave admitted.

Then Tony, a freshman in the Bible School, spoke up, "Let's pray."

We had been praying all day, prayed the day before, and had special prayer in the missionaries' prayer meeting the night before. But Tony was saying, "Let's pray!"

At that point I took charge. Since he seemed to have faith, I said, "Okay, Tony, you pray."

And Tony just talked to the Lord. He said, "Lord, you know that Ti Dave and Pastor Brown tell us that about all the pipe we've got is in the ground, and now this tool is in the ground and has got stuck. We need water, and if we don't have

128

this pipe and this tool, we can't get water. Lord, this is no problem for you...."

I got back in the jeep and started running the wench. The front wheels came up about 18 inches, and then all of a sudden, "Bang!"--down on the ground.

My first thought was that the rope had broken, but when I looked up I saw that the rope was intact, raising the bit up, up, up...

It was Tony's prayer, not Ti Dave's faith nor mine, that enabled us to have that good well at the Bible School.

When we were in Haiti for the Pastors' Conference in March 1998, I reminded Tony of that incident thirty years ago. It's not just a story—it's an event, a part of our history. The Lord answers prayer.

1968   BURNING HEART AT EMMAUS
By William A. Gillam

The visiting American layman, Don Turnidge, had just flown to Cap-Haitien in his small plane. All the way from Oregon, he had come to talk over plans for the future at the Emmaus Vocational Bible School on the Radio 4VEH compound. Already he had invested substantial sums of his own money in the first buildings. He had also rounded up a team of enthusiastic laymen from the northwestern states to construct those units.

Rightfully, his comment was more than justified, "I'm concerned about these young Haitians we are training. Will they really get the vision and accomplish the work that needs to be done?"

He and I were discussing this when the doorbell rang, and Tony, a tall, handsome young Haitian, stood there with his hand on his heart. "Pastor, will you pray for me?"

I invited him in, and as we sat down on the porch, his words fell over each other. Tony's stuttering was a handicap either in his native Creole or broken English. But I read him well.

"All this week my heart has been burning. I must do a work for God, which I have not done yet. Please pray that I may be filled with the Spirit."

We bowed in prayer. Placing my hand on his, we believed together for God's purifying work in Tony's soul. When we finished, his testimony matched my conviction that God had met him. His heart was filled with the peace of Christ's presence.

Encouraging this moment were several mornings of chapel messages brought to the Emmaus Bible School students at our Radio 4VEH center. I had recounted the thrilling chapters of Charles and Lettie Cowman's lives and highlights of OMS history. Intently, their black faces had turned upward for the touch of God's power. Tears had been mixed with earnest prayers. They had begun to see Haiti as part of a world vision.

One student said, "If young men like us could distribute the Gospel from house to house in Japan, surely we can do it in Haiti!"

Tony is one of more than thirty students who form the first two classes of the Emmaus Bible School. Working half-days and studying half-days, these young people are rising out of dire poverty and aimlessness into meaningful Christian vocation. The miracle of the New Birth is first...then the awakening of the mind, the cultivation of talent...and, supremely, the commission to witness and preach the unsearchable riches of Jesus Christ.

But what about the layman's question? Will Tony be a factor in changing Haiti? Where and what will he and the other students be five, ten, twenty years from now?

They are starting well. But all of them will be special targets of repeated satanic assaults. Strong temptations, subtle dissuasion, pride and pretension, discouragement, and even disillusionment will assail them.

Surrounded by a world of voodoo and acquainted with the power of evil spirits, they surely have a fight to wage.

That burning heart must be kept aglow! Fresh fuel for the altar, with continuous fire from above, is furnished through contact with the source of power.

Christ was aware of His disciples' desperate need of prayer if they were to stand the coming tests. He revealed the secret place of power in His statement, *"I pray for them: I pray not for the world, but for them which Thou hast given me."*

We, too, can intercede for these students, that their hearts be kept aglow with God's power as they spread across Haiti.

1968   HAITI CLINIC DEDICATED

On July 24, 1968, a dedication service for the Bethesda Clinic was held on the OMS compound. Scores of Haitians, dignitaries, and missionaries, as well as the summer Men For Missions International Crusade team, attended the event. Harry Burr, Executive Secretary of MFMI, brought the dedicatory message.

Begun in 1965, the clinic resulted from the vision of MFMI Crusaders who sensed the overwhelming physical distress of the Haitians and the inadequacy of the small carriage shed then used as a medical center. Since that time, largely through

MFMI, over $15,000 has been raised and much of the labor donated by work crews from various parts of the U.S.

Ten consulting rooms, a chapel waiting room, complete pharmacy, a records room, and two washrooms make up the two-wing complex. Hundreds of patients are treated each clinic day. Missionary nurses also conduct outstation clinics in the national churches for those unable to travel distances. Scores have accepted Christ through this ministry.

1968   A LETTER FROM DAD
By David Graffenberger (as told to Rachael Picazo)

One Sunday afternoon on the mission grounds at Vaudreuil, a telegram came informing me that I had to present myself in the office of the Department of Cults in Port-au-Prince the next morning. It seems several missions were being summoned for the meeting.

We were near Cap-Haitien on the northern coast of the island, and the trip to the capital took at least eight hours. At that time there were no buses running at night.

So I took off on the big blue NSU motorcycle that James Wallace had bought. I was moving right along when two things happened.

First, while I was running through the valley of Passe Reine, I came around a corner and there was a truck stopped right in the middle of the road with people everywhere around it. I don't know what I did, probably closed my eyes—but pretty soon I was in front of the truck without having hit a soul. What a big "Praise the Lord!"

At the following town, Gonaives, I bought my normal V8 juice and ham-and-cheese sandwich at the Shell station, then continued down the road. It had rained that afternoon but there was no sign of it on the blacktop, the heat having dried all traces of the water. In those days the paving ended at Pont Estere and the road from there was either dust or mud, according to the season.

As I drove off the blacktop, the second thing happened. Instead of coming onto a dirt road, I hit mud. The motorcycle slid every which way, spilling me onto the ground. I got up and felt myself. No bones were broken, the cut on my hand not serious. I looked at the motorcycle—it was mostly intact. So that was the second big "Praise the Lord!"

I tore my hanky into strips, used it to tie up some parts on the motorcycle and wrap around my hand, then got back on the motorcycle. I slowly navigated the muddy road across the Artibonite until the pavement started again at Pont Sondé. The sun had long set, and by this time in the middle of the night, I began to get sleepy. I was young back then, but I found myself falling asleep while driving. I finally decided it wasn't smart to try to keep going, so I stopped the motorcycle, laid out completely on top of it, and went sound asleep.

I slept for about an hour and 15 minutes, then proceeded to Hostin where I always had a room at William's mom's house. I slept the rest of the night there, then the next morning drove on 30 miles to the outskirts of Port-au-Prince.

There I stopped at the house of one of our truck drivers so I could change to my suit. I had to be properly attired for the appearance at the Department of Cults. My friend let me drive his car rather than take the motorcycle into the city for the occasion.

When my obligation was over, I returned by motorcycle to Vaudreuil without incident.

About three weeks later, I received the only letter I ever got from my father. Oh, my father loved me, but he just didn't write; he let my mother do the correspondence.

In his letter he said, "Son, I had to write you this letter. What were you doing on Sunday afternoon...?" And he mentioned the date.

"At two o'clock in the afternoon..." (which was five o'clock in Haiti when I got on the motorcycle) "...the Lord laid on my heart to pray. So Mom and I prayed until church started. We went to church and when we came home, we prayed another hour and a half..."

The time they were in church was the time I was sleeping on my motorcycle.

That was the only letter Dad ever wrote me. Oh, it was tremendous! It was a blessing.

1968   SOLOMON IN ALL HIS GLORY
By Marilyn Graffenberger

To get a bucket of water at Ti Bois meant an hour and a half trip, trudging down the mountain to the spring and back up again with the heavy pail. No wonder some of our pastor's eight children had "chic" in their feet. The disease had been transmitted by fleas from animals which the landowner allowed to run free in the courtyard where Pastor Lundi was renting a house, 8 x 12, with a dirt floor.

With no rain for nine months, the dust was deep and heavily infected with chic fleas. The barefooted children, infrequently bathed, were easy victims for the fleas which laid eggs in the pores of their feet, causing severe infection. Some could no longer walk.

With our year's furlough in the States coming soon, Dave and I had saved funds to replenish our worn-out and outgrown (for the children) wardrobes and purchase other necessities. But just now, the need for a larger, cement floor home for Pastor

Lundi's family seemed more important. We decided to use the money we had set aside for this need.

When the time came for packing, I wondered if we had been foolish after all, as I realized our clothes were unpresentable for use in the States. But no—we had decided to trust God for our needs.

No sooner had we arrived in Miami when we received a phone call telling us that money had been deposited in our account for whatever we needed. A waiting letter contained a check designated for clothing, and the next day a package came— new clothes for the whole family from friends who knew nothing of our funds diverted to the Ti Bois parsonage.

1968   4VEH OFF THE AIR

<u>Os Heinrich</u>: It was a beautiful, clear day that May 20, 1968, when I drove the seven miles to the Cap-Haitien airport with Rev. Don Price, who aired his program, "Family Altar of the Air," on 4VEH. He was on his way back to the States after a visit here at the station. I had my lunch with me because, as soon as I had seen the visitor safely on the plane, I would take my daily stint at Petite Anse, the transmitter site.

We waited and waited, but the plane never did come. I finally had to take him back to the compound so he could have his dinner there. While we were eating, Harold Brown came in with the news, "I was just listening to the Voice of America, and they announced that Haitian rebels have attempted an invasion in Port-au-Prince."

About an hour later three planes loaded with rebels landed at the Cap-Haitien airport. Some of them went immediately to Petite Anse, only a mile or so away, and took our radio guys hostage. I would ordinarily have been there!

The rebels demanded that they be allowed to speak on 4VEH. Our fellows told them it was not possible to broadcast from that location, that all the programs came by link from Vaudreuil.

Then they had Edner, one of our 4VEH operators on duty there, use our two-way radio communications link to talk with Hudson Hess, radio director at the time at Vaudreuil. The rebels demanded that they be allowed to speak on 4VEH, otherwise they were going to blow up the installation at Petite Anse.

Hudson replied, "Then you'll just have to blow the place up. There is no way to speak from there." Then he went on to explain that 4VEH was apolitical, not entering at all into the politics of the country.

Out at the Cap-Haitien airport, one planeload of invaders left that afternoon, but the rest stayed the night. The next day the Coast Guard came up and shelled the terminal, knocking big holes in the walls, damaging one of the two remaining planes and killing some of the rebels. The rest fled. I guess they realized that they couldn't do anything. Some went off into the mountains where they were later captured.

That's when 4VEH was accused of having sided with them, and the government closed us down. Both Petite Anse and our studios at Vaudreuil were locked on May 24, and soldiers were posted outside the doors.

The country was put on military alert and the roads guarded, so that everyone had to have a special pass to travel. In this confusion the Graffenberger family managed to get off to the States for their furlough. Those of us that were left were told to keep suitcases packed in case we needed to leave, because we didn't know what was going to happen.

Kathy Heinrich: As a missionary group, we had a lot of prayer meetings that summer—a lot of extra prayer meetings. We would meet in a home. It was kind of unnerving, having those guards there all the time and the station shut down, and we didn't know exactly what was going on. I think it really brought the missionary body closer together.

Os Heinrich: The Haitian police took Edner Hilaire, our main operator and watchman at Petite Anse, and put him in the Cap-Haitien prison. He had been there more than a month when his brother came to Hudson one day with a note that Edner had thrown over the prison wall, telling him that he was going to be executed that day.

Hudson and I rushed into town to the prison, where Hudson pled for Edner's life, assuring the prison warden that our employee had not had any part in the rebels' activity. The man said, "On my word, I promise we will not execute him."

He kept his promise. They finally released Edner.

Dave Graffenberger: We were ready to go to the States for furlough when this rebel invasion was attempted. We managed to get as far as Port-au-Prince, in spite of travel restrictions.   There we found that Eldon Turnidge and Bill Gillam had flown into Haiti because of the situation with 4VEH. The American Embassy wanted to see us, so the three of us went down and talked with them and filled out forms. Then we all left for the States.

Radio 4VEH had been off the air for several weeks when our OMS International Missionary Conference started at Winona Lake, Indiana, that June 1968. Bill and I left the conference to fly to Washington, D.C., where we met with the Haitian ambassador to the United States, Arthur Bonhomme.

Bill Gillam: Mr. Arthur Bonhomme, Haiti's Ambassador to Washington, was a tall, graying, intense man. He belonged to a renowned family and served his country well.   A fervent Christian, he was most deeply concerned about the communication of the Gospel. He boldly identified himself with the evangelical movement.

Thus, when Dave Graffenberger and I outlined the Radio 4VEH problem to the Ambassador in a seven-hour conference on

June 27 in Washington, we found ourselves talking to a man who "spoke the same language." Confidence is part of the Christian spirit. Our case was clear, our innocence was established, and he was ready to act.

He made an overseas call to the palace in Port-au-Prince, and as a consequence we were invited by the president to come and see him about the matter. (It likewise revealed the unique position in which this courageous man was serving God's purpose.)

We flew to Port-au-Prince immediately. Our ten-hour wait in the Yellow Room at the National Palace on July 2 was worth it. The long vigil vanished in a rewarding half-hour interview at seven o'clock in the evening. The president of Haiti quietly and simply stated his intention to order the reopening of the station, but he was careful to explain his decision. "I trust my ambassador in Washington," he said, "he trusts you; therefore, I trust you."

He urged us to continue our primary task of spiritual, missionary work, "...which," said he, "is what my country needs." (We had heard that hundreds of letters had come in to the prefect's office in Cap-Haitien from 4VEH listeners begging him to let the station start broadcasting again.)

President Duvalier handed me the keys to Radio 4VEH, and he telephoned the airport alerting them that we would be there the next morning to fly up north.

On July 3, with the keys to the transmitters and studios in our pockets, Dave and I landed at the Cap-Haitien airport. Civil and military authorities received and conducted us to the respective sites for reopening of the facilities.

Dave Graffenberger: When we flew into Cap-Haitien the next morning, there was quite a delegation to meet us, including the Haitian colonel; Os Heinrich, our radio engineer; our missionaries, and Haitian friends. We went over to Petite Anse and Bill Gillam made a little speech. When it was almost over, the colonel asked Bill Gillam, "When are you going to get the transmitters on?"

Bill turned to Os Heinrich. "Well," Os responded, "they've been down for six weeks, and we have to clean everything, warm them up, with all that moisture—and then, the engines have to be serviced, and we have to open up the studios and get our announcers and programs ready. There is no way we are going to get everything ready today."

The colonel ordered us, "We want you back on the air in two hours."

By this time it was noon. Everyone scrambled. But by two o'clock, I had to go to the military headquarters and beg for another couple hours of grace.

Bill Gillam: At 4:00 p.m., after forty days of silence, Radio 4VEH again took to the air with its sound of faith and salvation. On all station breaks that evening, the "Doxology" and the "Hallelujah Chorus" were played in a paean of praise to Almighty God. On July 6 I called Ambassador Bonhomme from Miami to report the happenings of that eventful week. His deep satisfaction came over the phone in a hearty "Praise the Lord."

Rachael Picazo Just hours before the Haiti presentation at our OMS Conference, Bill Gillam and Dave Graffenberger flew back from Haiti with the spectacular news that 4VEH was now back on the air! A thrill of praise ran through the conference, and the Haiti field presentation rode on wings of joy.

Our Haiti field was to raise funds this year for $15,000 still needed to pay for a 10,000-watt Bauer AM transmitter for Radio 4VEH. As we took our seats on the platform, Linda Ragsdale remarked to me, "Wouldn't it be nice if all the money came in today for the transmitter?"

In my own mind, I thought, "No way that will happen. Maybe a fifth, or even a fourth of it..."

I didn't say anything out loud, however. I didn't want to discourage her faith.

139

The Haiti field gave its presentation and the offering was taken for the new transmitter. Then a note was delivered to Bill Gillam on the platform. He took the slip of paper and read it aloud:

"I will give $1,000 towards the project if fourteen others will also give $1,000."

Bill was confused. He turned to someone and asked, "Does this lady need us to give her something?"

Dave Graffenberger took the note and began to explain it to Bill, and in doing so made it quite clear what it was all about. Three people stood almost immediately, even before he finished clarifying it, and pledged $1,000 each.

Then such a Spirit of giving came over the congregation that people jumped to their feet and with joy gave all they could. In a matter of 15 minutes, the Bauer transmitter was completely paid for!

Bill Gillam and Dave Graffenberger joyously embraced each other, and a deeply moved audience broke into spontaneous song, "Praise God from whom all blessings flow!"

1968   A RESERVOIR FOR HAITI
By Buss Rassi and Wallace Yoder

The idea came while we were on the work crusade in 1968. A water reservoir for the OMS compound in Haiti was an obvious and urgent need. And the location missionaries had in mind seemed perfect for a round water tank, using silo forms we had back home. We decided to pray about it. If the Lord wanted us to do the job, He would open the way.

At the OMS Conference at Winona Lake, Indiana, missionaries Dave Graffenberger and Harold Brown encouraged our venture.   Later Dr. Bill Gillam, Haiti director, gave the go-ahead. All we needed was money.

Shortly after the challenge was given to MFMers in our northern Indiana area, all the funds were in. In addition, two other laymen—Duane Laidig and Everett Tom, Jr.—sensed God's leading to accompany us to Haiti.

On Saturday, December 6, 1968, we were met in Port-au-Prince by missionary Mardy Picazo, a welcome sight indeed. The next day we boarded a Haitian "Greyhound" (truck with wooden benches) for the 4VEH compound. Bad weather had made impossible roads almost impassable. The 160-mile trip took 13 hours.

We found that Dave and Harold had all the work laid out for an early start on Monday. The cement mixer had been pulled up the mountain by hardworking Haitians. All the cement, sand, and other materials had been carried on their heads.

Although working conditions, equipment, and supplies were quite unlike those to which we were accustomed, the job moved along all week surprisingly well. The Lord showed us exactly how to build scaffolding with the materials available. By Saturday noon, six days later, the floor was poured and the walls completed—much more than we had thought possible.

The weather was another miracle. For two weeks prior to our arrival, it had rained; but the skies were clear every day we worked. Then, just as we finished troweling the roof, another deluge began. By the next morning five inches of rain had fallen.

The highlight of the trip was our daily devotional period. Every morning at 8:00, fifty to sixty men—Haitian and American—sat quietly on the mountainside for a time of testimonies and Bible study. Some, who would never enter a church, were challenged by the Word.

Fellowship with the missionaries was also a cherished experience. Duane and Everett received a new appreciation for

141

those called to the mission field, as well as a greater burden for the millions who have never learned of Christ. MFMI had gained two more enthusiasts.

The final seal was stamped on the project en route home. Though the plane was delayed five hours in Port-au-Prince, none of our connections were missed. And we can stamp "Tested and Proved" on Phil. 4:6: *"...But in every thing by prayer and supplication with thanksgiving let your requests be made known unto God."*

From start to finish, prayer had prevailed to provide a water supply for missionaries in Haiti.

1969   **DOMINICAN DISCOVERY**
By William A. Gillam

For the first time in his 18 years of missionary radio ministry, Mardy Picazo stood before Dominican audiences. Flanked by his son, Daniel, with his beautiful guitar, Radio 4VEH's director and chief engineer was in his element. He was experiencing the other part of Christian radio, the literal presence of the audience one imagines as he pours his heart and message into the microphone.

A few letters had slipped through the sealed frontier, but fewer in the past year or two. Senora Dina de Mehu, our dedicated Spanish program personality, had been having serious doubts. "Is anyone really listening to us over there?" she wondered.

One's first reaction could have been easily accepted--no letters, no listening. The increase of TV, less family life, and other reasons were plausible. But there was only one way to find out--go over and get the facts. Radio men call it audience research.

142

On three brief, previous visits to Santo Domingo we had met a group called "DELE" (Evangelical Literature Distribution and Editorial Agency), headed by Wilbur Kent and John Shannon, two enterprising young Canadians. We found a oneness of heart and similarity of vision. Moreover, they were able to arrange an effective week of itinerary in the areas 4VEH had major strength.

We were not expecting the packed-out crowds that jammed the meeting places—Santiago, Navarrette, Valverde, Villa Vasquez, Monte Cristi, Dajabon, Manzanillo, Loma de Cabrera, Elias Pina, El Liano, San Juan, and Santo Domingo. When we asked how many listened to 4VEH, generally a sea of hands was raised. More than 100 letters were collected before leaving the services, and hundreds more were promised.

"I never thought I'd live to see this day," commented elderly Senora Rivas in her humble little living room in Monte Cristi. She recited the list of Spanish and English programs to which she listens. "Radio 4VEH comes in here stronger than our local station," another stated. And a lay evangelist in Valverde with his own program uses the local station facilities to relay 4VEH announcements.

I talked with a fine young Dominican worker, who told us, "I know of a young woman of questionable reputation who found Christ through the 4VEH witness."

During eight action-packed days in the northwest and frontier sections of the Dominican Republic, we were convinced that literally thousands look to Radio 4VEH for daily spiritual food. Warm welcomes for return visits were extended by friendly missionaries and nationals.

Meanwhile plans are already in motion to add new hours of Spanish language broadcasts. And the closed Haitian Dominican frontier doesn't seem quite so impenetrable.

(On a recent visit to the Dominican Republic, Mme. Dina Mehu, longtime Spanish programmer on 4VEH, was told this story:)

143

"Twenty-seven years ago my little brother was introduced by a neighbor to your program for "little soldiers." (Spanish program for children by Dina Mehu.) He became an avid listener and was soon converted. He would not listen to any other station other than Radio 4VEH.

"My mother, however, was not a Christian and was very much against his listening to 4VEH. My brother had to take his radio outside behind a wall to listen.

"One day my mother demanded the radio to listen to dance music. When my brother refused, she took it and smashed it on the floor. My brother picked up the pieces, glued them back together, and made the radio work.

"In time I was converted, along with my other brothers and sisters. My brother is now grown, with a wife and four children. They are all fine Christians and listen faithfully to 4VEH."

When Mme. Mehu asked why no one had ever written to inform the station, he answered: "Why, Sister Mehu, nobody in our little town knows how to read or write. That's why you haven't heard from us!"

CASTRO LISTENS TO 4VEH
From Luis Palau

Luis Palau is the "Billy Graham" of Latin America. Wanting to hold a campaign in Cuba, Rev. Palau's representative went directly to Fidel Castro seeking permission. As he was presenting his plans, Castro asked, "Now who is the evangelist who will head up this crusade?"

"Luis Palau," was the reply.

144

"Luis Palau!" Castro exclaimed, "No! I will not give permission to this man to come to Cuba."

Then he explained. "I heard him give a message he called 'Cristo o Castro' (Christ or Castro?) on Radio 4VEH, and I would never give permission for this man to come to Cuba for a campaign!"

Permission was not granted, but the information thrills us that Castro was listening to Radio 4VEH and heard Luis Palau proclaiming the Gospel!

1970   THE MANNA OF MISSIONS
By Marilyn Murphy

In recent years Men For Missions International has used choral groups coming from Haiti, Brazil, Korea, and Taiwan to tour North America with unique presentations designed to transport listeners to the mission field.

Now it is music from Haiti again. But this time it will be to the British Isles—a first experience for OMS supporters there.

It is not accidental that the Morning Manna Quartet should have been chosen. Hundreds of visiting crusaders to Haiti have already been inspired by their singing.

Dr. Bill Gillam, scheduled to accompany the quartet, explains it this way: "Ever since my first visit to Haiti in 1954, this exotic little land has seemed to epitomize the whole cause of the Gospel. Its deep poverty dramatizes the famine of the multitudes who need the Bread of Heaven. And of course," continues Dr. Gillam, "there's the power of voodooism and the spirit world to be confronted. But we are convinced that no one can 'tell it like it is' better than the Haitian himself. That is, a Christian Haitian."

These four young Haitians will reflect their native culture, present a taste of folkloric music, share insights into their modes of thought, but, most of all, bear witness to the dramatic new life in Christ which made them key Christian leaders in Haiti.

When Harry Burr, executive director of MFMI, challenged them to consider such a tour, their questions and concerns were to be expected:

"How can just four of us from Haiti represent all the OMS work?"

"What will we do about language? Our English just isn't that good."

"Won't we freeze in the cold weather?"

"What will our families do while we are gone?"

But as Harry shared his plan and burden for letting British supporters see the results of their prayers and gifts, they began to understand. Doubts were laid aside, and preparation began in earnest. Miss Lula Mae Fuchs, Radio 4VEH music director, took over their training sessions—from 7:00 to 9:00 each morning, plus individual practice during the day.

From the start, too, there were problems. Some of the key people connected with the venture were affected. Norman Dudgeon, OMS secretary in the British Isles responsible for the quartet's itinerary, was hospitalized with a heart attack. But we praise God he soon recovered.

A few months later, Dr. Bill Gillam was suddenly taken ill in Haiti. Rushed to the U.S., he was given the diagnosis of cerebral malaria. Later they discovered that he had a brain malignancy.

Finding replacements in our radio staff was another problem. Claude Bazile, director of the French and Creole schedule, was responsible for no less than 40 radio programs per week.

Louis Inélus is the one who started the radio day at five o'clock each morning with his lively "wake-up" program and took his turn at the radio controls during the day.

Daniel Joseph had complete charge of the Bible correspondence courses in French and was a main control-board operator.

Maxwell Regis, although a full-time high school student in Cap-Haitien, gave weekend hours in the music department. But, eager to help, other staff members offered to add a few more tasks to their already heavily loaded schedules.

The Haitian quartet was started in November 1967. Valeene Hayes, then 4VEH music director, had approached Claude Bazile with the idea, and the members were prayerfully chosen from among talented singers. It made its debut on Claude Bazile's family worship program, Manne du Matin (Morning Manna). Thus it became known as the Morning Manna Quartet.

The quartet's first public appearance was at the MFMI banquet in Port-au-Prince, March 1969. The crusaders and their guests, prominent Haitian businessmen, were enthusiastic.

Haiti Field Director Bill Gillam encouraged them to extend their ministry beyond the radio audience. From then on the quartet traveled to conventions, youth conferences, and services in many parts of Haiti. Everywhere they went it was obvious God was using them.

Sponsored by Men For Missions International, the Morning Manna Quartet was scheduled for a nine-week tour to build interest in the work of OMS and show supporters in the British Isles the products of their investments. Both were accomplished. And as a bonus, God's love took root in many hearts—some for salvation, others for service.

Traveling with the quartet were Daniel Picazo (son of Haiti missionaries Mardy and Rachael), serving as guitar accompanist and interpreter, and Charles Lake, OMS youth director. Mr. Lake replaced Dr. William Gillam, Haiti field director, originally slated as speaker for the tour but detained due to serious illness.

The group conducted over 80 services, which had been arranged and promoted by OMS representatives Rev. and Mrs. Norman Dudgeon in the Manchester, England, headquarters; the Rev. John Hutchisons in the London area; and Rev. and Mrs. Brentnall at the Northern Ireland office. Giving special attention and assistance was Mr. Bob Logan, the MFMI representative for the British Isles.

Enriched by their experiences, blessed by broadened horizons, and assured of prayer support and faithful concern of many new friends, the Morning Manna Quartet returned to Haiti.

Their purpose had not changed. Knowing God's love in greater measure, they were even more determined to pass it on.

1970   **GRADUATION AT EMMAUS**
                   By Mardy Picazo

Shortly after his assignment to our section of Haiti, the agnostic military chief came to our compound and sought out Eldon Turnidge, our director. To our amazement, he asserted, "Americans send us food and clothes that last a few hours or days. It doesn't really do any lasting good. But you missionaries, now—you are changing people, giving us new citizens! That is what Haiti needs."

That is God's business—changing people. We use radio, churches, clinics, schools, and personal witnessing to show Haitians how they can be changed. But we must also train the national to reach his own people.

For this purpose David Graffenberger came to Haiti and started the Emmaus Vocational Bible School. In May 1970, we all rejoiced over the first fruits, a fine graduating class of 16.

These young people come from our churches scattered over Haiti. One is a converted witch doctor's son, and one young lady walks two hours after leaving the last dirt road to reach her village.

The big Vaudreuil church was packed with friends and relatives who came to see them receive diplomas, gained after four years of training.

What are they doing now? Four young men make up the Every Creature Crusade team started this summer. Four top students fill responsible positions in the radio station as music director, program producer, radio operator, and repair technician. One girl serves as chaplain in a children's TB hospital. The others have returned to their communities skilled in farming, woodworking, mechanics, and music, to make their own living while serving as witnesses and leaders in their churches and villages. Who knows what God will do through 16 Haitian young people who carry a burden to win Haiti for Christ!

1970   EXIT SCROOGE
By Rachael Picazo

Every seat was taken. Aisles and window ledges were filled. Still others stood outside, hoping to get a glimpse now and then. This was 1952, my first Christmas in Haiti, and my anticipation matched that of the crowd.

At last the program began. Dressed in penury's best, the children scampered to the platform for the usual little recitations and songs. And then the young people took over with the story of Scrooge. No one had memorized his role—evidently they had all learned the story well, and they made up their lines as they went along. What tremendous actors they were, exaggerating their parts and throwing in their own proverbs and idioms to spice up the performance.

The drama closed in a tremendous thunder of applause. I made ready to leave. But nobody else did; the evening was just beginning.

A play about the saints followed. To depict the marble statues, human figures stood with sheets draped over them. The climax came when one of the statues moved, frightening the poor worshiper right off the stage.

Then came the skit about the barber's first customer. The barber wielded his long straightedge razor just as the customer jerked the wrong way. Feigning a fatal slash of the throat, the customer sank to the floor. Soon the mother appeared, discovered the body, and went into a frenzy of wailing. The crowd roared with laughter at the barber's attempt to appease her.

Next, a series of little skits represented Bouki and Malice in Haitian folk tales. About 11 o'clock I slipped out, but the service lasted until well after midnight.

I missed something. Was it snow? Colored lights? No, they were not really that important. Then I knew. The real Christmas story had not been brought out—no reading of the Scripture, not even a manger scene. I wished desperately that some missionary would take it upon himself to help with the church Christmas program so that this sacred season might have a spiritual meaning to the Christians and significance for the nonbelieving community, as well.

But that wish did not come true for several years. The Christmas celebrations became no better; one year there wasn't even an attempt to have one.

Then Valeene Hayes came to Haiti and began to work with the church young people. About Christmastime, she approached me with the same burden on her heart. I had always produced a radio dramatization of the Christmas story for 4VEH.

She asked me if I could adapt these scripts for a stage production and translate them into Creole.

The request thrilled me. We could tell the real meaning of Christmas in a way the Haitians would understand and remember. With enthusiasm I began what became one of the hardest tasks I have ever undertaken. In retrospect, I realize this was a spiritual battle.

The script included eight scenes: Joseph and Mary; the angel's appearances to Mary, then to Joseph; the decree of Caesar Augustus; no room in the inn at Bethlehem; shepherds; the manger scene; and the wise men. Each scene took only two or three minutes. Valeene chose actors from her youth group.

That Christmas the usual program was given the children's recitations and songs—plus the new play. It took about half an hour. As soon as it ended, the pastor announced that now the serious part was over, we were ready for the fun. Skits of Scrooge, the saints, the barber, and Bouki and Malice were welcomed with loud applause.

Imagine our surprise the next year when the young people requested the Christmas play. In fact, they declared unanimously that if the play were not given they would not attend the program.

So, with happy hearts, we set up rehearsals. A scene was added about King Herod, costumes were improved, stage props refined. The play was still given only a minor slice of the evening's entertainment, but the church wanted it.

Several years passed. Last year our family returned after two Christmases away. We learned that the first year we were gone one of the Haitians directed the Christmas story. The second year it was not given at all, so we assumed demise.

But nobody reckoned with the Picazo kids. Rachel declared, "It isn't Christmas without the play in the church. Mummy, won't you direct it again this year?"

"They don't want it," I countered, "and besides, I don't have time."

Mentally I ticked off the jobs: secretary for hundreds of song request letters, daily radio programs for those requests, school supervision, and photographic work. But about the third time she asked, I began to hear the whisper of God's voice through hers.

Next she approached the church pastor. His reply was hesitant: "We didn't have the play last year, and something else is already planned for this time."

But one by one, Rachel gathered sympathetic friends and sent each to talk to the pastor about the Christmas play. Her scheme worked. Pastor Michel asked me to help with the Christmas play, and the Lord had me ready.

Later, to my surprise and delight, I learned that the Christmas play was to be the entire program. Even the special music between scenes was to augment the story.

I added a final scene to the play: One by one, the entire cast returned to the stage. As each approached the manger, an angel announced the coming of the Messiah, the Son of God, the Savior of man. The shepherds and wise men accepted the news gladly, of course, and took their places to the right of the angel. But the innkeeper, King Herod, and the scribes scoffed, so the angel signaled them to the left.

In a brief message Pastor Napo applied this scene to the great Judgment when all shall stand before the throne of God to be accepted or rejected.

The curtains closed, and an invitation was given. A downpour of rain on the tin roof of the church drowned out the voices. But God's Spirit was at work, and seven came forward for prayer.

Several lay pastors who saw the Christmas play at our main church asked for the script to use in their isolated outstations. Many copies were made to give them.

I can visualize a much different Christmas for Haiti. It will always have the shimmering of moonlight on the palm leaves, the splashes of wild poinsettias on the mountains. But some day thousands more in Haiti will also know how the Savior came in infant form on the first Christmas day.

Years later, in 1990, when we gave the Christmas play, somehow the local TV station in Cap-Haitien got word of the production and came with their cameras. But they felt it would be a better presentation if we could reproduce it just for their TV station. By this time it was in January, but they played it anyway and it was such an instant success that they repeated it several times.

We had also added the Garden of Eden scene, where Adam and Eve disobeyed God, thus plunging the human race into sin and the need for a Savior. Zita, the teenage daughter of two of our radio staff, Louis and Louisa Destiné played the role of Eve.

One day she was standing on the ocean boulevard in Cap-Haitien awaiting her ride from high school back to the radio station when a couple of teenage boys rode by on their bicycles. Suddenly one of them pointed, "There's Eve!"

He was so excited he didn't notice his bike heading for a deep pothole, and he was thrown to the pavement. Lying in the road, his elbow cut, he still had his finger pointed at Zita, wildly proclaiming, "There's Eve!"

1970   THE FIRST BIBLE SCHOOL ECC TEAM
By Alice Huff (as reported by Dr. William Gillam)

"Let's win Haiti for Christ," challenged Pastor Napo in Los Angeles in 1965 as he accompanied the Haitian Choir across the States and Canada. Audiences sensed their united concern and zeal for evangelizing their land.

OMS work was still new in Haiti, without a Bible school and with few trained national workers. Yet the group had a firm conviction that a divine plan was germinating. Today, five years later, that plan has burst into visible form.

Recently, in Cap-Haitien seven splendid young men were selected from the first graduating class of the Emmaus Vocational Bible School. They had been carefully briefed on the OMS' Every Creature Crusade style of evangelism, which would be adapted to the uniqueness of Haitian culture. From the seven, four would be chosen to make up the team working with a missionary crusader counselor and adviser.

Dr. Bill Gillam, field director, pointed the group to Acts 13:2 (NIV), which reads:

While they were worshiping the Lord and fasting, the Holy Spirit said, "Set apart for me Barnabas and Saul for the work to which I have called them."

"If the Holy Spirit spoke clearly concerning the selection of Paul and Barnabas," emphasized Dr. Gillam, "then here in Haiti He can reveal with similar clarity His choice for the crusade."

Each of the seven young men was asked to share his personal testimony. One told of a dream in which Dave Graffenberger and a visiting pastor from Montana appeared to him. Laying their hands on his head, they said, "Go and tell it." For him this was a call urgent enough to preclude studies in male nursing in preparation for ministry in the OMS clinic. It also meant delaying his marriage to a girl who was working closely with Christina Schwanke in our lab.

When the young men had finished, a circle of prayer was formed and they were dismissed. Ballots were distributed to the church committee and an almost unanimous vote revealed the four whom the Holy Spirit had prepared. A further seal was the willingness of short-term missionary, teacher, and pharmacist Zack Gill to step into the first phase as counselor and adviser.

With background in teaching the Word in the Bible School, he was a natural link to the new training program for the team. The men get together for prayer at 5:00 a.m. twice a week and spend two hours on Thursday nights in Bible study, training, and strategy. A strong sense of destiny prevails as they pray and plan together.

"It is as though we have been called apart. Our hearts are full. Every moment seems to be filled with a single thought—the coming crusade," says Zack.

For the most part, tonels (brush arbors) will be erected in areas where the Gospel has not reached. Campaigns of door-to-door witnessing and nightly evangelistic meetings will continue as the Holy Spirit directs. For Zack it will mean complete identification with Haitian food and life. In this land of voodoo and demonic action, a standard of salvation will be raised. The task ahead is great. But God is able to empower this Every Creature Crusade team to bring their people to Christ.

1970   **A CRUSADER'S LIFE**
                      By Helmut Markeli

Yesterday we visited two witch doctors who exercise great power in our area. The first one listened. But all the while his teenage child, running around wildly, cried repeatedly, "You will die if you become a convert."

Later we were told the witch doctor wept after we left. The other one wanted $20,000 for accepting Christ.

Every morning we visit homes, challenging the people to accept Christ. A typical excuse is the one a young man gave today, "I don't have a good shirt. I don't have shoes."

So, opening my purse, I took a out a 50 centime piece (ten cents) and held it out to him. "Can you not accept this gift because you have no shoes?" I asked.

Recently, while traveling, I became thirsty and turned to some huts near the road to ask for a mango fruit. I returned their kindness by offering eternal life through Jesus. The farmer accepted in front of family and neighbors. At a later visit, the grandmother surrendered, too.

While most people say, "Pita" (later), the crusade team has won 130 people for the Lord in this village of Norman—all within the last three months.

ECC TEAM AT DESARMES

To the morning evangelistic services held by the Every Creature Crusade team in Desarmes, Haiti, a ten-year-old girl came with her feet cracked open like parched ground. Although bandaged and prayed for regularly, the condition seemed to show little improvement. One day, as the child neared unconsciousness, the mother was advised to put her in the hospital.

Sometime later, the team saw the girl on the street, her feet completely well. When team leader Helmut Markeli asked about the healing process, she shyly radiated, "After you prayed for me and I was converted, my feet healed up."

The ten-year-old was but one of 83 converts in the Desarmes crusade effort from mid October through November 1972.

The 1970 Morning Manna Quartet

1970, the first graduating class at the
Emmaus Vocational Bible School

Three wise men at the Christmas play in 1970

The first ECC team from the Bible School in 1970

1971   **PORT-AU-PRINCE CENTER**
OMS Outreach

In rap sessions conducted by the Mardy Picazos for young people of the elite in Port-au-Prince, Haiti, seven have turned their lives over to the Lord. Roland Elie, one of the first inquirers, now witnesses to classmates and feels God wants him to be a minister. At the MFMI banquet in March, his father was the first of six influential men to respond to the Gospel challenge. And in rapid succession, his mother and younger sister have come to Christ.

1971   **IT COULDN'T BE DONE**
By Howard Young

Piercing the clouds over the salt flats along Haiti's coast, a giant radio tower monuments a chain of miracles. Only God could have dovetailed all the men, the means, and the equipment, which brought it together in a two-year sequence. Experts said it could not be done. But it's there, proof positive of the powerful message it beacons from 4VEH to nations across the Caribbean. In an interview, Ray Pottschmidt, one of the 12 work crusaders who finalized the project, gives a few insights.

Q. Ray, how tall was this tower and how was it erected?
A. It was 270 feet high and weighed 11 tons. We built it section by section, hauling each piece up with a winch to be bolted in place by a climber.

Q. Did you have experienced climbers for a job like that?
A. Actually, missionary Phil Chandler was the only one experienced in erecting a tower. A veterinarian from Indiana

had climbed some in college but never higher than 90 feet. Then we had a truck driver and a rancher who were brave enough to try it.

Q. Did the weather create problems?
A. It was normally the rainy season, but it didn't rain once in the five and a half days we worked. The farmers at the mission coop farm were praying for rain, and the tower crew was praying for clear skies and no wind. Our last day, as it was getting late, most of the crew wanted to quit and finish up the next day at a leisurely pace. But one fellow persuaded us to stay and complete the job. A few hours later it began to rain. So the Lord had sorted out the prayers and answered both.

Q. People all over the world were praying for the safety of the crew. Were there any accidents?
A. None, even though all of us were doing dangerous jobs we had never done before.

Q. Did you have any expert advice on the job?
A. The president of the company which provided some of the equipment came one day and said, "It's not possible to put a tower up that way, but they're doing it."

Q. How do you account for that, Ray?
A. When God is with you, you can do anything.

1971   **THEY STUMBLED**
By David Graffenberger (as told to Rachael Picazo)

We needed to build a parsonage for the Ti Bois church, situated in a mountain range south of us. So I encouraged some of the Christian construction workers around Vaudreuil to form a work team, like a Men For Missions Crusade, and travel down to Ti Bois to donate their time and expertise in building the house. They had observed and helped the Americans in Men For Missions Crusades to Haiti, so they knew what I was talking about. I approached the trucker who hauled loads for OMS, and he consented to transport all the men free to Hostin 140 miles south of us. From there we would walk the ten miles up to Ti Bois.

We planned to build the parsonage out of dirt blocks, so we sent a couple of men ahead to make them at the building site. A few days later, I decided to go see how things were progressing. I had traveled to Port-au-Prince on mission business, so on the way back I stopped at Hostin where I usually stayed at the home of William Bertrand's mother.

I had bought a lantern for the workers to use at Ti Bois, so I decided to deliver it to them that night. It was already nearly sundown, so Mrs. Bertrand tried to persuade me to wait until morning since it gets dark suddenly in Haiti once the sun sets.

But I had already decided to go that evening. I walked through banana fields for an hour and a half, mostly on little trails under the trees, until I came to the road that leads to the foot of the mountaot of the mountain one ch Ti Bois.

We had taken Men For Missions groups, and even the choir, on our bus along this road as far as it went. Then we had all gotten out and climbed the rest of the way up the mountain on foot. The man who lived at the end of the road was friendly and kept the bus at his house while we were gone. He also allowed us to store building materials there until we could find people or donkeys to carry them up the mountain.

It got dark while I was walking, and I thought I met some Haitians among the trees, but I couldn't tell for sure because it was so black. Nobody used flashlights, and I didn't

159

have one either. As I walked along, I thought I heard people crashing into the trees, rattling the big banana leaves. When I got to within a quarter-mile of the end of the plantation, I heard people behind me.

The banana fields ended abruptly at a little knoll about the size of a two-story building. As I came out of the trees and started up this hill, somebody called out. I didn't pay any attention, not knowing if it was me they wanted. I just climbed the hill until I got to an elevation of about 50 feet. There was a flat clearing on this knoll, and when I reached it, the voices yelled again. This time I stopped, and as I turned—Whoosh! Twenty men surrounded me with machetes, and sticks and other weapons. They told me I was under arrest and they were taking me to jail.

At this moment the moon came over the mountain range and lit up the whole scene. I looked around the group and recognized the man who had the house at the end of the road.

I began talking to him in Creole. "You know me. Remember, I am the one who leaves the bus at your house when we go up to Ti Bois. Remember when we brought the choir here to sing?"

The man stared at me, then nodded his head.

"You keep building materials for us at your house," I reminded him. "Why, you have cement stored right now for the parsonage at Ti Bois."

Hesitantly, the man admitted, "Yes, I know who you are."

I shook his hand and included the rest of the men in my conversation, "We could use your help in hauling it up the mountain for the parsonage at Ti Bois. There is a lot of cement, so if any of you has a donkey, that would be great."

There was murmuring around the group, the men clearly confused.

"Before long there's going to be a group of Haitian carpenters and masons from Vaudreuil coming to donate their time to build the parsonage," I told them. "This is to help the pastor right here at Ti Bois."

I shook hands all around and then continued my journey. I walked another hour up the mountain and spent the night at Ti Bois. The next morning I visited with the men who were making the dirt blocks, left them the lantern, and came back down the mountain.

When I returned to the house of William's mom, I found her very concerned for my safety. Had she been praying for me? I collected my gear and went back north to Cap-Haitien.

A few days later, we returned with the carpenters and masons and built the parsonage. The Haitians enjoyed giving their time and the budget paid for their food. On that trip they were just like other "MFMers." Many even wore MFM shirts and hats and carried MFM bags.

One year later, two American couples sent their high school sons to Haiti to spend a couple of weeks with us. Our friends were concerned that their sons weren't enthusiastic about Christian activities and thought maybe working in Haiti would help them.

I decided to give them a good introduction, so I brought them from the airport right out to Hostin where we spent the night at William's mom's house. I told them we had to be up the next morning at five o'clock because we were attending church on top of the mountain. We walked two-and-a-half hours up to visit the service. At Ti Bois we sat in the audience while the pastor preached on the power of prayer and faith.

He said, "You remember last year Frère (Brother) Dave was up here with the Haitians from Vaudreuil, and we built the parsonage. But he made one trip by himself beforehand to get the work started."

Then he went on to relate, "The next day after he was here I went down to Hostin, and some of the local men said, 'We were planning to kill that white stranger, but we couldn't catch him. Every time we'd just about get to him, something would trip us and we'd fall down.'"

(I remembered hearing the people in the darkness crashing into the trees, yet I knew that Haitians run through the dark constantly without stumbling. They were behind me, calling as I came out of the plantation. They would have killed me if they had caught me!)

The pastor continued, "These men said, 'We couldn't get near the white until he got out into the open where he could see us.'"

(That was it! I had to be able to recognize the man who guarded our bus, so he could vouch for who I was. I couldn't do that while we were in the darkness under the trees. Even after we got out into the open, I couldn't distinguish who they were until the moon suddenly illuminated their black faces.)

The pastor went on to explain, "They were afraid of Frère Dave because of rumors that were going around that the whites were kidnapping black babies. They saw that white stranger walking through the banana plantation, so that's when they decided to kill him."

He encouraged his congregation to have faith that the Lord was with them, remembering what had happened with Frère Dave.

Suddenly I recognized that my trip to Ti Bois that night had been a tremendous experience of God's protection.

Jeremiah 20:11 (NIV) *But the LORD is with me like a mighty warrior; so my persecutors will stumble and not prevail.*

The radio staff at 4VEH in March 1970

Dr. William A. Gillam
(ca. 1971)

Yvone and her mother
(ca. 1972)

Pastor Doucet Alvarez with two of his children in 1972

1972   VALERIE ANN GRAFFENBERGER
May 22, 1965 - October 7, 1972
By Alice Huff

"We'll do our best for your daughter," said the anesthesiologist as she attempted to reassure Dave and Marilyn Graffenberger. Their six-year-old Valerie was on the verge of surgery for a brain tumor. Dave answered firmly, "We know that God can heal, but He did not heal everyone when He was on earth. If it is His will and for His glory, Val will come through fine."

"I guess I don't need to talk to you anymore," the medic replied. And she was right, for Someone had already talked to them. Tenaciously they clung to His words:

"Rejoice evermore. Pray without ceasing. In everything give thanks: for this is the will of God in Christ Jesus concerning you." (1 Thessalonians 5:16-18). Divinely-given peace reigned. At the conclusion of Valerie's surgery in Oregon on July 21,1971, the medical report was grim. A massive, malignant tumor could not be completely removed. The portion of her brain controlling peripheral vision had been cut away to allow for expansion of the remaining tumor. X-rays were recommended to retard the rate of growth. But the prognosis was obvious—healing for her would have to be a miracle.

Speedily Dave, Marilyn, and Valerie experienced the priceless gift of supporting prayer. The news was sent to Haiti, their place of OMS service; all OMS fields; regional and Commonwealth offices; and World Intercessors prayer secretaries. Those who supported them were informed. The IntercessoGram, sent from the World Intercessors department (over 10,000 copies) bore the prayer need around the globe.

Within a short time Marilyn reported, "Valerie's recovery from surgery is rapid and unbelievable in every way. A few

163

hours after surgery she was completely alert and asked for a Popsicle. Cobalt treatments, five days a week for a month, brought no ill effects."

After 17 days, the bright, cheerful patient was released from the hospital and went swimming that afternoon. She had energy to ride her bike, played hard, and entered school in September. Through the months since, only God's ledger has the full account of the accumulated prayers. Certainly supernatural intervention was evident.

Often Dave and Marilyn express, "Thank you for your prayer support. Continue to pray with us that as a family we may be a blessing and a witness for Christ. We praise the Lord for our fantastic experience with Him through Val's illness. Hallelujah!"

Genuine and noteworthy are those words—another proof that God's grace, dispensed by the Spirit, energized by prayer, can turn hurts into hallelujahs.

On October 7, 1972, seven-year-old Valerie, daughter of Haiti missionaries David and Marilyn Ann Graffenberger, completed her earthly assignment. Into 19 months of mystifying symptoms, then critical surgery, and subsequent decline from brain malignancy, Valerie crowded a lifetime of Christian outreach and triumph. Her cheerful endurance of pain, unwavering acceptance of divine purpose, and pointed personal witness scored eternal impact on all whose lives she touched.

Her parents, David and Marilyn Graffenberger, her brother Brian, and her grandparents give radiant testimony and grateful praise for God's sustaining grace and the uplift of praying friends across the world.

A memorial fund for the advanced education of Haitian students and leaders outside Haiti has been established in Valerie's name through OMS International.

1971   DR. WILLIAM ARTHUR GILLAM
February 8, 1914 - June 29, 1971
By Alice Huff

A loud thud sent Mary hurrying to the bedroom. There, on the only straight stretch of floor space in their small trailer home, lay Bill, unconscious. A few hours earlier (Tuesday, April 7, 1970), everything had been normal for the Gillams. As director of the Haiti field, Bill had been busily executing his heavy responsibilities. At noon, however, severe nausea had sent him to bed.

Now, at about 6:00 p.m., Mary summoned the staff nurses. It was more than an hour before they succeeded in reviving him. They knew it was something serious.

By Land Rover, Bill was jostled over the miles to a hospital in Limbé. With limited equipment, the doctor could give only a partial diagnosis: cerebral thrombosis (blood clot in the brain) or cerebral malaria. He could not prescribe medicine. Yet a clot could be fatal at any moment or cause irreparable damage. Speedy and proper treatment was urgent, but no plane for the U.S. would leave for three days.

Without panic, Bill and Mary flung themselves confidently on God. At Bill's request, fellow missionaries and longtime friend, Byron Crouse, anointed him and prayed for healing.

The Haitians, esteeming the Gillams highly, poured extraordinary love and prayer on them. An outstation pastor walked five miles, dropped on his knees beside Mary, and petitioned God.

Mary, who could have been exhausted from the strain and hurried packing, was relaxed. "The Lord's strength and peace surround me," she said.

On Friday, the weather prevented the plane from taking off. This meant a delay until Monday. Bill continued to have more attacks.

[The following was written by Suzanna Picazo, 14-year-old MK in Haiti who stood by watching as missionaries tenderly placed Dr. William Gillam in the car bound for the airport. He would be flown to the States and for the next several months be treated for his brain cancer. I think they all sensed this was goodbye.]

It was with a heavy heart I watched them drive away. It all seemed so mixed up that my mind couldn't quite grasp what had happened. The car had just left, bearing the half-conscious body of one whom I had grown to love and admire so much.

My Haitian friends turned to me suddenly and said, "What's the matter with you? Haven't you ever seen a man like that before?"

Had I ever seen someone like that before? Had there ever been one who, no matter how busy he was, would take time to talk out problems with young people? Had I met one who was so Spirit-filled that to hear him pray tore your soul with a burden? Had I heard anyone sing with such meaning that it could rip the rock bottom out of my own heart?

To my surprise, I found myself weeping. I turned to my friends and answered them quietly, "No."

They were silent. Then the leader of the group, a sarcastic cynic, led the discussion. "Neither have I. You know, so many people come here and they do so much and work so hard, but you know, Pastor Gillam...he loved us. He really did. He was always smiling and shaking our hands and putting his arms around us."

"And to hear him sing," another added, "he didn't even need a microphone, and everyone in the area could hear him. We didn't know the English words he was singing, but by his face and the way he sang, we knew he believed in it."

A member of the Manne du Matin quartet joined our party, the ones with whom Uncle Bill was to go to Great Britain. The last words Uncle Bill had spoken before the car had driven off were, "Christians, I'm praying for a revival in Haiti...I'll see you fellows in September."

"Even when he was sick he was thinking of us." There were tears in his eyes as he looked around at our small group. "We'll go to England anyway; we'll see that dream accomplished. But who's going to keep praying for our revival?"

By Alice Huff: During April and May, the OMS prayer sheet, the IntercessoGram, requested prayer for Bill. When it went to press, the crisis was not known. As it reached over 25 countries, thousands of prayers were marshaled and then transferred by the Spirit to meet the specific needs.

In addition, the Spirit alerted particular individuals. One shareholder wrote them, "The weekend previous to April 7, I was impressed to pray for you. As the weekend slipped by, this burden greatly increased. I found myself in almost a continuous state of prayer, especially in the area of your health. It wasn't until Thursday (April 9) that I understood why this unusual burden to pray."

As Bill was taken to the Indianapolis hospital, OMS friends formed an all-night chain of prayer.

Their four children, scattered in Japan, California, New York, and Kentucky, also found peace during days of uncertainty.

B. H. Pearson wrote "No regrets! No regrets!" were almost the first words I heard Dr. William A. Gillam speak after he was transferred to the City of Hope, a center for cancer research in southern California. These were remarkable words to be spoken by a man cut down in the prime of life.

A few weeks later, during a family rendezvous that brought his children and grandchildren to his bedside, Bill told his son, Richard, and son-in-law Tom Madon, "Fellows, the greatest thing in the world is to know the mind of God."

In these words Bill Gillam was sharing one of the deepest secrets by which he lived—he sought to know the mind of God.

The day before leaving the City of Hope—an admission by that noted research center that they could do nothing more for him—Bill Gillam still had strength to say clearly to Dr. Roy Adams, who was a frequent visitor at his bedside, "We are more than conquerors."

How amazing that never did a word of complaint, fretfulness, or impatience spring from his lips. Again and again he said to those visiting him, "I love you. I love the doctors. I love those who care for me. I love the OMS. I love everyone."

He did.

He loved the world.

Bill Gillam is gone. But to those of us who knew him, he will never be forgotten.

At the keyboard, the conference table, the microphone, the platform, the baptismal pool, the brush arbor, the magnificent church, the desk— wherever God put Bill Gillam—in Colombia, Haiti, the Orient, the homelands—he performed with perfection and power, masterfully reflecting the Master of his life.

1971   **WHATEVER IT TAKES**
                          By Aldean Saufley

1,000 Converts by ECC Evangelism in Haiti
Elite in Capitol Respond to the Gospel
Haiti More Open Than Ever Before

After almost a year of furlough and a certain loss of contact with the field, these headlines, shared by a newly returned fellow missionary, brought us tremendous excitement. Such success thrills everyone involved in missions, be he missionary or homeland supporter.

But there is another side. Those who attended our OMS Missionary Conference at Anderson, Indiana, last year cannot forget Dr. William Gillam's powerful address on "Whatever It Takes." His portrayal left no question that a price must be paid for spiritual conquest. Perhaps not even he envisioned how costly it would be.

Let me trace a series of happenings on the Haiti field-- Full of enthusiasm, the Gary Bailey family arrived to fit into strategic vacancies. Gary worked in construction and Virginia in the clinic. Before their first term was completed, however, they were forced to return to the States. Gary, after months of critical illness, is still unable to work and faces serious surgery.

Dr. William Gillam and his wife, Mary, moved to Haiti in the fall of 1968, where he assumed the leadership of the field. Prefaced by a heavy prayer burden for the spiritual needs of the nation, Bill initiated an Every Creature Crusade. In the midst of prayer and planning sessions, however, he was stricken with frightening symptoms. In April 1970, he was flown to the U.S. and is currently battling for his life following two surgeries for malignant brain tumors.

Wayne and Edith Hodges from Oregon joined the staff. Wayne became head of the automotive and diesel maintenance shop. Edith took over the direction of the "Children's Corner" broadcast in addition to other duties. From the start this family had severe physical problems. Recently Edith had to return home for medical help. Now, because of her complications, Wayne, as well, has had to leave the field.

In January, Francis and Iris Muia became the delighted parents of a baby son. Soon after his birth, cataracts were discovered on both eyes. This necessitated an interruption of ministries as they flew him to Florida. Barring God's

169

intervention, little Alan will require delicate surgery in the future.

Five-year-old Valerie Graffenberger was seized with blackouts and convulsions during February. When available treatment failed and attacks increased, her father flew her to the USA. Presently she is undergoing tests for an illness puzzling a team of specialists.

And to this lengthy list, other tragedies happened among our Haitian personnel. Last fall the Haitian radio quartet toured the British Isles and France. During that time, another young man filled in for Claude Bazile, French program director for 4VEH. In a bicycle accident, his life was snuffed out—a great loss.

One of last year's graduates at the Vocational Bible Institute had become Dave Graffenberger's right-hand man in the agricultural department. A few months ago he was driving the tractor when it turned over on a bank, taking his life.

Why relate all these sad stories? To present a clearer picture of the "*wrestling not against flesh and blood, but against principalities, against powers, against the rulers of the darkness of this world, against spiritual wickedness in high places.*"

Remember the first headline: "**1,000 Converts by ECC Evangelism in Haiti.**"...These converts came from the most devout voodoo area in Haiti. Satan's choice territory has been invaded and these have been snatched from his grasp. Therefore, his retaliations are not weak or few. Success, yes, but not without high cost.

Ellen and I will soon return to Haiti. At times, the thought of stepping into the conflict frightens us. Certainly, we have a tremendous need for God's enabling—to build a shield and produce overcoming strength against Satan.

"Whatever It Takes" is our commitment. We go armed with God's promises.

YVONE
              By Valeene Hayes (as told to Sue Oiler)

I was only a visitor in Haiti, but I felt like a typical missionary with my pith hat, trudging up a steep mountainside. Then we walked through a village full of children, and I prayed, "Lord, if You'll let me return to Haiti, I'd like to tell boys and girls like these about You."

God did send me back as a full-time missionary. But with my tongue still stumbling over Creole words and phrases, how could I tell children about Christ? Yet, how could I not tell them?

Then I became friends with a young Haitian woman named Claudette, who earned her tuition for school by working in missionary homes. Her only free time was Saturday mornings, yet she was eager to help me start Good News Clubs. I taught her the Bible stories and showed her how to arrange flannelgraph figures on the board. She already knew lively Sunday school choruses, and she also knew a little English, so she could translate for me into Creole when I spoke.

The first Saturday morning we made our way through the brush to La Fleau, a village halfway up the mountain behind our missionary grounds. There, 25 bright-eyed youngsters heard of Christ as they sat quietly under a mango tree. And they only let us go when we promised to return the next Saturday.

Along the trail home, we glimpsed three tiny huts up a little pathway. I thought aloud, "I wonder if there are any boys and girls up there."

"Let's go see," she encouraged me.

Two small girls shyly emerged from one of the homes as we approached. Their faces were clean, but dust from the bare ground where they played coated their thin legs.

"Would you like to hear a story?" we greeted them.

The light that sparked in their eyes was answer enough.

"Call the other boys and girls, then, and we'll begin."

But there were no other children; the other two huts had been vacant for some time. So, keeping our promise, Claudette and I told a story and taught them a chorus. We learned that the older child was named Yvone.

It was still early when we left them, so we followed a path to another clearing where a number of boys and girls gathered. And we repeated the story of Christ's birth—the third time.

The next Saturday a caravan of children from around our area tagged along. Even before we reached La Fleau, strains of the chorus we'd taught the week before floated from the top of the ravine, where a large group stood waiting.

As we left La Fleau that day I said, "Let's not stop at Yvone's house. It hardly seems worth our time for just two."

For the next month we held Good News Clubs in the two villages. The fifth week, as we hurried down the path, someone came running breathlessly from behind. It was Yvone. As she caught up with us, the pained look in her seven-year-old eyes took me by surprise.

"Miss Valeene, aren't you coming back to tell me another story?"

I was speechless.

"I'm so thirsty for a story," she confided as two big tears spilled down her cheeks.

Without exchanging a word, Claudette and I knew we must go to her house. Right now.

Too eager to bother sitting down, Yvone and her sister stood right in front of the flannelboard as Claudette told about the wise men and how they loved Baby Jesus. With joy on her face, Yvone said, "I want to love Him, too!"

I had explained that God had sent His Son to earth. But in the story we told them, He was still a baby. So I put off Yvone's desire to let Jesus come into her heart with a promise, "We'll come again and tell you more about it."

The next day I saw a woman pulling a little girl across the mission grounds. It looked like Yvone! Yes, that was the same threadbare dress she had been wearing yesterday.

"Are you Miss Valeene?" The irate woman blurted as she approached. "I want you to stay away from our house."

When I asked the reason, the mother shrieked, "All Yvone talks about is Jesus, Jesus, Jesus! She says she loves Him. We have our own religion; we don't need yours. And she's too young to love Jesus."

"Is she too young to love you?" I questioned.

"Well, I'm her mother."

"Don't you know that God loved Yvone even before you knew her? He loves both of you and is waiting for you to love Him, too," I tried to tell her.

But she cut me off, and I reluctantly agreed not to return.

"I want to hear the stories, Miss Valeene," sobbed Yvone. "But Mama won't let me love Him."

Inwardly I asked the Lord to intervene. And immediately the thought came, "Ask if Yvone can go to La Fleau. Tell her you'll pick her up on your way."

Amazingly, Mama agreed to this arrangement. Yet didn't she realize Yvone would still be hearing about Jesus?

So each Saturday Claudette and I called for Yvone, not daring to come closer than the banana plants around the house. She was always ready and eager to go, but we noticed she stood apart from the other children. And each time the invitation to accept Christ was given, tears rolled down her cheeks.

Finally, Claudette asked Yvone why she wept. "My Mama won't let me love Jesus," she answered simply.

Four weeks later as Claudette gave the invitation, I felt little arms around my legs. Yvone had made my feet her altar as she prayed for Jesus to come into her heart.

A few minutes later her face was radiant as she declared, "Now I won't have to cry any more: Jesus is in my heart."

"Did your Mama say you could..."

"No, but Mama will love Him, too. I'm going to pray and do everything at home to help her find Jesus," she pledged.

Yvone became a little missionary on that mountainside. Every week she brought new boys and girls to the Good News Club and sang in the children's choir over Radio 4VEH. She also kept her promise to be useful at home. Her mother commented to others of her new attitude of helpfulness.

A year and a half later I was preparing to return to the States for my scheduled year of furlough. The day before I left, a very agitated Yvone came running into the radio studio.

"Miss Valeene, come! Mama wants to see you."

"What's wrong? Is she sick?" I asked.

"No, no, but come. She is waiting for you," Yvone urged.

Dropping everything, Margaret Bonnette, our nurse, and I followed Yvone up the hillside. In the doorway of her tiny house Mama stood with her hand over her heart. Perhaps she was ill, after all. But in a penitent voice she called out to us, "I want Jesus to forgive my sins and come into my heart, too."

Influenced by the prayers and Christian life of her daughter, Mama also found peace with God. Yvone's joy was exceeded only by the angels in heaven.

EPILOGUE

During the year I was away from Haiti, Yvone and her mother carefully obeyed what they learned the Bible taught. One Sunday when Mama wanted to work in the garden, Yvone insisted that they honor God on that day. Later they testified in church that God had rewarded their faithfulness with a bigger crop than they had ever had before.

At this writing (1972) Yvone is now 15 and in the fourth grade at the day school run by our 4VEH church. She serves her Lord by washing the instruments in the clinic and helping with Bible clubs near her home.

1972   **FREE INDEED**
                       By Wayne Hodges

Plaine-du-Nord, a little town about four miles from our compound, is known throughout Haiti as an important devil worship center. Believing the spirit of St. Jacques lives in the ugly polluted pool there, people come from all over the island to make sacrifices.

Last year the Every Creature Crusade worked in this town for several months and a church was started. Tony Paul, a member of the team, stayed to establish the Christians and develop the church.

One day Tony decided to hold a service in the local prison. He received the necessary permission and after the message gave the men an opportunity to accept Jesus as Savior and be freed from sin. Several men responded and truly asked Christ into their lives.

Seeing this, the burly prison guard, with tears in his eyes, said, "If God has set you free, I cannot hold you," and he released them.

Then the rest of the prisoners clamored to "accept Jesus," too. But their chance was gone.

MOUNTAINS AND ALL
By Celia Rigby

My heart sank as I finished the letter from OMS headquarters. There was good news; I had been accepted as a candidate for Haiti. But then the blow. Before I could begin my missionary career, all my support must be raised. The amount was enormous.

"I'll be an old-age pensioner before I get there," I told myself.

My parents had been missionaries in India, so I knew something about trusting God. And then my thoughts turned to Bible school days in England, when God had challenged me through the story of Caleb to take Him at His word. Like Caleb, I had covenanted to claim every mountain in my pathway. So now, letter in hand, I cried, "Lord, here is a mountain. Where am I to start climbing?"

To my amazement, pastors responded overwhelmingly. Soon I had so many meetings I wondered if I could fill them all. Then it hit me; what was I going to say to all those people? Again, the Lord's promise came: "Behold, I have put my words in your mouth." I studied as much as I could about Haiti and the OMS work there, then left the rest with Him.

I wasn't receiving a salary from OMS as yet and had just finished college, so I did not have a cent to my name. "Lord, here's another mountain," I prayed, "but I believe You are going to provide."

He did. Every week without fail God sent the exact amount I needed and sometimes enough to help others.

At a meeting one night the Lord whispered, "Celia, a missionary in Colombia has a greater need than you. Send her the seven dollars in your purse."

When I got to my room, my second thought was, "Maybe I'm just getting emotional." But I couldn't sleep until the money—all I had—was in an envelope addressed to that missionary.

The next morning I reminded the Lord that He was pretty rich, and I was rather poor at the moment. I had just gotten up from my knees when a knock came at the door. As I opened it the little boy from next door said, "Mommy wondered if you'd like to come and eat with us today?"

I had never had a meal with these people before. And that evening while I was speaking, God challenged a young man to give me sufficient funds for the rest of the week. Another mountain was mine.

Several months later, a trip from north to south England forced an overnight stay at a youth hostel. A bed for the night took my last penny. I had had nothing to eat so decided to read a book in the lounge to forget my hunger. In a short while I felt a tap on my shoulder. A complete stranger asked, "Are you a Christian?"

I answered, "Yes, I am."

The young girl exclaimed, "I have been praying God would send another Christian along. I am the only one in the hostel and need to talk to someone like you. Would you come to my room for coffee and cookies while we share together?"

God used that evening to speak to both our hearts. After prayer I said goodbye and was about to leave when she said, "Wait a minute. The Lord told me to give you this money. I don't know your needs. But here it is."

She handed me enough for my journey the next day and to keep me going the next week. It has been less than a year since that letter came from OMS. I have left the British Isles and am on my way to Haiti. Walking with Jesus is exciting-mountains and all.

GALILEAN CHILDREN'S HOME
OMS Outreach

December 31, 1972, marked the long-awaited day for Pastor Doucet Alvarez of Hostin, Haiti. Friends, family, missionaries, and supporters gathered for the dedication ceremony of his new children's home. Among them were Dr. Edward H. Boyce and Rev. Ira Davison, pastor and assistant from New York's Manhattan Holy Tabernacle, who had flown in for the occasion.

Fifteen years ago Pastor Doucet began gathering orphans about him, housing and feeding them in his own home as he trusted God to provide. With a heart too big to exclude a homeless child but facilities too small to take them all in, he soon knew something had to be done.

In 1968, the late Dr. William Gillam, then director of the Haiti field, visited Dr. Boyce's church and later wrote him about Doucet's orphanage. An enthusiastic supporter of OMS for 30 years, Dr. Boyce urged his people to take on the project. Their gifts of $8,000 supplied materials for new facilities to house 100 children.

Missionaries, MFM work teams, NOW Corpsmen, and visitors contributed construction skills and labor for the two-story central building and two dormitory wings, now completed.

Told by a lawyer that orphans never amount to anything, Pastor Doucet vindicated his efforts by enumerating achievements of children from his Galilean Orphanage. His dedication message also included, "I've decided to change the name to "Maison Galilean" or "Galilean Home." I told the children they are not orphans. Only children who have fathers live in such a nice home. And they must have a very rich Father to have provided so bountifully for them."

"We seek first to lead each child to a personal knowledge of Christ as Savior," Pastor Doucet added. The children pray

178

Painting the towers every two years (ca. 1972)

Listening to Radio 4VEH opens a window to a
whole new world (ca. 1973)

People who visit Haiti generally want to return (ca. 1974)

together, then go out to invite neighborhood friends to Sunday services. Through their efforts nine community children have accepted Christ, including those of a witch doctor.

1972   HIGH ON MISSIONS
By Claude Beachy

"If I were a writer, I'd do an article on this for the MFMI *Action* magazine," commented Bob.

"If I were a writer, I'd entitle the story, 'Fellowship at 275 Feet,'" replied Fred.

The setting was atop the tower of Haiti's Radio 4VEH. MFMers Bob Castanien from Ohio and Fred Stolzfus of Florida, assisted by missionaries Dave Graffenberger and Claude Beachy, plus Haitian operator Edner Hilaire, were painting as they swayed in the wind high above the tidal flats of Petite Anse, the little Haitian village by the tower.

For five consecutive days, at promptly 9:00 a.m., the power of the two 10,000-watt transmitters, which feed the tower, was cut off. The men started their ascent, a 25-minute climb to reach the top.

While slapping paint, they shouted encouragement to one another and shared what God had done in their lives. Several times tears mixed with the paint in the salty ocean breeze as they marveled at His love and mercy.

Bob Castanien, a truck driver, had climbed the tower before. Last year when it was built, he volunteered to help assemble it in the sky. He remembered how the Lord had poured in the strength and allayed their fears. Now he experienced the same energy and reassurance.

When word came over shortwave that Bob was again one of the climbers, his wife Georgie, back home in Canton, Ohio, wasn't surprised. But each day she committed him to the Lord. Added to her prayers were those of many French and Creole 4VEH listeners, who each morning were urged to pray for the safety of the painters.

Then, too, every morning before starting up the ladder of six-inch bolts extending from one corner of the three-foot triangular tower, the men paused for prayer. Novices at climbing and unaccustomed to heights, they realized their peril.

After painting for three hours each day the men descended from their precarious perches, and power was reapplied. The gospel voice of 4VEH again flowed to over 2,000 pre-tuned radios scattered across northern Haiti.

For the MFMers it was a never-to-be-forgotten experience. And for the engineers of Radio 4VEH it was a tremendous lift.

Now the tower stands newly painted—protected against salt corrosion and rust. But like our lives, which need regular infusions of God's protection, the tower awaits another crew a year or so from now.

1973   TO DON DON BY HONDA
By Claude Beachy

Mile after mile, I carefully negotiated the rutted trail, constantly aware of the delicate electronic equipment strapped to my motorcycle. Without doubt, the road ranked the worst I had traveled in Haiti. My destination was Don Don, a town planted in the mountains. But as the route grew more treacherous and exhausting, I seriously debated the wisdom of continuing.

Spurring me on, however, was the clear-cut purpose of the venture. To plan our radio strategy for reaching the interior with gospel broadcasts, we must know the strength of our radio signal there. Making that test was my assignment.

Dodging the hundreds of Haitians, who trekked the narrow route with market wares balanced gingerly on their heads, not only impeded my progress but also demanded precision driving. At one point donkeys loaded with fruit and charcoal actually wedged me off the path.

Suddenly a rut, well over a foot in depth, trapped the Honda's wheels, hurling me to the ground along with the bike and its precious cargo. Shaken, I righted my vehicle and surveyed the damages. To my surprise, only a bruised knee remained as evidence of the accident.

At last I arrived at Don Don. No destination could have been more welcome or gratifying. Advance announcements over Radio 4VEH had prepared the Haitians for my visit and testing experiment. Hundreds gathered immediately, completely encircling me. Fortunately, the police arrived as well—to keep back the crowd and silence their blaring radios so I could make my measurements.

When my mission was completed, I remounted the Honda for the three-and-a-half-hour journey back. By then, my arms cramped and my fingers ached from working the throttle and brakes. Frequently loose gravel threatened to send me down precarious drop-offs. But, finally, the mountains were behind me and I hurried along the last 13 miles. Usually this broken blacktop with its potholes and wash-overs seemed rough, but compared to what I had just been over, it was a super highway.

At home with Edna and the girls, I flopped into a chair to reflect on the Lord's care. Why wasn't the instrument damaged when the cycle flipped in that 18-inch rut? What held me from tumbling down the mountain when the front wheel struck shifting gravel?

Just then my glance caught our Prayer Dime Calendar. Drawing it closer I saw that our family was pictured to receive prayer that very day. How tremendous! Could those who had prayed possibly have realized the important role they played that day?

Enthusiastically I write to remind you that prayer does make a difference for your missionaries. OMS publishes a Prayer and Praise Guide featuring a missionary for each day, which thousands of loving pray-ers use. As you join with them in perhaps just a sentence or two of intercession, that missionary senses some special thrust of divine provision or protection.

1973   4VEH AUDIENCE SUDDENLY MULTIPLIED
By Mardy Picazo

Haitians, like people everywhere, like to gamble. Cockfights and the national lottery were the main ways in which their few coins were spent. The problem was that they cost too much for common people.

Then one day, an enterprising person came up with a unique way of gambling that almost anyone could afford. He started selling chances to win all sorts of prizes such as a bicycle, furniture, or other very desirable things— at only ten cents a ticket. The number to gain the prize was the last four digits of the winning ticket on the national lottery, which could be heard by radio, broadcast from Port-au-Prince. Anybody who had a little transistor radio could become a lottery master.

This started in the capital and spread like wildfire throughout the country. People were selling off their chickens, little plots of land, or anything they had of value to be able to buy radios that could tune in the station from Port-au-Prince.

Ten cents was not so hard to come by, so tickets sold easily and in quantity. Before long, as we traveled down the main roads, we saw table after table under the trees, everywhere in the country.

Most of the radios were bought in Port-au-Prince, where the wholesalers were inundated with orders. When our 4VEH people wanted to buy eight or ten for our distribution program, they told us they had several orders pending for two or three hundred units each order.

Then the situation suddenly took a serious turn. The government discovered that these "Borlette" tickets had seriously depleted the sale of the 60-cent government lottery, and they were losing thousands of dollars weekly.

A warning was circulated that "Borlette" tickets could no longer be sold. But when the sales continued here and there, the government suddenly issued an edict that "Borlette" tickets were forbidden and that anyone found selling them would be arrested and put in prison. Anyone found with tickets in his pocket was subject to being beaten.

Suddenly thousands of radios all over the country were no longer needed for the numbers game. People had the radios, so they tuned in the loudest station... which happened to be 4VEH!

Overnight, Radio 4VEH acquired tens of thousands of new listeners who would not have heard the Gospel otherwise.

1973   **PRESSURES OR PRIORITIES**
By Margaret Bonnette

It was a full day at our outpatient clinic. An unusually large number of very sick Haitians had come from long distances. So we were trying to help them with the best we had and also get them on their way as soon as possible. Obviously Pierre, a 16-year-old boy, was critically ill. He had been carried on his father's back into our consulting room. The mother had come along, too.

While waiting for his laboratory analysis, we placed him in a bed in the injection room with a national worker to watch over him. I continued seeing the sick. But I couldn't forget Pierre. My constant prayer was for God's wisdom in how to treat him. Finally, the Lord got through to me that Pierre was too ill for our treatment and needed to be hospitalized.

A short time later, the Holy Spirit reminded me to check on Pierre's condition spiritually. This meant leaving many others, but I knew I must obey that inner prompting.

Pierre's parents were beside his bed, so I told them the test results and the urgency of getting their son to the government hospital five miles away. Then I asked Pierre if he knew Jesus Christ.

"I'm Catholic," he said.

After a time of explanation, I used the Wordless Book to tell the salvation story. Pierre responded quickly and prayed the prayer of repentance. His mother did the same. (The father accepted Christ three weeks later.)

Just outside our clinic gate, however, while waiting for the bus, Pierre died. But other Haitians told us he had witnessed to those passing near him of Jesus and how they, too, could have life eternal.

1973   **A WINDOW**
By Rachael Picazo

Delivoir always had a smile. I'm sure it helped him get odd jobs around the missionary compound. But what everyone appreciated most was his honesty and willingness to stick to a job until it was done.

One day when I asked Delivoir about his health and family, with face aglow he began to describe his weekend trips to an isolated community, three hours' brisk walk from the nearest road, up and down hills, and across a dozen streams. There nobody had ever heard about Christ. So Delivoir and a friend were giving their weekends to tell them the Good News of salvation, and people were responding.

But in the remote sections of Haiti's mountains, where nobody knows how to read, how can new Christians mature in God's ways? They have been under the influence of voodoo for generations, and their minds have been steeped in its superstitions.

Delivoir was finding it a losing battle. One Sunday a man would accept Christ as Savior, but, having no knowledge, would slip back into old habits before the next weekend came around.

Rather than give up, Delivoir hit upon a plan. He decided to take one of 4VEH's little pre-tuned radios and leave it there for daily instruction.

It worked! The radio was a thing of wonder, a little box that could speak in Creole, or sing, or play heavenly music. No one was so busy but what he could take a few minutes a day to listen. Devotionals taught them how to be converted and live honest, moral lives; songs told of heaven and God's great glory; and readings quoted God's actual words to man on earth. Even simple health instructions were given, teaching that sickness is caused by little "beasties" so tiny one cannot see them, rather than by a curse from one's neighbor. Delivoir also started a class for new believers in Christ. They would be baptized to form the nucleus of a church at Grande Ravine.

Then the Christians built a little shelter where they could worship God together. They asked Delivoir to show them how to read, so they could study the Bible for themselves. A schoolteacher for their children was requested, and a nurse to help their sick. No more witch doctors; God's peace far surpassed the fear that pervaded the voodoo religion.

Each day they paused by the radio to hear what more it had to teach them. They arranged chores so they could listen to their favorite programs. This talking box was a window into a new world.

1973   **WHY I AM A MISSIONARY**
By Marilyn Murphy Shaferly

Why am I a missionary?

It's a question not easy to answer. Certainly, I never intended to be one of those odd individuals.

Restless and searching for deep satisfaction and meaning in life, I graduated from college to begin what I loved—secretarial work, on my terms.

But God had something else in mind. And I guess this is really the key to why I am a missionary.

Secretarial work? Yes, God planned to use that. But not where and how I had planned. Through His leading, as clear as if He had spoken aloud, I went to work at the OMS headquarters, then in Los Angeles.

Months later God spoke clearly concerning the need for a secretary at Radio 4VEH in Haiti. I knew I should go. And with mingled excitement and misgivings I obeyed. Perhaps there is the second key to why I am a missionary.

A bigger question in my mind is why God chose me to be a missionary. I know why I obeyed—I was afraid not to. I knew that only in God's will would I find joy and peace.

But looking back over almost two five-year terms of missionary service, I understand some of the things God had in mind. He has taught me to know and love Him more, as well as to care more about other people and their needs. He has also given me a longing to see others come to Him. Extra bonuses have been a wonderful husband, whom I met on the field, and now a beautiful son.

I am a missionary, first of all, because God chose me. I will remain one as long as I know it's what He wants. Whatever abilities I may have are His, with the prayer that their use will result in others finding Christ.

As I serve God as a missionary here in Haiti, it is always with a sense of inadequacy—realizing I am learning more than I can ever teach, that surely others could do better—but also with a sense of awe that He has chosen me. I have chosen to obey.

1974   WHY HAITI?
By Howard Young

People ask me over and over, "Do you go to any countries besides Haiti?"

"Are there mission fields anywhere else?"

"Why do so many go there?"

Of course, Men For Missions does take crusaders to other countries. But, yes, the majority do go to Haiti.

Perhaps the low cost lures some. Haiti sits just a few hundred miles from Miami, our main jumping off place, so airfare is low. And the Haiti crusades last only seven days, a period almost anyone can spare. But perhaps the real reason lies much closer to the purpose of God.

Most Americans and Canadians visualize a mission field from already known facts. Because of a history of mission activity on the continent of Africa, they picture black people, lush jungle, sticky weather, thatched roof huts, voodoo, and malnutrition. But since most of us can't afford to go to Africa, the Lord has brought Africa close to us. In Haiti, our African stereotypes come to life, and God uses the sudden switch from our affluence at home for a culture shock profound enough to get our attention.

On a Haiti crusade, culture shock ebbs and flows like a Caribbean tide. The first surge hits as humid air blends with the smell of burning cane fields while crusaders deplane. It ebbs when they meet the missionaries and take in nature's beauty, then flows as cobblestones of the main road north literally shake the affluence out of North American bus riders. When white crusaders pack into an already full church and Haitian Christians begin to sing, it builds again.

By week's end, however, the shock is gone. In its place the Holy Spirit plants deep love for a people not so different, after all.

At the beginning of a recent crusade, Field Superintendent Dave Graffenberger said, "I'm praying God will smash your heart while you're here, then put it back together His way."

It happened. And apparently the rebuilt hearts leaked a little, for tears trickled down crusaders' cheeks as they boarded their departing plane.

Why Haiti? For many, a trip to Haiti has turned stereotypes into flesh and blood and stretched horizons across a world.

1974　　UNDER HIS CONTROL
By Dick Brown

It had rained for four straight days, and a stationary storm front hovered over Cap-Haitien. Eight days remained until high tide—which would put our tower site several inches under water.

With sunbaked clay turned into soft oozing mud, work would be impossible. How would we ever complete the job?

God knew about these problems, just as He'd known a tower base plate, the one item needed to start the whole project, would arrive in Haiti just two weeks earlier. He'd known about the mud and water when our Haitian workers dug a hole for the concrete foundation two weeks before. He was also aware that a boom had to be built from scratch and that at the last minute it wouldn't work without alterations. Not one of the little matters surrounding the erection of a tower—to beam a powerful Radio 4VEH signal into Cuba and the Dominican Republic nearly twice as strong as before—had escaped His attention.

That's why the rains stopped the night the work team arrived, and the tide waters were delayed for six more days as God's ten chosen men worked in 110-degree sun erecting the tower.

The ten chosen men, from ten different but divinely prescribed backgrounds, converged in Haiti late in April. At least 1,000 miles away from home on "vacation," they had left their families and jobs, relying on the Lord for funds. And as they worked in the blistering heat, painted with sunburn lotion like Indians ready for war, they rejoiced for the opportunity to serve Him.

And that is exactly how that job was completed. God was in control when the chain-hoist, supporting an 800-pound gin boom, slipped. Sliding only six inches, it stopped when one of the last links caught in the pulley. Had it dropped, cutting guy wires in a thunderous 270-foot descent, the tower would have toppled, carrying six men to certain death. Maybe you prayed that day (May 6).

God was also in control when a five-inch bolt fell 200 feet, sinking into the ground six inches and missing a crusader by only a foot. God was still in charge as His ten men knelt for prayer—their job completed.

When you go on a Men For Missions trip to Haiti, you're assured excitement and fulfillment, along with God's blessing and miracles, if you give Him the chance.

1975   **BECAUSE GOD CARES**
                   By Lea Ullom

Spend a morning with me at Bethesda Clinic.

A waiting crowd greets our arrival: crying babies, mothers, fathers, the elderly and the young, some well dressed, some in rags—but all clean and in their "best." In their hands many hold gospel tracts. Already our Haitian pastor has held a service.

My first patient is a teenager, his abnormally enlarged chest wheezing and straining for air. We'll give him several injections throughout the morning and hope by noon he'll be able to return home.

Next, a child about five years old shows signs of malnutrition, his once black hair now a reddish color. We've given him vitamins and powdered milk several times, but his mother is a city beggar, unable to help him. Today, for the first time he smiled—an indication of life and personality within his frail body.

Nurse Flo Boyer calls, "Lea, do you remember this man?"

Yes, I remember him well. A week ago he was helped into the clinic, his eyes severely infected. He had walked a long distance and was very weak. They had tried lemon juice first and his eyes got worse. "So we put white sugar in them, and that didn't help either," he and his wife explained.

Today he's much improved, thanks to antibiotics we gave him.

On and on it goes. We pray for strength and wisdom...to show them we care...because God cares.

1975   GOD AT WORK IN HAITI
By Rachael Picazo

On June 2, Radio 4VEH celebrates its 25th Anniversary.

As one Haitian informed us, "Everyone—converted and non-converted, radio owner and non-owner—knows what 4VEH is and stands for."

"My radio is on 4VEH from sign-on in the morning to signoff at night," write the people of northern Haiti.

"4VEH provides a unique service," declared one, "for it is a tool—a tool of information."

It speeds emergency messages to families scattered over Haiti or the United States, tells of happenings across the world, gives health instruction, explains scientific marvels, dedicates Christian songs to loved ones and friends. But most of all 4VEH serves as a tool in God's hand to penetrate barriers of class, illiteracy, religious prejudice, superstition, and hopelessness. This tool borne on radio waves reaches into the grass-thatched cottage and the luxurious mansion, into the city, the remote mountain recesses, and across the broad desert plain.

"I cannot explain my thanksgiving for this station to which I have listened almost every day," translates a letter in French. "One day it led me to repentance. That's why I can never forget this source of help and the change it made in me."

"Please pray for me," requested another from Cap-Haitien, "because since I have been listening to your broadcasts, I have felt drawn nearer to my Creator. I am a Catholic and my parents are very severe with me concerning Protestantism. Pray for them, also, and help me to find the way of happiness."

When 4VEH first went on the air 25 years ago, comparatively few receivers existed on the island. Not many Haitians could afford the short-lived batteries, much less the radios. But with the coming of transistors in the late '50s, radios appeared which required only flashlight batteries, available anywhere in Haiti. In an effort to help more hear the Gospel by radio, 4VEH bought 2,000 kits, made them into radios pre-tuned to the station, and placed them in strategic homes.

Just a few years later, the cost of transistor radios dropped within reach of many thousands in Haiti. Almost overnight our radio audience mushroomed. The necessity for more programming became evident.

In 1967, 4VEH went to dual broadcasting. One set of transmitters carried programs in French and Creole all day long for Haiti. Over another set English or Spanish broadcasts went to the West Indies islands. This actually doubled the program hours, as well as our need for personnel. God heard our pleas and handpicked for us choice, well-educated Haitians. Now a graduate of our Emmaus Vocational Bible School capably supervises the French programming department. Other well-trained Haitians serve as secretaries, announcers, control operators, newscasters, program producers, transmitter operators, and technicians. Since few programs are available in French and Creole, our Haitian staff produces 79 percent of the Haiti broadcasts.

Haiti sits in the hub of the Caribbean, surrounded by the other islands of the West Indies. Sharing the same island is the Dominican Republic, while on the other side, just 50 miles across the channel, sits Cuba. With its newly completed directional tower array, 4VEH targets these two Spanish-speaking areas.

Recent letters verify its effectiveness: "4VEH...now is heard so clearly it seems to be in our back yard," declared a listener in the Dominican Republic, and a 19-year-old youth in

Cuba wrote: "I have listened for the first time to 4VEH on medium wave...Please send me your program schedule."

With this powerful thrust, God uses 4VEH to reach many behind the Sugar Cane Curtain in Cuba. We marvel that such letters as these, translated from Spanish, filter out of that neighbor island: "We are under great persecution. We have no church, but in my house I gather my neighbors, that they may have a chance to hear the voice of my Lord by means of Radio 4VEH."

And another: "It is with joy that I inform you that a family of 12 persons has been converted as a result of your programs." One of our broadcasters estimated that 75% of his listener letters from Cuba are written by children and young people. Pray for our neighbor, Cuba!

The fourth language used on 4VEH is English. A large percent of the West Indies islanders speak English. To them 4VEH is "their" local station. Some live on small isolated islands where radio forms a vital part of their lives: "In our little island (Salt Cay), whose area is nine square miles, your programs are listened to by nearly the entire population. I can assure you of the souls who are speaking of their decision for the Lord Jesus Christ."

"The people of Turks and Caicos Islands cannot survive without Radio 4VEH," declared another from Grand Turk.

It is God's light set aflame through the tubes and towers of 4VEH that has established this beacon in the heart of the Caribbean.

But 4VEH also suffers setbacks. The fuel crisis recently dealt us a blow. Our budget could not keep pace with the 300% rise in cost of diesel oil which runs our electric generators. We had to cut back broadcasting time and reduce the number of programs to the Dominican Republic and Cuba. Our number one radio prayer request is that we might find a solution to this problem.

Radio 4VEH is perhaps the best known of the four closely knit departments of OMS International working in Haiti: radio, church, clinic, and vocational Bible school.

THE EMMAUS VOCATIONAL BIBLE SCHOOL

The Emmaus Vocational Bible School is training Haitian youth to become capable spiritual leaders. Besides filling key roles in the Radio 4VEH staff, they also hold responsible positions in the clinic laboratory and pharmacy, the day schools, and churches. Last year all ten finishing at Emmaus entered full-time Christian work directly connected with OMS in Haiti. Since the first graduating class in 1970, 89% have remained in Christian work.

THE EVANGELICAL CHURCH OF HAITI

Twelve congregations and preaching points have been started by the Every Creature Crusade teams since they began in Haiti some five years ago. Three teams now blanket other areas of the island.

New Christians, as well as older ones, must know God's Word to grow. But how is this possible if one cannot read? Radio 4VEH provides some help, yet new Christians soon experience a keen desire to read the Bible for themselves. Thus the natural outgrowth of the church in Haiti is the school. There are not enough government schools in Haiti for all its children, and the required fees are more than the average peasant can pay. Thus, in almost every church, an elementary school has been started, where Christian teachers give daily instruction in Bible along with basic academic subjects.

Here, however, Haiti's language problem comes into sharp focus. Though French is the language used in the schools, most Haitians speak only Creole, a dialect just recently reduced

194

to writing and without any significant body of literature other than the New Testament. Thus, in learning to read, a Creole-speaking child in a Haitian school must also learn French. No solution has yet been adopted for this dilemma.

BETHESDA MEDICAL CENTER

OMS from the first has provided a clinic to minister to the sick of the community. Even when it was only Miss Flo Boyer working from a little clinic room remodeled from the old plantation carriage shed under a giant almond tree, the people were deeply grateful. They considered it of vital importance.

In the early days, a woman became desperately ill in the night. Afraid she would die before morning, she got up, saddled her donkey, and headed for the witch doctor. On the way she became unconscious; but, by some miracle, the rough wooden saddle supported her slumping body so she did not fall, and the donkey trudged on and on. At last he stopped—not at the witch doctor's house, but at the gate of our OMS compound. The watchman peered through the gate in amazement, then rushed to get the nurse. Lowered gently from the back of the donkey, the woman was given care that brought her back to consciousness and, eventually, to health.

Today, a Y-shaped clinic includes a chapel and two long wings housing a laboratory, x-ray, pharmacy, and consulting rooms. A couple of other attractive outlying buildings serve for dentistry and obstetrics. Every patient first has an opportunity to hear the plan of salvation, as a different pastor each month holds daily services in the chapel. Many respond to God's tug on their hearts.

One well-to-do man kept coming from a long distance. The nurses knew he could afford a private doctor's care, so finally asked him why he always came to this clinic.

"I feel better after coming here," he asserted. "Even if you only give me an aspirin, you do it with prayer and Christian love, and it does me more good than all the expensive medicine I could get from the doctor."

A badly wounded man once told the nurse, "Just do what you can with me, and if you can't help me, I will go home to die. I will not go anywhere else."

So the three nurses (plus three part-time nurses who are missionary wives) and one dentist do what they can, with prayer. Amazingly, God enables them to treat an average of 1,400 patients a month, giving health instruction and preventive inoculations, caring for all manner of dental problems, delivering babies, and treating the mothers.

We are engaged in battle here, and you, "staying by the stuff," through your prayers and gifts share equally with us in what God accomplishes.

1977 **JUST AN OLD STRAW HAT**
By Harry Naylor, Brownsville, TN

Over a period of years I'd encouraged laymen to go on MFMI crusades and visit overseas mission work. But when I urged my friend Reggie Smith to go to Haiti, he called my hand.

"Sign me up," he said. "But that means we go together."

Since he'd put me in the corner, I made reservations for us both on a Men For Missions crusade to Haiti four years ago.

The welcome we received in the homes of the Haiti missionaries was out of this world. But what we saw among the people broke our hearts. Their love for us, and hunger to know Jesus, caught us off guard. We could hardly take it.

On Sunday morning we were sent to a little country church with a dusty dirt floor. The preacher brought a stirring message, and an offering was taken to put a concrete floor in their place of worship.

Only $119 was needed. But they didn't get enough the first time, so the ushers passed the plates again.

Sitting behind me was a Haitian man, a Christian, doubtless delivered from the darkness and superstition of voodoo worship through Jesus. He wanted that floor in his church very much. But he had nothing to give—except his hat. To our amazement, he placed it on the offering plate.

The hat might have been worth four or five cents. It was used, not new. But the pastor held it up and said. "We'll sell this hat and put the money it brings toward the floor."

Like lightning, the Lord spoke to my heart through His inner voice, "You buy that hat and take it back to the United States."

I jumped up like a bargain hunter at a grab bag sale and reached for the hat before somebody beat me to it. As far as I know, no one else was interested, but to me it was important. And I'm sure that pastor felt well paid when I handed him $20 for the hat.

I really didn't know what I was getting into, but I brought the hat home and began telling people about it. The first man I told was so stirred by the story he went to the bank, borrowed a thousand dollars, and gave it to me for Haiti.

Later I was in a Lay Witness Mission for which Reggie Smith, my traveling companion, was the coordinator. He had me speak on Saturday noon at a bank. I told the story and showed them the hat.

"If one of you has $5,000 and wants to buy this hat, I'll take your money...but I'll keep the hat."

They laughed. I did, too. But a man came into Sunday school the next morning and handed me a check for $1,000. And his church pledged $2,600 more for Haiti mission work.

Nell Mayo, a 77-year-old Christian lady, wanted to go on a crusade, but she took ill and died before her dream came true. She had questioned me earlier about making her will. We found out later that $7,000 had been designated for Haiti.

Many others have sent in various amounts. The best estimate we can make is $20,000 to $25,000 sent in or willed to the OMS work in Haiti just because of that old straw hat.

I've often wondered what that Haitian man would think if he knew his hat had inspired people to send thousands of dollars to his country. Maybe he wouldn't even know how much that is. And I think it's just begun. As more people hear this story, I believe other things will happen.

One lesson I've learned from this is the importance of obedience. It is so easy when we have such impressions to think, "Oh, that's just my mind running off." But because a Haitian peasant obeyed God and gave his straw hat, and because I for once obeyed God's nudging and bought it from the pastor, not only did their church get a new cement floor, but also dozens of people have been stirred spiritually and thousands of dollars sent to aid in spreading the Good News. Rather like the boy with fish and bread in his lunch who went to hear Jesus, five thousand people were mighty glad he didn't refuse to hand it over to the Master.

1977   HAITIAN RADIO DIRECTOR
By Rachael Picazo

In May 1977, Mr. Gaudin Charles, 33, was installed as the first Haitian manager of Radio 4VEH and honored by a dinner at a Cap-Haitien hotel attended by the provincial prefect. In his inaugural speech, Gaudin stated, "What decides the worth of a man's life is not the title that he bears, but the calling to which he responds."

Haiti Field Director David Graffenberger declared, "This ceremony is not a foreign concept to OMS International as it functions in many countries around the world. One of the basic goals of the Mission has been to train leadership in each country. It is a pleasure to have Haitian young men such as Gaudin who are prepared to accept roles as leaders."

Associated with the station for 13 years, Mr. and Mrs. Charles returned to Haiti last winter after they had both earned B.A. and M.A. degrees from Azusa Pacific College. Gaudin's master's degree was in business management. This day fulfilled a vision and many prayers for the day when 4VEH would be administered by a godly Haitian leader.

PROFILE OF A MAN OF GOD
By Marilyn Shaferly (written in 1989)

Gaudin Charles arrived at 4VEH in 1964, a typical young man in search of a good living. His intention was to make enough money at Radio 4VEH to enter the School of Law. But after one year working with 4VEH engineer Mardy Picazo at the transmitter site, Gaudin had an experience which forever changed him. "An experience with the Lord," he says. Alone in the control room, listening to a well-known Haitian preacher, Gaudin became profoundly convinced that underlying every person who was influenced or converted through Pastor Luc Neree's messages, an entire network—the recording technician, the radio operator, the radio station—all shared in the event.

It was then Gaudin knew that God intended for him to be a part of the network. His "job" became a ministry. "I am a link," Gaudin says... "In every person who comes to know Christ or whose life is changed through 4VEH, I have a part.".

Gaudin is now director of Radio 4VEH, and also produces some of its best-loved programs in a land where Christ and His principles are unknown. For 20 years the "Sunday School" lesson has been aired uninterrupted, even during Gaudin's four years at Azusa Pacific University in the States. Gaudin literally worked night and day to record four years of programs in advance.

One man, a professor for 44 years, has followed Radio 4VEH broadcasts, including "Sunday School" since 1954. This past December 1988, Gaudin received a letter from the professor. The man reported, "On September 24, 1988, at 9:00 p.m., I decided to receive Christ as my personal Savior."

Gaudin knew God had chosen Christiane Marcelin to be his wife. But she refused all his attempts at courtship. She was studying to become a nurse and was determined to let nothing deter her. So for two years he made no attempt to develop the relationship. As the nursing program neared completion, however, Gaudin made his proposal. Christiane accepted.

After the arrival of their first son, Gerald, severe postpartum depression left Chris helpless to care for him until doctors finally ascertained the proper balance of medication. There was a repetition of the same after the birth of their second son, Ronald.

Then Gerald developed asthma and at the age of four died from a doctor's overdose of medicine.

Later Ronald became hydrocephalic. He was on his way to surgery when the Lord miraculously healed him after a Men For Missions group in St. Petersburg, Florida, prayed for him.

Their third son, Gary, suffers from sickle cell anemia, which also plagues Ronald.

A Christian heritage is doubly important in Haiti where moral values are often diametrically opposed to biblical standards. Gaudin's own father, now 90, has walked faithfully with Christ for 53 years.

Christiane's father, too, defied custom and braved criticism to stand for what he believed. Without doubt, much of the Christian character and maturity evidenced in the Charles' home can be traced to their Christian roots, which they, in turn, are giving to their children.

In spite of his full schedule, Gaudin followed through and obtained his law degree. "With the Word of God in one hand and the law of the land in the other, I am equipped to serve my country," he states.

"What makes Gaudin so different?" someone asked. The answer lies in his sense of mission. On one occasion when he had been working all night in the radio studios, one of the missionaries urged him to go rest and let someone else take his place.

He gently explained, "I want you to understand I'm not working for the OMS, nor even for 4VEH. I am working for God, and He will provide all the extra strength I need for today."

1979   BETTER THAN MAGIC
By Gaudin Charles (as told to Marilyn Shaferly)

Louis Inélus could hardly believe his ears. As a part-time taxi driver for tourists arriving in Cap-Haitien on luxurious cruise ships, Louis was accustomed to strange demands and odd reactions. This lady, however, surprised him.

"Take me," she told him, "to the nearest and best witch doctor. I'm willing to pay $200 for someone to tell me the future and help me with my problems."

Ordinarily Louis tried to accommodate the whims of foreign visitors. This time he could not. As a Christian and a popular personality on the Radio 4VEH staff, he immediately recognized the challenge and opportunity this American lady unwittingly presented.

Carefully choosing his words, Louis agreed to find help. With his troubled passenger in the back seat, he threaded his way through the milling crowds of vacation-clad tourists, insistent street vendors, and honking taxis. Arriving at a corner shop where a small dance combo was luring tourists inside, he stopped. With pleasure Louis' passenger noted the bright red and white sign "Magic Shop."

"Wait right here," Louis told her. Then he hurried to a nearby school where 4VEH director Gaudin Charles was teaching an evening English class. Gaudin listened, astounded, to Louis' breathless tale. The class, though most of them were non-Christians, enthusiastically dismissed Gaudin, who rushed back with Louis to the Magic Shop.

The anxious tourist agreed to accompany Gaudin to his home, no doubt believing she'd found a renowned witch doctor. Even when Gaudin began to pray, she thought it the beginning of some ceremony.

But as Gaudin shared with her the Good News of Jesus Christ, the Holy Spirit accomplished His miraculous work in the woman's heart. Tears streaming, she exclaimed, "I have never heard Jesus Christ presented this way before."

After a few moments she bowed her head and trusted Christ as her personal Savior.

That night when the majestic tourist ship sailed out of the harbor, there was at least one new person aboard. While watching the lights of Cap-Haitien fade, perhaps she fingered the Bible Gaudin had given her and recalled his parting words: "Begin reading this very night, and when you return home to New York, remember the decision you made tonight here in Haiti."

The fellows depend on God's protection as the
tower goes up

Mr. Gaudin Charles: broadcaster, 4VEH Director

Haitian staff recording a Parol Vivant Bible drama in 1980

Pastor Tony Paul in front of his church in 1980

1979 PAROL VIVANT (The Living Word)
By Rachael Picazo

I consider the Bible the most exciting, relevant book in the world. And I love drama—always tried out for a part in grade school, high school, and college plays. I had heard radio productions called "The Greatest Story Ever Told," which touched on characters we read about in the Bible, but they were fictional, "made up" from the imagination. I thought someone should put the actual Bible stories into skit form, using the details given in Scripture. It would be especially good for children.

We were working at Radio Station WMTC in the mountains of eastern Kentucky when I decided to write one myself, my first attempt being of the boy Samuel when God spoke to him in the night.

We chose characters from our radio staff. Ran Boggs, the control operator, an accomplished musician who knew the record library of the station, found mood music to enhance the story. It was an instant success, so the radio Bible drama became a weekly feature. When we left WMTC in 1952, someone else was assigned to continue the series.

After we came to Haiti and our 4VEH staff grew, I began writing Bible dramas again as a feature of the weekly "Children's Hour." I carefully researched each story with cross-references, comparing various translations, pouring over the commentaries, dictionaries, maps.

This time Aldean Saufley, a skilled organist, provided mood music and help with background noises in the show. Mardy Picazo, my husband, was always there to narrate the production and take other parts as well, and others from our missionary staff freely gave of their talents and time. Often when we had visiting MFM Crusaders, they would also take part, providing crowd noises...etc. We called the stories, "The Doorway into the Past."

As more programming was needed for the French and Creole broadcasts, we decided to translate the dramas into Creole. Pastor Napoleon Etienne became one of our enthusiastic champions for the Creole programs. Not only did he translate the scripts, but he also took the main part in its production-- served as the narrator, chose the cast of Haitian actors, and even took other character parts. We called the Creole dramas "Parole Vivant" (The Living Word).

Haitians love a tale, and they immediately applauded these narratives from the Bible. They proved to be good actors, sometimes identifying with their parts so completely they got carried away with the story.

One day we were recording the parable of the prodigal son, as found in Luke 15:11-32. The session was progressing nicely to the point when the son came home. Then, suddenly, in the studio, the "father" ran away from the microphone and threw his arms around the "son," and they both began to weep and laugh together. The other actors danced around the studio clapping their hands and rejoicing. Sitting in the control booth, I had to wipe the tears from my own eyes before I could see how to push the buttons to stop the recording. That day we caught a glimpse of how "*.... there is rejoicing in the presence of the angels of God over one sinner who repents*" *(Luke 15:10b NIV)*.

We have produced hundreds of these dramas over the years, using various translators, organists, and narrators. Yet the power of God's Word still remains fresh and powerful through these programs as they are rebroadcast over and over.

LISTENER RESPONSE

"Have you ever heard the story of Moses?" a friend asked 4VEH Director Gaudin Charles.

"Of course, many times," he responded.

"But have you ever listened to 'Parole Vivant' telling the story?" the 4VEH listeners probed.

"Yes, I've even taken the part of Moses in the story," Gaudin assured him.

"But," his friend persisted, "have you ever sat down and listened to the story as it comes over 4VEH? *Mes amis*, it is formidable! It is powerful when you make it really come alive over the radio!"

1980   **PASTOR TONY PAUL**
By Rachael Picazo

Tony, named Jean Berthony Paul, was one of 11 children. Like most in their community, the family's affairs were ordered by the local voodoo witch doctor. There was never quite enough food to really satisfy his hunger. When his father's crops yielded a good harvest, the witch doctor always came by and extracted payment for a sickness or demanded that his father put a charm on the land so the crops would be good next year.

In a family that large, it was not possible to send all the children to school since they could not afford the uniform each child had to wear, buy the books, and pay tuition each month. So the oldest son, not Tony, was chosen as the one in the family in which to invest such precious funds.

Tony was a lad of 14 that day in 1952 when two young men from the Vaudreuil Church came by his yard.

"Good afternoon, son," they greeted him, "May we come in and read to you from the Bible?"

Tony was horrified. "No!" he backed away. "The witch doctor has forbidden us to even talk to you. You'd better go before my father sees you!"

The young men smiled pleasantly and replied, "At least come visit the church at Vaudreuil. There are many young people there, and you would be welcome."

The young men often came by Mr. Paul's yard, and each time they saw Tony they extended the invitation to visit the church.

One Sunday Tony did go to the tabernacle and stood at the window, where he could watch and hear the people sing. He noted their happy faces and warmed at their friendliness. The next Sunday he came back. And the next also. He began to look forward to those visits. Finally he felt at ease to come inside the building, where he sat with the young people and heard about Jesus Christ, who can save from sin.

At last he plucked up courage to approach his mother. "Mama, I have visited the church at Vaudreuil. They sing bright songs and are very friendly. They seem happy. I would like to become one of them."

His mother turned on him. "Tony! What have you done? Don't ever talk about such things again!"

Tony was truly sad at that response. But he had not been specifically forbidden to attend the services. In fact, there had come a deep longing to know the God these people knew.

As time went on, Tony's mother noticed how despondent her son had become. By now he was 16 years old. One day she astonished him with the declaration, "Tony, if you truly want to become a Christian, then I will become one with you."

At these words Tony ran the mile and a half to the church. Arriving breathless he urged the pastor, "Come quickly! My mother wants to become a Christian with me!"

Gathering other Christians to help them pray, the pastor and Tony hurried back to the house, where the mother and son believed in Jesus Christ. There was celebration in that home and rejoicing in heaven that night.

Then the two witnesses from the church were invited to come read the Bible in their home. Over a period of six months, Tony's father and all ten of his brothers and sisters also, one by one, accepted Jesus Christ as their Savior.

As a healthy, growing "babe" in Christ, Tony wanted to study the Bible for himself. So He prevailed upon his more favored pals to teach him how to read. He became friends with some of the missionaries at Vaudreuil and got jobs working at the missionary compound. Even though he had a severe stuttering problem, Tony believed God wanted him to become a pastor to teach the Gospel to his people. (God later healed him of his stuttering.)

When he heard of the Emmaus Vocational Bible School about to start at Vaudreuil, Tony determined to apply for admission. He got his friends, Haitian and missionary, to tutor him so he could pass the entrance exams. He prayed, and he talked Bible School. As the staff set up entrance requirements, they had Tony in mind and set them at a level they knew he could pass. So Tony was in that first class of the Emmaus Vocational Bible School in January 1967.

At his graduation three years later (May 1970), Tony was one of four chosen for an Every Creature Crusade team. These four, along with a young missionary leader, traveled to different places in Haiti. There they lived for a few months, witnessed to each person in the area, held nightly evangelistic services, and taught the Bible to new believers.

After six months, the team came to Plaine du Nord, a center for voodoo worship. There they met with strong opposition. One night, as they were holding their evangelistic service, ruffians began to throw stones into the congregation. They hit one young man in the face, knocking out some of his teeth. A young lady was hit in the head, the blood from the wound splattering her clothes. (Later these same ruffians

207

accepted Christ and on their knees begged forgiveness of the congregation.)

At other times the ECC Team was brought before the local Haitian magistrates and falsely accused.

But many in that city heard and believed, and from that number 40 were baptized. When the time came for the team to leave Plaine du Nord in March 1971, it was Tony Paul who was left in the town to nurture the new congregation.

Filled with the Holy Spirit, Tony was eager to win his people to God. Daily the church grew as more believed in Jesus Christ.

After three months, Tony challenged the new believers, "Let's go to the next village and tell them what God has done for us."

Fourteen young Christians walked with Tony two miles across fields and creeks to Bredar. There they witnessed God's saving power. At once, many believed. They said, "Now we have a chance to know the God preached over Radio Station 4VEH. Come back next week and teach us more."

Soon there were seven outlying villages being visited regularly by the Christians of the Plaine du Nord church. Now, nine years later, two of these will soon have churches with buildings and pastors of their own.

Tony's heart ached for his people, for they were so very poor. He felt the answer to their poverty was in God's Word. So he taught them, "Give your tithe to the Lord and He will prosper you. For God has said in Malachi 3:10, 'Bring ye all the tithes...and prove me now...see if I will not open you the windows of heaven, and pour you out a blessing, that there shall not be room enough to receive it.'"

One woman, who earned her living by peddling merchandise, decided to try it out. The next day she brought her tithe to Pastor Tony, which was two cents. She told him, "Take this now, so I won't be tempted to steal from the Lord and spend it for myself before next Sunday."

The next week, when she brought a day's tithe, it was four cents. Little by little God began to bless her, so that some months later, she brought one day's tithe of a dollar!

Tony was single and he wanted a good wife, one who could also help in the work of the church. A beautiful young lady named Marie, teacher in the Catholic school, visited Tony's church. There she listened to the Gospel and accepted Jesus Christ as her Savior. Tony knew this was the one to become his wife.

Commonly throughout Haiti, a man and woman will live together and even have children, without ever marrying. Even some who claim to follow Jesus observe this practice, because they are so poor. A wedding entails so much expense they consider it unattainable. They say, "We don't have money for wedding rings. We can't give a reception for guests. And where could we get new clothes for the affair?"

This troubled Tony. So as they were planning their wedding ceremony, Tony suggested, "Let's make our wedding an example that our people can follow. We will not buy any new clothes, nor give a reception. Let's take our vows with our hands on the Bible rather than exchanging rings."

And so their wedding cost no more than the few gourdes required for government papers. Through later years Pastor Tony has made a practice of performing this kind of simple wedding for couples who have no means, in the presence of the Christians gathered to fast and pray on Thursday mornings under the trees near the town. These weddings are awesome in their beauty because of God's blessing.

Tony was also concerned about the people's inability to read. "How can they know the Word of God when they cannot read?" he reasoned.

In due time he organized a school in the church building. He chose Christian teachers, who taught the Bible along with their regular classes. To pay the teachers, he charged each student a few pennies per month.

Then the Haitian government decreed that schools must be separate from churches. So as Tony set about to construct an independent school building, God sent Christian laymen from far countries of Canada and the United States to help build it. At this writing in 1980, there are 580 children now learning to read the Word of God in Tony's school, under the instruction of 12 dedicated teachers.

The city of Plaine du Nord is called a capital of voodoo because of the Festival of St. Jacques each year, July 23-25, when thousands of adherents come to bathe in a filthy pool they consider sacred and worship Satan with every kind of evil orgy. Pastor Tony was grieved for his people. He passed out tracts; he preached to the incoming visitors.

But finding that the Christian young people from his church were tempted to be drawn into the evil practices, he organized a spiritual retreat and took them away from the town for the duration of the festival. It is Tony's constant prayer, "O Lord, make this city which is called 'The Capital of Voodoo' to become 'The Capital of the Gospel'!"

Early on in the growth of Tony's church, he saw that he needed help in conducting its ministries. So he chose godly men to pray with him, to help him make decisions, spearhead outstation evangelism, teach the Word, and direct the services when he needed to be away. He now has nine such men carrying leadership roles in the church, which has 880 baptized believers, and whose average Sunday School attendance is 500.

Pastor Tony also ministers at the clinic, speaks on the radio, conducts open-air meetings, and is active in evangelistic efforts throughout Haiti. Haiti is a better place, and heaven has been enriched with many souls because of Pastor Tony Paul.

Eutrope Samson, saved through 4VEH, teaching
electronics (ca. 1980)

More than 1,000 people helped 4VEH celebrate its
30th Anniversary

The radio 4VEH staff in 1980

1980   **30th ANNIVERSARY OF 4VEH**
By Marilyn Shaferly

In the early '60s, Radio 4VEH personnel began placing pre-tuned transistor sets in Christian homes. The Marcelin home was one. Up on the window ledge went their radio, volume turned high so neighbors could hear. Music was the favorite. Programs on hygiene and nutrition made their impact too. Villagers soon learned that shorter fingernails and soap and water baths improved their health as well as the quality of their lives. They discovered how to prepare the nutritious foods which grew all around them.

In another home, with an extremely ill husband and no one to help, a desperate wife told her children to turn on Radio 4VEH. "Maybe," she said, "we will hear something to help us."

Early morning gospel music and devotionals poured over the air. As the family listened, the ailing father sensed faint stirrings of faith. Before long his health was restored. Later the entire family found spiritual healing through Christ and is now active in a congregation.

Teenager Eutrope Samson yearned for an education. Every morning before dawn, he'd slip outside to study under the street light. His neighbor, a businessman, owned a radio. By 5:00 a.m. it was on, and Eutrope heard music and devotionals from Radio 4VEH. Even while he studied, the 4VEH message took root. One day he gave his heart to Christ.

Today Eutrope is not only a respected leader in the church, but also founder and head of an electronics and typing school in Cap-Haitien and the director of our OMS vocational Bible school. Another student, convinced of 4VEH effectiveness, bought three small radios for a village which had no church, few Christians, and no radios. Though some could afford them, they felt that such a wonderful instrument belonged only in wealthy houses.

"No," argued the young man, "if you have a radio, it will help you have a better home."

And so a father, the only Christian in his household, agreed to take one. His entire family now serves the Lord, and one son teaches in a Christian school.

The other two radios brought similar changes. Villagers, transformed by the Gospel, soon ended their common-law status by marrying their mates. Others cleaned up their homes. And when Christians arrived to begin a church, they found the people prepared.

Wherever Radio 4VEH is heard, Christians are strengthened and nurtured. One pastor put it, "If you see a strong church, you can be sure its strength is the result of Radio 4VEH's ministry."

Even time has taken on new meaning. In a country where most people were illiterate, time meant very little—until, that is, Radio 4VEH took hold. As announcers told the hour, villagers ran to see what it looked like on their clocks. They learned that a program announced for 5:00 was aired at 5:00—not 5:05 or 6:00. Eventually this carried over into punctual church activities. In most communities, if you don't have "4VEH time," your watch is not correct.

Thus, with joy and victory, more than 1,000 friends of 4VEH gathered in Cap-Haitien last June 2 to celebrate 30 years of Christian broadcasting. Haiti's leaders expressed enthusiastic gratitude for the station's contribution to the social and spiritual life of the nation.

Today 4VEH broadcasts in four languages with combined power of all frequencies totaling 25,000 watts. Directional antenna systems increase its effective output to 50,000 - 75,000 watts of power beamed to specific areas.

Countless Christians across the West Indies, Cuba, and in over 20 other nations date their salvation to a broadcast from Radio 4VEH. Millions seek solace and spiritual food from a little box which daily brings "The Evangelistic Voice of Haiti."

1980   **THE GOAL IS SOULS**
                  By Warren Hardig

Ever miss your destination but reach your goal? I did. It was last summer.

As director of a witnessing crusade in Haiti, I planned a "day of witnessing." The target, a little settlement called Grand Ravine, had figured heavily in my involvement in missions on my first crusade in 1970. Now I was anxious to go back, this time for door-to-door witnessing.

To get there required hiking for an hour and a half plus fording a stream five times. After several hours of visitation we'd hike the same wet, winding trail back.

Dividing the crusaders into teams, we supplied them with tracts, assigned an interpreter for each group, and started them up the rugged trail.

My team brought up the rear. But before we started, someone gave a tract to the Haitian lady carrying our water. She listened with interest as they explained the plan of salvation. But when asked about accepting Christ, she said, "Sometime...Not now."

So we started our hike. We hadn't gone far when another Haitian lady came running to us. Though we couldn't understand what she wanted, we handed her a tract. Looking at it a moment she spoke the Creole words for "Jesus Christ." Immediately I sensed the Spirit's nudge and called Pastor Jacques, who is a professor at the OMS Bible School. He came at once to serve as interpreter.

The lady continued to speak rapidly, gesturing broadly with her hands. Through the pastor we learned she wanted us to pray for her son who was sick. And she wanted to become a Christian. After our explanation of what it means to follow Christ, she led us through a thorny cactus fence to find a chair. Then, seating herself, she prayed to receive Christ.

To ensure adequate follow-up, Pastor Jacques took out his pen, unzipped his Bible, and wrote down the new believer's name. Then he sent someone to get her son. After we prayed for his healing, the boy asked if he, too, could be saved. So, like his mother, he sat in the chair and prayed for God's forgiveness.

Out came the pastor's pen again to record his name. Thrilled over two conversions in the matter of a few minutes, we resumed our trek. But we hadn't gone a hundred yards until another woman stopped us. She, too, wanted to know Jesus, found a nearby chair, and sat down to pray the sinner's prayer.

By this time, all of us were overwhelmed. Never had we seen such hunger for salvation. As Pastor Jacques again took out his pen, one of the crusaders expressed all our sentiments with, "Wow! I feel like we're watching as names are written in the Book of Life."

But the chairs. Why had each one wanted a chair?

The explanation endeared these peasant people to our hearts. Since Haitian churches seldom boast altar rails, sometimes seekers sit in chairs placed in front of the congregation. Apparently these people were familiar with this custom.

The Holy Spirit, however, wasn't limited to chairs—nor to meeting the heart needs of ladies only.

As our journey continued, a man approached us. He was rubbing his stomach and told Pastor Jacques how little he'd had to eat.

Our hearts went out to him, of course, and I prepared to share my sack lunch. But I didn't want him to equate Christianity with receiving a hand-out. So, with the pastor's help, I explained that food could satisfy only temporarily. By accepting Christ he'd have eternal life. Then I shared how God had saved me from a life of sin and gave him instruction from the Word.

Right there in the middle of the trail, the man accepted Christ. Pastor Jacques was ready with Bible and pen. And my lunch became a feast for both my new brother in Christ and me. About this time missionary Les Babcock informed us we'd have to start back soon. So we turned aside to a small OMS church, which had a brush arbor school-room in the back. There we presented the claims of Christ to the students, and several received Him as Lord.

Remember the lady carrying our water supply? After watching the others accept Christ, she eagerly gave her heart to Him as well.

We didn't get to Grand Ravine that day, but a number of Haitians came into the Kingdom of God.

And that's what a witnessing crusade is all about. More than a sightseeing tour in a foreign country, it's sharing your witness with people who don't know the love of Christ. Our goal is to win souls.

1981   **OBSTETRICS WING**
By Marilyn Shaferly

Nurse Ruth Gamber arrived at our Bethesda Medical Center in 1972, enthusiastic with the vision of training Haitian women in midwifery skills. There was already some

215

maternal/child health care offered, but with the dedication of the new obstetrics wing in 1975, opportunities expanded.

Ruth chose four promising young women from the community and started with the basics: how to read a thermometer and scales, which end of the thermometer to use... Gradually the girls assumed more and more responsibility. They learned to foresee potential medical problems, prescribe routine medicines, and take care of babies and mothers until they were discharged.

Ruth spent her first furlough from Haiti earning midwifery certification at the Frontier Nursing Service in Kentucky. Back in Haiti, Lynn Patterson, another nurse who had just completed the same training, joined her. Together they and their four assistants minister to the needs of the 20-25 expectant mothers who crowd into the waiting area each day. Many are young. Most come from communities around the clinic, where without the care offered by Ruth and her staff, they would probably give birth at home, attended only by a local midwife.

In the weeks preceding and following her baby's arrival, each mother receives instruction in nutrition, hygiene, and child care. She is also included in the clinic chapel service, where the plan of salvation is presented clearly.

Mme. Jean-Baptiste, who had already delivered her baby, developed a high fever. Since the clinic at that time had no resident doctor, responsibility rested on Ruth. She prayed for wisdom, then prescribed medication for bacterial meningitis. As the medicine took effect, Mme. Jean-Baptiste began to improve.

Mme.Jean-Baptiste was not a Christian although her family was. As they, the Haitian students, and Ruth talked about spiritual matters, she accepted Christ as Savior.

What a joy to see her now! She still comes regularly to the clinic, not for consultation, but to do what she can for

216

other patients. Sometimes she brings food or does a patient's laundry. Sometimes she just comes to visit. But always there is a light in her eyes, gratitude to her newfound Lord.

1982   **MOUNTAIN ROAD**
By Hudson Hess

Skirting the coast, a chain of mountains called Matheux often fascinates first-time visitors to Haiti. I was no exception that Sunday morning in 1964. Riding with Pastor Napo to my first rural church service, I pondered the barren, silent, inhospitable peaks.

A sadness gripped me as I realized that these mountains, now so dry and desolate, had once proudly carried vast forests of hardwoods and pine. Could any human being exist up there? It seemed impossible. Yet, trails curled up the slopes.

Not long after, Pastor Napo asked Dave Graffenberger and me to accompany him on a visit to one of his mountain churches. We were delighted.

I shall never forget that first trip to Ti Bois. The trail, strewn with rocks and boulders, stretched almost straight up. With relentless fury the sun glared down at us. Even the path became our enemy, radiating absorbed heat like an oven. With no shade nor place to rest, our heads throbbed and perspiration poured.

"Lord," I prayed, "if you want us to reach these people for you, give us a road someday."

Since then I have become accustomed to the peaks and made the trip countless times. Once I hiked 130 miles in a week to visit our churches there. I have learned to respect the sun and not compete with mountains at midday. Yet, on every trip, prayer and planning for the road continued.

217

Many times our Field Director Eldon Turnidge would fly me over these ranges in his small plane, while we surveyed the rugged highlands. We saw mountain crowded upon mountain, so inaccessible that, though villagers saw lights of Haiti's capital blinking at night, many had never fought their way down the slopes to the city.

I learned that sixty thousand farmers, among the poorest in Haiti, scratched an existence from these steep, sun-baked slopes. Gardeners lugged scanty produce to the city over tortuous footpaths, brushing rock walls on one side to avoid gaping ravines on the other. When sickness struck, sometimes death overtook them on the trail en route to help.

In 1970 a fulltime assignment to church ministries meant I could visit the area more regularly. Without a penny for the project I began hiking around the mountain, looking for the best approach to construct the road. One day in a desolate region well off the beaten path, a local peasant asked why I was there. My reply evoked little encouragement.

"I've watched goats on those hills since I was a child," he said, "and there's absolutely no way a road could go through." Today the road runs right by the spot where that conversation took place.

At this crucial point, the Lord sent a man to help me. Julien Lundy, our little pastor at Ti Bois, took interest in the project. He was a man who didn't know what it means to give up. First, he accompanied me on survey trips. Then he began preparing the people for a united community effort. Wherever he went, he talked road.

The people thought Julien crazy. In one meeting a lady stood up and declared, "My grandchildren will all be dead before anything like that happens."

Most just knew it couldn't be done. But Julien, not dismayed in the least, kept right on, as confident as though the road were already built.

218

Sometime later, while conversing with a business friend in Port-au-Prince, I mentioned the project. His interest flared into a check for $100—enough to purchase some hand tools and send Julien for two weeks of training in road building techniques. Learning well, he returned to stake out our road.

Help came from other quarters. Church World Service promised food for workmen, an MFMI group in Ohio sent hand tools, and the American Embassy gave a small grant. Ground breaking began in March of 1972.

It was slow at first. The men lived distances away, were more interested in their gardens, and figured their time wasted anyway on something that could not be finished. But Julien came every day and the road inched forward.

Then, in October, tragedy struck. As Julien pulled onto the main highway with his motorcycle, a passing auto struck him. He was rushed to the hospital more dead than alive. Besides internal injuries, his left eye had been cut, a wrist badly broken, and his left kneecap smashed. Even if he pulled through, it was doubtful he would walk again. The work came to a complete halt.

During this low period, the Lord gave new encouragement. Friends of OMS in Australia sent their Christmas offering—around $3000—for the road project. So we secured another man to head up the workmen. And four months later, a miraculous healing brought Julien back to climb the mountains as before. Now Julien worked on layout while Nicola handled the work crews. Progress speeded.

Then a second near-fatality occurred. At an especially difficult spot, a large boulder above the workmen broke loose without warning. As it thundered to the roadway, the men frantically scrambled out of the way—just in time. But the impact caused a section of the road to give way, propelling one worker down the steep slope with the boulder.

"He's finished!" everyone cried. Hurrying to his side, the workmen found him badly lacerated—but still alive. We knew only the hand of God had kept him from death. Yet, for nearly two months, most of the men refused to work.

"The devil doesn't want the road," they asserted. "He's going to kill somebody for sure if we continue."

But leaders from Leger, a community in the center of the mountains, heard about the road. "If the people at Ti Bois are not interested in continuing the road," they said, "don't stop for them. We'll send 100 men a day to get it up here."

And with increased rations from World Service, the task took on a completely new dimension.

REPORT IN *ACTION* MAGAZINE

In 1973 when a huge rock blocked construction, Hudson asked MFMI for a bulldozer operator. Bob Pipes and Clyde Bowman of Ohio and Floridian Bob Wittig volunteered their mountain-dozing experience and cleared the rock with a rented bulldozer. As skilled operators, they did in a week what manual labor could not have accomplished in months.

Bob and Clyde longed to return the following year and presented the idea of purchasing a bulldozer to the Butler Council in Ohio. Nearby councils in Bucyrus and Morrow County helped, and Russ Burbick located a used D8 Cat for $8000. Following restoration by Keith Franks in 1977, the dozer was dedicated by Dwight Ferguson, founder of MFMI. A few days later it was en route to Haiti.

The first time Bob and Hudson took the dozer to Ti Bois (halfway to Dupin), hundreds of people appeared, to witness the arrival of the first vehicle. Hudson translated while Bob spoke to the crowd. Tears filled his eyes as he declared, "Only in God's economy could a Catskinner like me become a celebrity."

MFM crusaders began arriving on the scene. Here was a job made to order for "earthmovers." Though the highest peaks, at 5,000 feet, aren't much as mountains go, sometimes the machines teetered on the edge of nothing. More than once the snorting monsters rocked enough to frighten even guardian angels.

More than 20 men—usually two or three at a time—made up the teams to Haiti. Clyde Bowman and Bob Pipes, both of Bellville, Ohio, returned often. With the primitive and the modern working together, a track 20 feet wide began snaking back upon itself again and again, climbing the gulch-pocked range.

Missionaries Dave Shaferly and Les Babcock took turns supervising work teams until Bill and Janie Glace joined OMS in 1978. Bill briefed each team about the dangerous work and warned them about tarantulas. The men slept on a pastor's porch, ate Spam sandwiches, and took baths in a drainage ditch.

A road grader from MFMers in Kansas arrived that same year, and World Vision helped the project by purchasing fuel. They also selected the project for their nationwide television fund-raiser. Bill spent a day with TV personality Art Linkletter, as Art interviewed team members and Haitians in preparation for the broadcast.

After reaching Ti Bois, Bill identified Leger, nine miles distant, as their next goal. The terrain was hazardous and hard on equipment. But God sent Forrest Cammack of Oregon, who could fix broken machinery.

As the mountains surrendered before the onslaught, missionary and national evangelistic teams plodded ahead on foot. Consequently, road builders arrived to find congregations already established by the vanguard. And better roads mean better attendance at services.

In March 1982, ten years and 28 miles after the project started, Bill Glace, Bob Pipes, and a weary crew of MFMers chugged into Dupin.

This was not the first time MFMers had invaded Dupin, however. Years before, even without a road, MFMers from the Richmond/Winchester area had accepted the challenge to build a church there. Members of a Brazil, Indiana, church were involved in financing it. The MFMers had poured two weeks of love-labor into the rugged church where the Christians of Dupin worshiped.

Now, with the road reaching into their village, a grateful crowd of Haitians cheered the completion of this "highway," their outlet to the world. The MFMers, standing around the bulldozer, praised God.

Government dignitaries, missionaries, and thousands of people held a huge celebration with a ribbon-cutting ceremony and a feast of goat meat followed by speeches. Since then countless Haitians have come to salvation.

Hudson stated, "Of this I am sure. The One who said, I am the way, the truth, and the life, is interested in a way for the truth and the life to penetrate the mountains of Matheux. It's great to have a small part in His plan."

The road will always be etched on the hearts of those who helped build it, for God exchanged their effort for Haitian lives, now rerouted for eternity.

1982   **FM STEREO 95**

Radio 4VEH added to its varied presentations when FM Stereo 95 went on the air just in time for the Christmas season, 1982. This is the first FM Stereo station in northern Haiti.

222

Its director, Valeene Hayes, received several weeks of intensive training at Radio WCMR in Elkhart, Indiana, under the supervision of its manager, Edwin Moore. As a help in starting this Good Music service in Haiti, WCMR donated copies of several thousand classical and gospel records from their library.

Reactions to 4VEH's new FM Stereo 95 are enthusiastic. A businessman in Cap-Haitien exclaimed, "Now I know where to keep my radio tuned!"

1983　　　　　　　　**THE MYSTERY LADY**
By Gaudin Charles and Valeene Hayes
as told to Rachael Picazo

In was in the spring of 1983 that a lady telephoned Radio 4VEH and asked for the manager. Her impeccable French indicated that she was well-educated; her voice on the phone was cultured, refined.

"What is your name?" our radio manager Gaudin Charles inquired.

"I will not tell you my name," she replied, "but I listen to 4VEH and enjoy hearing the music. Why don't you put on more of it?"

"We do have more, on our new Good Music channel that started last Christmas," Gaudin informed her. "That's the FM channel, stereo 95. It is mostly music from noon until 11:30 at night."

"How do I tune it in?" she expressed interest. "We have a very good radio in the house."

Gaudin explained how to find the station, and thus she became an enthusiastic fan of our FM Stereo 95 broadcasts.

Gaudin carefully worded a question to ask if she were a Christian. This brought a sharp retort, "I don't want to talk about those religious things. I am not a believer."

"Please tell us who you are," again Gaudin entreated. "We would like to get to know you."

"You would not want to know me," she remarked, "I am not a nice person. You know about Mary Magdalene? Well, that is a picture of my life."

"Yes, I know the story of Mary Magdalene," Gaudin assured her, "and you know what happened to Mary Magdalene..."

"I have to go," she interrupted, and hung up.

What happened to Mary Magdalene of the Bible was that Christ transformed her life.

At our daily staff devotions, Gaudin asked that we pray that this woman might be helped through the 4VEH programs to come to know God. Since he didn't know her real name, he referred to her by the term she used to describe herself, "Mary Magdalene."

A few days later the mystery lady telephoned again, deeply troubled. "I don't want to live," she confessed, "but I am afraid to die. I have a place picked out on the ocean bay where I can walk out and take my life, but I am too frightened."

Gaudin talked to her of God's love, read scripture, and encouraged her to listen to the radio programs.

Again, she broke off the conversation suddenly. It became a pattern, as if she were interrupted and didn't want to be overheard.

Realizing that this woman was suicidal, Gaudin urged her to phone him anytime she needed help. So the mystery lady began to call several times a week. When Gaudin was unavailable, Valeene Hayes, our FM Stereo director, talked with her in English, which she spoke without hesitation.

When Mary Magdalene called Gaudin at his home, sometimes his wife, Christiane, talked with her. The conversations always turned into Bible lessons, often lasting half an hour or more. And they all continued to ask her, without success, to reveal her name.

One day Mary Magdalene asked Gaudin, "What are those code numbers you use every time you read the Bible?"

"Do you have a Bible?" Gaudin asked.

"No," she admitted.

"Would you like to have one?"

"Oh, yes!" she quickly assured him, "one just like yours."

"I will give you a Bible. Tell me where I can bring it. Or give me your name and address and I will send it to you."

"I will not tell you my name," she refused. "You would know who I am if I mentioned my name. You would know my husband, too."

"Then you know me?" Gaudin asked her.

"Oh, yes! I know you. I see you in town sitting in your white Peugeot waiting for your wife or driving your children to school at College Practique du Nord."

"You have seen my wife?" he was astonished. "Where?"

"At the hospital where she is a nurse."

"My wife and I would like to know you in person. Let us meet somewhere, or come to the 4VEH studios, so we can get acquainted."

"No!" she asserted, "Maybe sometime, but not now. I do want the Bible. I will send my chauffeur to pick it up at the radio station, but don't ask him any questions."

"I will have it for him tomorrow morning," he promised.

The next morning a stranger appeared at the radio studios asking about the Bible. Gaudin greeted him, peering out the window to see if he could recognize the car. But the chauffeur had parked well out of sight. Gaudin gave him the French Bible he had ready and tried to engage the man in conversation so as to get a hint about his employer. But she had instructed him not to talk, so the identity of Mary Magdalene remained a mystery.

That evening she called to thank him for the Bible. Gaudin had her open it while he explained about the "code numbers," pointing out the books, their chapters, and verse numbers. He helped her to find the Gospel of John in the New Testament and urged her to read there first.

Gaudin was especially concerned that she might take her own life. So one day he confronted her with the two eternities: the one with God and the one without God.

He gave her a picture of heaven with Jesus, who declared, "In my Father's house are many mansions... I will come back and take you to be with me that you also may be where I am."

He read the description in Revelation 21:4... "He will wipe every tear from their eyes. There will be no more death or mourning or crying or pain, for the old order of things has passed away."

Then Gaudin showed her the eternity without God, which Jesus described in Matthew 13:4-42, "The Son of Man will send out his angels, and they will weed out of his kingdom everything that causes sin and all who do evil. They will throw them into the fiery furnace, where there will be weeping and gnashing of teeth."

Gaudin warned her, "I want you to understand clearly what will happen if you die now without having accepted Christ."

Mary Magdalene was frightened. "I need more time," she hedged.

"Life is fragile," Gaudin reminded her, "but today you can accept His salvation."

"No!" she cried out, "You are pushing too much."

Then for many weeks she did not call at all.

It had been a year since her first contact with us at 4VEH when Mary Magdalene remarked to Gaudin, "Valeene plays the same song every night on FM Stereo 95."

Gaudin asked Valeene about it. She replied, "It must be a theme song. Ask Mary Magdalene what time she hears it."

Since she heard it around 10:30 every evening, Valeene explained, "That is the end of the "Night Sounds program" by Bill Pierce. He always closes two or three minutes early, so I chose Dino's piano rendition of "The Savior is Waiting" to fill in the time until the 10:30 station break."

"Does it have words?" Mary Magdalene wanted to know. "Every time that song is played something happens deep inside of me."

"Yes, it does have words," Valeene told Gaudin. "I will type them out for you."

Gaudin offered Mary Magdalene, "I will bring you the words to the song. Tell me where to deliver it."

"No!" she gasped, "I will send my chauffeur to pick it up at the radio station."

That night instead of playing the instrumental rendition, Valeene chose a choir to sing Ralph Carmichael's song.

The Savior is waiting to enter your heart
Why don't you let Him come in?
There's nothing in this world to keep you apart,
What is your answer to Him?
CHORUS
Time after time He has waited before
And now He is waiting again,
To see if you're willing to open the door.
O how He wants to come in.

Used by permission from Sacred Songs, Inc. Renewed 1986 Ralph Carmichael. Assigned 1987 to Spirit Quest Music

The next morning Mary Magdalene telephoned 4VEH.

"I heard it," she told Valeene. After a pause she added, "You really do care. You folk really do care."

In another conversation with Valeene, Mary Magdalene questioned, "Why do you have the news on at 11 o'clock at night? Here we are listening to soothing music, and then comes the news—sometimes not very good news. Why can't you just finish the day with music?"

Valeene explained, "The director said that it was necessary to put the latest world news on at 11 o'clock."

"But I thought you were the program director of FM Stereo!" she objected.

"Yes, I am" Valeene replied, "But I am under Mr. Charles, who is the manager of all of the 4VEH broadcasts."

"Well, I just don't like to hear that kind of news late at night. Why can't you put it earlier and not interrupt the music?"

"I am sorry," Valeene was firm, "but everyone is home at that hour, and it has been requested that the news come on then."

"Well, I'll just turn my radio off at 11:00," she decided, "and then I'll turn it back on at 11:15."

One Saturday night Valeene was sitting at the FM Stereo controls when the electricity went off. Again.

The blackouts were becoming more and more frequent, hindering schedules for recordings and broadcasting. It got so intolerable that finally we bought powerful battery-operated UPS (Uninterrupted Power Supply) units which could immediately supply electricity to operate the essential components of the station for a few minutes until our own big diesel generator could be turned on to give full power.

But that Saturday night was before those conveniences. The blackout frustrated Valeene to the point that she felt overwhelmed. What time was it? Almost 11 o'clock. Left in total darkness, she froze to her swivel chair. How long would it last? What should she do? It was so dark she didn't have to close her eyes to pray, "Father..."

Suddenly a firefly flashed. It was the first time she had seen one in Haiti, so bright the light reflected off the office walls visible through the control room window. As she watched its glow around the room, her spirit soared.

"Father," she continued her prayer, "You always bring light into our dark situations." She lost track of time as she praised the Lord there in the isolation of the darkness with its bright firefly.

Suddenly the power came back on. It was almost 11:15... too late to put the news on now. As she punched the buttons putting the station back on the air, she sensed an inner prompting, "Put on the news."

"You don't put the 11:00 o'clock news on at 11:15," she reasoned. But that inner nudge persisted...and she obeyed it.

At the end of the program newscaster Gaudin Charles gave his "nugget," generally a scripture verse. But since it was Saturday night, he gave the appeal, "Remember tomorrow is Sunday, a day of honoring our Creator. Attend the church of your choice and worship Him. Don't let anything keep you from the most important part of your life—your relationship to God."

Valeene sat spellbound, as God's presence seemed to electrify the words lingering in the air.

Monday morning at staff devotions, Gaudin again asked that we pray for Mary Magdalene's salvation. He himself led the prayer, and he became so earnest in his petition that he knelt prostrate on the floor. Then the telephone rang.

One of the secretaries interrupted the staff devotions to call Gaudin to the phone. "It's *her*!" she whispered as she handed him the receiver.

Some time later, Gaudin came to the FM control room where Valeene was working.

"Why did you put the 11 o'clock news on at 11:15 Saturday night?" he queried. So Valeene explained the situation.

"Well, I have a story to tell you. Mary Magdalene just called to thank me for my strong words Saturday night," he said. "You know she doesn't listen to the 11 o'clock news, but turns on FM later for the music. She said when she turned on the radio last Saturday night at 11:15, there was the news. She listened and, after hearing the nugget that followed, went to her closet to see if her Sunday dress was ready to wear. She said she hadn't been to a service in years, as she had had nothing to do with religion or anything like that."

"I did what you told me to do," Mary Magdalene had related. "I went to church. I walked into the Cathedral and the sun was coming through the stained glass windows and it was beautiful. I said, 'God, I want to feel your love.' Mr. Charles, does your choir sing 'Gloria'?"

"Yes," Gaudin told her.

"The choir was singing 'Gloria'," Mary Magdalene continued. "I sat down there and I wanted to feel God's love. So when the service was over, I went home and read in my Bible, John Chapter 14. I spent the rest of the day in John 14, and I have some questions to ask you."

So Gaudin answered her questions, explaining the Scriptures.

Many months passed before the mystery lady telephoned again. Gaudin was away, and Valeene, taking the call, barely caught herself from bursting out, "Mary Magdalene!"

"Oh!" Valeene greeted her, "we were just talking the other day how we have not heard from you for so long. We have missed you."

"You have?" Mary Magdalene was surprised. "I thought maybe I was becoming a nuisance."

"Oh, no," Valeene assured her, "in fact we have been wondering what has happened to you."

"Well, you know," she said, "I had to call often because I was leaning on you for what my heart needed. But I want you to know that I now lean on the Savior. I have asked the Lord Jesus into my heart, and He is helping me. He even helps me find things I misplace."

The more she talked, the more Valeene realized how changed this woman was now. Even her voice was different.

"Your English is beautiful," Valeene observed.

"Thank you," she replied.

"Do you do any translation work?" Valeene asked.

"I do some. I love it."

"We have been praying for a translator."

"Well, I want you to pray, Valeene, that the Lord will direct our meeting. We are going to meet each other, but I want it to be the way the Lord wants it done."

That meeting is yet to take place.

Our acquaintance with Mary Magdalene spanned about three years, then she was gone. Once she called from New York, back in 1986. We miss hearing from her, but we are delighted that FM Stereo 95 and its staff had a part in helping this mystery lady to become like Mary Magdalene of the Bible-transformed by Christ.

1983   **A TIME TO BUILD**
By Gladys Gaskell, Horton, Kansas, USA

We were overwhelmed. How could we accomplish everything in two weeks? Our group came from Kansas, Nebraska, and Alberta, Canada, and was led by David Gaskell. We had come to Haiti to assist in constructing the new Vaudreuil church.

Designed by a Haitian architect and built by Haitians, the building waited on the mission compound for us to stabilize the walls, raise six trusses, build wooden purloins, and finish the roof with corrugated steel sheeting.

Because it was Mardi Gras, the boss of a construction company working on the Cap-Haitien harbor allowed us to use a large crane to hoist the steel trusses into place. This came in response to prayers of church members, work crusaders, and missionaries. The crane would be lent only when not in company use. And the 1700-pound trusses could not be raised any other way.

So it was a stimulating morning when the crane arrived at the building site. A large crowd gathered to see the first truss lifted into place. The North American volunteers and Haitian workers, with the use of the crane, made light work of the 3/4-ton trusses. Others fixed purloins in place as the Vaudreuil church took shape. At the end of the two weeks, the building was under roof.

Our group of workers participated in the first service held in the new construction. In preparation, women swept debris from the dirt floor, moved benches in from the brush arbor (a building of poles and thatch in which believers had been worshiping), and decorated the altar area with palm leaves and flowers. That evening 800 people attended a praise service celebrating this giant step towards the completion of their new church.

After we arrived back in our homes in the States and Canada, we learned that wind and rain had demolished the old brush arbor the next week. God's timing was perfect.

The initial work on the road to Du Pin was done
by hand in 1982

The borrowed crane hoists the steel trusses into place
(1983)

The Finished Evangelical Church of Vaudreuil in 1983

Frere Marcial, a beloved prophet in Haiti in 1985

1984   THIS REALLY HAPPENED IN ENGLAND
By Rhoda Banks

At the close of the service, a little old lady lifted her expectant face to the OMS missionary-to-be, an eager question mark in her fading eyes, her hand warmly gripping his.

"I really enjoyed the meeting," she smiled, "but I'm afraid I didn't hear a word. You see, I'm very deaf. What was it you were telling us?"

So at the door of the church, the missionary meeting began all over again, in precise form. The young man enunciating distinctly, eagerly repeated the challenge of his calling to go to Haiti.

There had been little apparent interest or rapport with the congregation, and the missionary's enthusiasm had met with something approaching indifference.

Now the little old lady reached into her purse and pulled out her checkbook. "I'm nearly blind," she informed him, "so you will have to fill it in for me."

"Certainly," he replied. Somewhat hesitantly he wrote, "OMS International."

"Uh...what would you like to gi...how much...what shall I...."

"Just put £1,000, my dear"   (about $2,800).

"A th...a thous.... Oh! right....a thousand pounds." His shaking hand did not hinder the next entry, and her shaking hand signed the almost unbelievable document.

Is it too much to assume that this little senior citizen had a new name added to her prayer list from that night forward, the new missionary had a heart-lift, and a record was entered in heaven's archives?

1984   THE EVANGELICAL CHURCH OF HAITI
By Rachael Picazo

In 1984 the Evangelical Church of Haiti separated itself from the parent organization, OMS.   Then followed a time of stress.   Things were said, actions taken that distanced OMS personnel from the pastors of the Haitian church.   Once during this period, I started to complain to the Lord and wanted to ask Him to rebuke one of the pastors.

There came such a feeling I don't know how to describe— like a restraining hand gently cautioning me against going forward with those thoughts—along with the distinct message to my own heart, "These are my children."

1984   THE BRIEFCASE
By Harold Brown, as told to Rachael Picazo

I had gone to Port-au-Prince to pick up the Fowlers, a new missionary couple.   Steve Scholes and I were driving a jeep back up north to the mission grounds.   We had three briefcases sitting between the two front seats and the Fowlers were sitting in the back.

In my briefcase was some money I had changed from dollars to gourdes for the mission, but not a great deal.   I was also bringing up for another missions staff in the North, a sealed envelope containing their payroll.   Mary's and my passports and airline tickets for the next week were in there.

In the struggle we were having at that time getting our legal right to stay in the country, I had written a letter to the four top ministers of the country: the ministers of Interior, Justice, Social Affairs, and Foreign Affairs.   Pastor Nerée had helped me write the document, which stated that we could no longer be responsible for The Evangelical Church of Haiti and from that date on, Rev. Nerée would represent OMS before the government as the recognized Haitian pastor representative. In my briefcase were letters from three of the departments acknowledging our dispatch and confirming that it was fine.

It was already dark by the time we reached Puilboreau Mountain, and there the jeep had a flat. Steve and I got out to change the tire and had a problem with the jack so we were working quite a while. The Fowlers stayed in the machine. But when we got back into the jeep to resume our journey, we noticed that both my and Steve's briefcases were gone.

The Fowlers had been in there the whole time, and the doors had been locked most of that period, but nevertheless our two briefcases had disappeared.

I went to the house closest to the road and woke up the man inside. It turned out that he was an Adventist lay pastor. I explained the situation to him.

"The briefcases are gone. They had money in them, and we don't expect to get any of it back, but I would like to have the documents, passports, and all the other things."

"Well, there is a wake on the mountain," he said, "and I'll be going up there. After that, I will send people out across the mountain to explain that the briefcases belong to a 4VEH pastor and that we need to get them back."

This happened on Thursday night, so on Friday I started doing what I could to replace the passports and tickets that had been lost as Mary and I were to leave the next week.

On Sunday noon coming back from church, we saw the Adventist lay pastor was sitting by the gate as we drove onto the grounds. He had ridden an hour on his motorcycle from Puilboreau Mountain.

"I just came to tell you," he said, "yesterday morning when I got up, those two briefcases were sitting at my front door. I don't know where they came from. I didn't open them, and they are in my house. Whenever you want to, come and get them."

That afternoon I went to his home, and in his presence we opened the briefcases. Steve had left his billfold in his case with a little cash in it, and that was gone, as well as all of the money from both.

But all of the documents—the important government letters that we desperately needed, the passports, and tickets— were there. Everything truly essential had been preserved. We even learned that the payroll for the other mission was covered by insurance so we were fortunate in spite of the thieves. That was one of those incidents we knew that the Lord had intervened in the situation. We still have that briefcase with its broken lock.

1984   4VEH IN THE FLORIDA ORANGE GROVES

Radio Station 4VEH is experiencing strong response to their new shortwave broadcasts beamed toward the west end of Cuba and southern Florida.

Reports pour in from central and northeastern U.S. and Canada where delighted expatriate Haitians once again hear their favorite station. Listeners call the Cap-Haitien studios to express their joy and to give messages and requests. One Florida pastor reports that Haitians picking fruit work with a radio blaring gospel music from 4VEH.

NEAR SCANDINAVIA

A small group of Haitians, as crew members on a ship in the icy waters off the Scandinavian coast, stumbled across 4VEH on the shortwave band of their radio. They were so excited they threw a party aboard ship.

1985   **A PROPHET IN HAITI**
By Rachael Picazo

Sitting there at the funeral, I thought how different it was going to be in Haiti without Frère (Brother) Marcial. Why, he was an old man, nearly 80, when we came to Haiti more than 30 years ago!

That summer he was up in those 60-foot trees with the younger men, trimming branches to make charcoal. He was an active lay preacher and effective soul winner, out visiting one or another of his regular preaching points every week.

We were delighted with his enthusiasm in our church services. If the singing wasn't quite loud or lively enough, he would stand and give a pep talk until the singing became a "joyful noise unto the Lord," fairly shaking the rafters!

One of the first Haitian women I came to know in those early days in Haiti was a frail little Christian lady who helped me with our laundry. She became ill one day, and when I inquired as to where she lived, they told me she was at Frère Marcial's house. There she was, in a tiny room scarcely long enough to squeeze in her cot, barely wide enough for her wee table and chair. There were only three or four of these little rooms in that thatched-roof home; but each was occupied by a woman with her children, who had recently become a Christian and thus, banished by her family, had no place to go. The yard was full of children and the cooking fires of the women.

It was not long before we came to know Frère Marcial personally because he considered each missionary his special prayer concern and the recipient of his tithe in fruit and vegetables from his garden, brought by one of the children or ladies who lived at his house.

Frère Marcial did not often come to our house so I was surprised that day when I welcomed him in. He sat in the chair nearest the door, politely removed his hat, and came immediately to the purpose of his visit, The Lord had told him to come pray for Pastor Picazo (my husband Mardy).

He did not inquire about him nor ask to see him; he just dropped to his knees and began to intercede for Mardy's health. In a few moments, he concluded his prayer with thanks to God for answering, got to his feet, sang a song with me, and quoted John 3:16, then taking his hat he started for the door.

Mardy was at that moment lying in bed very ill with puzzling symptoms. Within a few hours the doctor discovered Mardy had diabetes, started him on treatment, and then was most amazed at how quickly it was all under control. Mardy was soon up again and feeling fine.

Later, we learned of other incidents: the time Marvin McClain had a massive heart attack, Frère Marcial appeared at his door, informing them the Lord had sent him to pray for Marvin. As with us, he made no inquiries, but just did what God sent him to do. He prayed right then and there. Later when Marvin was able to travel, a missionary doctor in a nearby city was astounded. All the evidence showed that that heart attack should have been fatal, yet Marvin was recovering nicely. Eight weeks later in the States, an extensive physical examination revealed that all damage from that attack had healed.

Then I began hearing comments from the Haitians them-selves, of times when they knew they were facing death—until

Frère Marcial appeared, saying the Lord had sent him to pray for them.

Who was this man Marcial? A simple, unassuming peasant, who had childlike faith that seemed to bring him into God's presence "face to face," as is said of Moses.

He did not even know how to read or write, yet he had committed hundreds of Scripture passages to memory. On one occasion in our radio staff devotional time, he asked the Radio 4VEH director, Gaudin Charles, to read Isaiah 48, beginning at verse 16. Gaudin began reading in chapter 49 by mistake. He had read only a few words, when Frère Marcial interrupted him and gave him the reference again.

In like manner, after the scripture reading, he asked that we sing number 62 in the song book. While staff members were finding the page, he led out with the song from memory.

Only on a few occasions had Frère Marcial asked for anything from us. Yet this country is largely populated with the poor living on the bare edge of existence. Begging is often taught to children and considered an accepted way of life by the impoverished.

That first occasion was when we were living in the capital, 170 miles from Frère Marcial, and our daughter Suzanna was getting married. Frère Marcial wanted to come to the marriage of this child he considered his own, for she had been born there in his community. So, lacking the four dollars needed for the round-trip fare, he went from house to house of the missionaries and explained that he wanted to attend that wedding.

He was there for that beautiful occasion, having ridden the bus on a fatiguing, bumpy ride about ten hours to get there. During the service, Frère Marcial was asked to speak a few words. He told us that he had just passed his 100th birthday the January before, and at that time the Lord had appeared to him in a dream and told him that he was going to give him another ten years!

We moved back to the radio station and were again in Frère Marcial's community when he approached his 110th birthday. This was another rare occasion that he asked for help-- this time to make a trip to the southern part of Haiti (again on one of those crowded buses, mind you, at 110 years of age!) so that he could visit the place where he was born and see his father's family once more. "For," he said, "they need to know about God."

Then we heard that the Lord had revealed to him on his 110th birthday that He was going to add a little time to his life. He also said the Lord showed him that Radio Station 4VEH was in danger from evil forces and that he was to intercede and, further, to come once a week to lead in the radio staff devotions. That involved walking about half a mile each way but he came faithfully.

He told one of our missionaries who was visiting him, "Isn't God good to us? He gave us His Son, Jesus Christ. He gave us the Bible so that we can hear His Word and listen and understand. He even gave us Radio 4VEH!"

The time came that Frère Marcial could no longer walk to the station. When we went to visit him, he would be lying down, generally on a mat under the trees in the yard. He would sit up and talk with us, always asking one of us to read a scripture and another to pray before we left. His mind was alert and he was eager for any news from our children, especially our son Daniel, a great favorite of his who was in the States on furlough.

Hurricane Kate was in the area, bringing rain on that Friday morning when Frère Marcial decided he must walk to the radio station once more. By the time he arrived at the back fence he was soaking wet, and his feeble legs could carry him no further. He sent word for the staff to come, which they did, talking to him over the fence. But he became chilled, fever followed, and five days later he went to be with his beloved Lord. In another six weeks he would have been 112 years old.

Yes, sitting there at the funeral, I thought that this should be a time of rejoicing. He lived a fulfilling life and now his home-going should be crowned with joy. Yet tears were falling unbidden down my cheeks.

"I'll miss his prayers," I realized, "prayers for us, for Radio 4VEH, for Haiti."

I was bereft—Haiti was bereft—of a prophet. And the plea rose in my heart, "Please, Lord, raise up another prophet for Haiti."

1986   **MONEY AND THE MOB**
                By Mary Brown

One of the consequences of the expulsion of President Duvalier from Haiti in 1986 was that for a time the government was practically nonexistent. In that turmoil, the roads became a place for thieves and robbers.

I remember one time we were going down the other side of Puilboreau Mountain when we saw a mob coming up the road. I said to Harold, "Let's roll all our car windows up."

But he said, "No, I think we shouldn't. If I roll up my window, they're going to think that I am afraid."

Well, I rolled up my window, but as we drew nearer, they crowded in, completely surrounding the car. They were total strangers, probably drinking, and, of course, they wanted money. One guy stuck his machete actually against Harold's throat, but we didn't have enough sense to be afraid. It wasn't until later that we heard about the killings on the highways.

About that time, a car came in the opposite direction, up the mountain, loudly tooting his horn as he plowed into the crowd. The windows in that car were tightly closed except for a narrow crack through which somebody was throwing paper money.

The money distracted the mob, and as they scrambled to retrieve it, we just went right on down the road with no problem.

We began to learn that when travel was necessary, we needed to venture forth with fervent prayer. Also we should make sure the car was in good condition, that our horn was loud, and that we had a good supply of small-denomination paper money.

The Lord's faithfulness is there, even in troubled times.

June 1986   **PRAYER LETTER**
                      By Mardy and Rachael Picazo

These have been months of great trial for the Haitian people, with the change of national leadership and its ensuing problems of keeping order. There have been demonstrations, violent and peaceful. Perhaps you heard of the killing of 600 Voodooists here in Haiti by violent mobs who were striking out at everything having to do with the former Duvalier regime. Many of the militia and some government officials were also killed. Voodoo is a powerful cult in this beautiful tropical island, and we believe it has been largely responsible for the dire poverty, darkness, and fear in which the masses live.

With that as background, you can see that here is a tremendous spiritual struggle. Thus Radio 4VEH is airing a whole new series of programs with a spiritual emphasis as never before.

Prime time at the noon hour, previously French cultural programming, is now leading the Haitian people in prayer over the air. The new Haitian Bible is being read all the way through, a portion each day. The Hour of Comfort encourages those who are frightened; powerful testimonies are aired, along with inspiring songs. The Lord is using Radio 4VEH to channel healing to a needy people at a needy hour.

1986   **THE CAR REFUSED TO GO**
By Mary Brown

It was during the time when Harold (Brown) was having to go back and forth to Port-au-Prince because no missionaries were stationed there, and all our official business had to be conducted in the capital. Traveling on the roads was dangerous. Gangs of rowdy young men set up roadblocks and demanded payment to pass, while others just outright robbed the travelers. Several people were murdered on the highways. Travel must be during the daytime, so we set out in the morning to be sure to arrive before night. The journey took about six or maybe eight hours.

As we were on our way to Port-au-Prince, our old white Peugeot began to sputter on the Limbé hill, the first of several mountains on the way to Port. Harold petted it, doctored it, and messed with it, so we kept climbing bit by bit.

The same thing happened on the mountain the other side of Limbé. But in trying to go over Puilboreau the car finally quit. We had to turn around and coast down again. We managed to make it back to Limbé, where David Hodges looked at it for us and found something wrong that he could fix. But by that time it was so late we knew we couldn't get to Port-au-Prince before dark, so we returned to the mission compound.

The watchman stopped us as we entered the gate.

"Oh, Pastor Brown," he greeted Harold, "God sent you back!"

In looking back, we realize now that that day was a crucial point in our struggle to keep the grounds for OMS. Those were amazing times.

1986   DESHOUKAY--UPROOT!
By Rachael Picazo

Haiti's government was badly shaken in 1986 when their president was expelled. Then celebration followed throughout the country. People congratulated each other with the declaration, "Now we have liberty. We have freedom to do anything we want without the police stopping us."

What resulted was anarchy. Mobs began to *deSHOUkay* ("uproot") anyone who owned anything, nice house or prospering store. The old Haitian word took on a new meaning to describe what happened when a mob would converge on a home or business, break in its doors and windows, pillage and loot everything inside, then destroy the building. Sometimes they would burn its owner by encircling his neck with an old tire, pouring gasoline on it and the person, and setting them on fire.

The instigators of this violence used local radio stations to announce who, where, and when they would *deshoukay* next. But when they demanded that their announcements be broadcast over Missionary Radio Station 4VEH, we refused to cooperate with them. Thus 4VEH was written on their "Hit List" to destroy.

It was a good thing that 4VEH was located seven kilometers (five miles) outside the city. Though the Haitians are noted for walking long distances, we hoped it might detain them a while. But we knew that, unless God intervened, before long they would certainly carry out their threats.

Those of us on the radio staff did not know from one day to the next if this would be our last to broadcast. Each night we carried home with us certain items we would normally leave in the studio--a couple of expensive new microphones, some personal cassettes, and CDs. I lay awake far into the nights concerned about how I would react if the mob chose to *deshoukay* our home or maybe attack us missionaries as they had some of the city merchants.

During that period, reading the Psalms was a great comfort to me. Some of them seemed to express how I felt, especially Psalm 37. And then one day the promise in Proverbs 3:25,26 (NIV) just seemed to rise out of the page in bold letters to grab my attention. I knew God had put it there for me (and anyone else who needed it):

> *Have no fear of sudden disaster*
> *or of the ruin that overtakes the wicked;*
> *for the LORD will be your confidence*
> *and will keep your foot from being snared.*

After that it was not so hard to surrender to sleep. Many times I was repeating this wonderful promise as I drifted off.

The Haitian people also expressed their discontent by creating road-blocks on the highway. In the five miles between our location and Cap-Haitien, sometimes there would be as many as twenty piles of tires being burned, fallen trees, or rubbish dragged across the road every few hundred yards. Travel by vehicle was virtually impossible, so our Vocational Bible School and Clinic had to close. Those missionaries involved went back to their homes in the States and Canada until Haiti's government should be stabilized. Other organizations all over Haiti also sent workers home. Even in our local church, night services were canceled.

The only ministry still involving missionaries was the radio station. Even there we had to cut back broadcasting hours because the price of fuel for electricity doubled, then tripled, in price. The French and Creole programs for Haiti had been broadcasting 17 hours each day; they were cut to five hours. The English/Spanish programming, which had been broadcasting eight hours a day, was dropped completely. The FM Stereo service, being of low power, was able to keep its schedule of programming in French and English from noon until 11:30 p.m. With the cutback in English programming involving missionaries, only a skeleton staff was left, and we were told to pack and be ready to leave on a moment's notice, should we need to be evacuated.

We were allowed 40 pounds, so we tried to think of essentials-- passports, check book, a supply of American dollars (make a point to change a bunch of Haitian gourdes into U.S. currency), a sweater for air conditioning on the plane (in the tropics, anything below 80 degrees is "cold"). That bag had to be kept ready to go on a moment's notice. So we set it in the middle of our bedroom. Just in case we might need it next day, we let it stay while we walked around it... for a week, a month, several months.

There were only six of us left out of a normal staff of around thirty. At every prayer meeting we missionaries asked each other, "What do we do?" The American Ambassador had urged all U.S. citizens to return home. But we wanted to keep 4VEH broadcasting every day possible. We finally agreed that the next week we would take a vote.

The decision to stay was unanimous. Each missionary had his own reason for his conviction, but the scripture Marilyn Shaferly brought expressed our combined view the most precisely: Jeremiah 42:7-22 (NIV)

...the word of the LORD came to Jeremiah. ...He said to them, This is what the LORD, the God of Israel...says: "If you

246

stay in this land, I will build you up and not tear you down; I will plant you and not uproot you (!!!)...Do not be afraid of the king of Babylon, whom you now fear. Do not be afraid of him, declares the LORD, for I am with you and will save you and deliver you from his hands....

"However, if you say, 'We will not stay in this land,' and so disobey the LORD your God...."

And so we stayed.

October 31, 1986   PROVERBS 16
By Rachael Picazo

Louisa Destiné is a Haitian programmer and receptionist at Radio 4VEH. One Thursday around noon she came directly from the regular fasting and prayer service, held under a nearby grove of mango trees, to find the studios empty because of lunch break. She sat at her desk and began typing the song requests for her next program. Unexpectedly, she heard her name called, "Louisa!"

Thinking that someone must have come through the office, she glanced around. She didn't see anybody—maybe the person had walked through and out the other door. So she forgot about it as she continued her work.

A second time the voice spoke, "Louisa!"

This time she was quick to look up. She scanned the room. Nobody was there! Shivers of fear ran through her. Then the third time came the clear utterance, this time in a command: "Louisa, get your Bible."

She was shaking so much her legs wouldn't cooperate, and while she hesitated the voice urged, "Right now!"

Louisa stood and walked to the cabinet where she kept her Creole Bible. Holding it upright between her hands, she asked simply, "What shall I do with it?"

"Open it," came the reply.

"Where to?"

But there was no answer. So she tilted her hands away from the edges, letting it fall open where it would. It lay in her palms opened about the middle of the book, and her eyes lighted on Proverbs, chapter 16. Suddenly a visible hand appeared over the pages of the Book, and one of the fingers pointed to the first and then the last verse of the chapter.

Proverbs 16:1 reads in Creole:

Lèzom fè lidé nan kè yo.

Min, dènié moa nan min Bondié.

Men make plans in their hearts,

but the last word is in God's Hand.

Proverbs 16:33 reads in Creole:

Moun tiré kat pou yo konnin sa pou yo fè.

Min, désizion as sé nan min Bondié li yé.

Men draw cards to know what to do.

But, the decision: that is in the Hand of God.

No matter what the mobs might try to decide about 4VEH, the final outcome was in God's Hand! Radio 4VEH was not *deshoukayed*. The decision about her future: That, too, is in the Hand of God. Amen!

1986   **THE LETTER NEVER SENT**
                    By Harold Brown

I had received an official letter from our OMS headquarters in Greenwood to pass along to the president of the national church. So I took it down and dropped it into the mailbox of our local system. We had a little post office there on the mission grounds, where each missionary family had a box, as well as those Haitians living on the grounds or connected with the local church.

A few days later I received urgent word from our OMS headquarters that the letter addressed to the president of the national church must NOT be delivered. It would be tragic if he received it because it had been written by someone who had a wrong understanding and did not express the stand of OMS.

So I went down to the post office to see if by chance the letter had not yet been taken out of the church box. I could unlock the door of the post office and look into the backs of the boxes. I saw that the one for the church was empty.

I went home very concerned and told Mary, "The letter is gone. I don't know what we're going to do. This letter can upset the process of negotiations and totally undo what has been accomplished to this point. It puts into writing, with a signature, a policy that is not good." Even though I knew it was too late, I asked God to somehow intervene.

There was no response from the church leaders. Two or three days later, I discovered that the faulty letter I had posted had fallen behind the container which receives the letters to be distributed. The one putting out the mail had not noticed the letter, so had not placed it into the church box. I retrieved and destroyed the letter, and my praise overflowed to our wonderful God who answered my prayer even before I knew I should pray!

October 3, 1987,   (Thanks to a listening Lord)
THE *HALT!* IN HAITI IS CHANGED TO
FORWARD... MARCH!
By Marilyn Shaferly

Nestled against the foothills, the OMS mini-community includes the medical and dental clinics, Bible school, Vaudreuil church, 4VEH studios, and homes of the OMS staff. Some have called this the evangelical capital of northern Haiti.

For the past several years, however, satanic forces, abetted by a chaotic political climate, have provoked division in this little community. Conflicts threatened to totally annul its Christian witness. Differences between OMS and its Haitian church seemed to defy solution.

Now, at last, the signal is *"Forward . . .March!"*

On October 3, 1987, leaders of the Evangelical Church of Haiti and OMS—after years of attempts at reconciliation—signed an agreement which now paves the way for increased witness and an even greater impact on northern Haiti. Evangelism can once more assume priority in OMS' overall strategy for reaching Haiti's millions.

Were it not for the miracle of October 3, the "Forward...March!" command would still be "Halt!" And were it not for mighty, prevailing prayer, there would have been no miracle. Throughout the years of tension, friends in the U.S. and around the world interceded.

Friends in Haiti prayed, too, at regular Thursday morning prayer and fasting services under the trees and in early morning prayer meetings in local churches. During the particularly tense period between June and December of 1986, a group of Haitian women met every night under one of the street lights on the OMS compound to claim those grounds for God's continued blessing.

The Haiti team joyfully seeks to obey the "Forward ... March!" command. We're more aware than ever before that

250

persistent prayer must be the underlying support. With fervent and unrelenting prayer, effective witness is guaranteed.

1988   RADIO 4VEH: OVERWHELMING CHOICE
By Rachael Picazo

A prosperous storekeeper in Port-au-Prince recently made a trip to Cap-Haitien. He hoped to increase his business by offering a better feed at a lower price to the hog farmers in northern Haiti. So as he crossed the high range of mountains which divides southern from northern Haiti, he stopped in every little village and town along the way to ask the people what radio station they listened to. He intended to advertise his product so everyone would know about it.

By the time he got to Cap-Haitien on the northern coast, he knew over which station he wanted to advertise, Radio 4VEH! Ours was overwhelmingly the station everyone listened to.

When he came to us with his proposal, he was thwarted because, being a missionary radio station, we do not carry commercials. But our station manager listened to his sales pitch and decided that awareness of his product would be good for the growing number of hog owners here in Haiti.

So he interviewed the man on the air and thus the information was given. In his turn, the businessman had done us a favor by canvassing the countryside as an outside neutral person. He confirmed the many other reports we had received, that Radio 4VEH is listened to far and wide across Haiti. And wherever Radio 4VEH is heard, the Gospel also is heard.

1988   **LISTENER RESPONSE**

(The November 17, 1989, edition of the French newspaper,
"Le Septentrion," published in Port-au-Prince, Haiti,
included this excerpt in an article outlining the role
of various radio stations in Cap-Haitien)

"We also need to pay tribute to 4VEH, the Evangelistic Voice of the Antilles, which does not give political news, but prefers rather to offer comfort through their hours of prayer, songs, and meditations, of which we have so much need in these especially difficult times in which we live."

1988   **LISTENERS RESPOND**

("A Talk with the Pastor" is a regular weekly
feature on 4VEH, hosted by a local pastor.)

A Haitian pastor urged his church members to settle a dispute peacefully, but they were intent on taking their disagreement to court.

In yet another attempt to settle the matter, the pastor pleasantly discovered the affair already resolved. Upon asking what part of his advice had helped them, he was told: "Oh, Pastor, it wasn't you who helped us decide. We heard the program, 'A Talk with the Pastor' on 4VEH. It showed us that it's wrong to go to law among Christians!"

1990   **4VEH CELEBRATES 40th ANNIVERSARY**
By Rachael Picazo

We had great anticipation, but also forebodings, as we planned the 4VEH 40th anniversary celebration. Threats and negative comments were painted in black across the studio building twice, and once on our new yard sign. Our staff painted over the graffiti, but we knew this was the surface eruption of a deeper, more sinister plot to hinder our widely publicized celebration.

Our staff was much in prayer, and we alerted OMS headquarters in Indiana to send word to praying friends around the world.

I was still praying as I entered the Vaudreuil Church, which was soon crowded with some 1200 guests from many points in Haiti, as well as Canada and the United States. Several hundred more stood in doorways and at the windows. But, best of all, the presence of God was so evident, I wanted to shout with joy! He not only protected, but also blessed and anointed the whole event!

The service in the church was broadcast live on 4VEH, and to our surprise, all the other stations in Cap-Haitien went off the air in deference and honor to our special occasion. The entire program was video taped as well as covered by TV Channel 7 from Cap-Haitien. Yet, the program moved so well we hardly noticed that five and a half hours had gone by!

Among the highlights were thrilling letter excerpts from listeners, commendations from Haitian dignitaries, awards given to staff members for meritorious and long-term service with 4VEH, and a drama about the station's beginnings. Emma Achille Placide, world-reknown Haitian soloist, communicated powerfully through her testimony and music. God made her a spark of blessing as she credited 4VEH for launching her career.

A highlight for the missionary team and all who helped pray us through the crises of the past few years was the testimony of a leader in the community. The short, thin man with graying hair explained that when asked to participate in the ceremony, he decided not to attend. But, in the night, God compelled him to come and deliver a message.

"What you see here at Radio 4VEH has come at great cost to the missionaries," he said with tears. "They have suffered tremendous persecution and loss because of this community. You remember that when Aaron and Miriam persecuted Moses, God struck Miriam with leprosy. Then Aaron asked Moses to pray for him and Miriam. So I want to request two elders of the Mission to pray that God will forgive this community for all they have done." The two he chose, Pastor Mardy Picazo and Gaudin Charles, our 4VEH director, went to the platform and lovingly petitioned God to accept the plea and bless the Haitian community. It was a strangely moving moment.

A cantata by the 4VEH staff chorale, trained and directed by Valeene Hayes, crowned the program with an overflow of thanksgiving for God's faithfulness. None who attended will soon forget the profound blessing with which God honored and protected the celebration of our fortieth year on the air as 4VEH, La Voix Evangélique d' Haiti (The Evangelistic Voice of Haiti).

4VEH's 40th ANNIVERSARY
By Os Heinrich

I was excited about returning to Haiti. For 12 years I'd been a staff member of Radio 4VEH. Now friends had paid my way to attend the 40th anniversary celebration of the station.

As the DC3 of Missionary Flights International took off from Florida's West Palm Beach, my emotions overpowered me. I was going back home!

Much has been written about Haiti—its poverty, hunger, sickness, AIDS, violence, anarchy, failed elections, government coups, removal of foreign aid programs, and the exodus of missionaries. But when we landed in Cap-Haitien after a beautiful four hours over colorful Bahamian waters, it was the culture of Haiti that hit me with force. The orderly confusion of clearing customs, dust from three months of drought, odors from garbage, unpredictable drivers, and masses of people clogging the roads and byways—it seemed that nothing had really changed except that my Haitian friends looked older, and some had died-- one of cancer, another of AIDS, one trying to reach Miami on a small Haitian boat, several in the political upheaval. Those remaining talked of frustration, hopelessness, and despair in the present Haiti situation.

What a contrast, however, as we gathered for the June 2nd anniversary service! When Haitians celebrate, they really do it right. In the brightly festooned Vaudreuil Church, I enjoyed every minute of the five-and-a-half hour program—even wished it were longer! Appropriately, the theme was "Oh Eternal, How Great is Thy faithfulness."

Each message, testimony, and song evidenced that truth. For 40 years, God had greatly used Radio 4VEH to reach across Haiti and the Caribbean with the light of the Gospel.

I thought back over my 12 years in that land. Certainly He had proven His faithfulness to me through the joys of two children born there, the tears of losing a grandmother and a father-in-law while away from home, the suffering and distress of hepatitis, and the frustrations of broken transmitters. As I surveyed the crowded sanctuary and hundreds scattered across the grounds (including 70 MFM Crusaders from the United States and Canada), obviously He'd also been faithful to all who had invested funds, prayers, tears, and labor to make 4VEH a mighty force for Him.

When Aldean Saufley played "Amazing Grace," the theme song which always opens and closes the broadcast day, the lyrics amplified in my soul, "How sweet the sound that saved a wretch like me. I once was lost, but now am found, was blind, but now I see."

The Haitians sing, "I was on the garbage heap, but the Lord found me and made me one of His children."

It was so true in my life and for countless Haitians...because of God's faithfulness through 4VEH!

Suddenly I realized that the Lord was showing me a different Haiti—a Haiti in which the Son of the Gospel was shining brightly...a Haiti He had not forgotten...a Haiti in which He had innumerable children He was taking from grace to grace, conforming them into the image of Himself...a Haiti He refuses to leave and where He is not willing that any should perish. Truly, where darkness abounds, grace abounds so much more!

When Field Director Harold Brown and I shook hands at the airport, we used the common Haitian expression, "Pran courage" (Take courage). That said it all. Our hearts were rejoicing and at peace because God is changing Haiti and we are co-workers with Him.

The Scripture of the celebration still rings in my spirit, "It is good to praise the Lord and to celebrate your name, Oh Most High, to announce your goodness in the morning and your faithfulness during the night...You make me happy by your works, Oh Eternal One. And I sing with thanksgiving."

(Os Heinrich is currently computer operations manager at OMS World Headquarters where his wife, Kathy, is hospitality hostess.)

256

1990   **PRAISED**
By Valeene Hayes

We hit a mountaintop of rejoicing on our 40th anniversary June 2, 1990. Right after that, all kinds of breakdowns, illness, and personnel problems added to the political confusion of the country that affected us at 4VEH.

One midnight in Haiti I saw the word "DESPAIR" in large letters on my wall. It was during a blackout and I was in bed. So I got out of bed, sank to my knees, and holding my Bible close, prayed that the Lord would keep me from falling into despair. The Lord did not remove the word on the wall, but the letters began to fall into different places, spelling "PRAISED."

I sensed God speaking to my heart, "Have you praised Me? I am worthy to be praised!"

I went to my desk with my flashlight and matched letters to see if I was really seeing right. Could the letters in "despair" be rearranged to make the word "praised"? YES!

I have never forgotten that moment of God's intervention...and its lesson continues to encourage me today!

1992   **THE REST OF THE STORY**
By Dr. Vernon Hall

Two days after last September's *coup d'etat* that forced deposed Haitian president, Jean Bertrand Aristide, to flee for his life to Caracas, I received a call from our front gate. I was needed at the clinic immediately. Putting on my shoes, I hurried to the emergency room. There a pool of blood encircled the feet of a 30-year-old man clutching a heavily bandaged arm.

As soon as I removed the crude wrapping, blood gushed from an ugly slash. Quickly applying a pressure bandage, I took

257

a look at the young man's head wound. Since it was not bleeding, I returned to the arm, just as one of our employees came to see if I needed help. Cautiously we released the pressure bandage, but again blood spurted profusely. I knew then I would need Lois, my wife/nurse, for this major situation.

Answering the emergency call, she came from her ladies' Bible Study to help determine if we could save this seriously wounded patient. Our probing revealed an open fracture with complete severance of the muscles and tendons controlling his little finger and, partially, his ring finger. What to do? Was it possible to reconstruct this mess?

We tried, layer by layer, putting the muscles back together with four packages of sutures internally before I could start on the skin. Only time would tell, if he survived, what function he would have.

Though very weak and thirsty from loss of blood, the man spoke clearly and intelligently while we worked on him. Only twice did he complain of pain, although I'd used no anesthetic. He told us his father had cut him up.

The father waited outside, his actions and breath evidencing alcoholic intake. When he showed me a superficial wound on his arm, I told him rather curtly, "You'll have to wait till we finish with your son, whom you've treated so brutally."

After further examination of the young man's head, I almost decided it was indeed time to give up. An oblique gash in the scalp about five inches long went all the way to the skull.

Again, we did our best, cleaning out the bone chips and sewing the laceration layer by layer. With Haiti completely shut down at the time, it was impossible to take the patient elsewhere for treatment. So after the three-hour ordeal of our best reconstructive surgery, we gave him antibiotics and sent him home, uncertain whether we would ever see him again.

I then turned to the father, sewed up his arm without anesthesia, and released him, too. Through my cold, professional manner, the father knew we didn't think highly of him.

The next day the son returned, weak and feverish. We gave him more shots and pills, and within three days he showed improvement. The fever was gone, but a slight neurological dysfunction remained on his face and the medial side of the hand and wrist still had no motion.

Our staff nurse, Mike Van Dervort, then asked him about his relationship with God and if he wanted to become a Christian.

"I've thought about it," he said, "but I'm not ready to make a decision."

The next day, however, he requested us to pray with him, and he accepted Christ. Presenting him with a Bible, we encouraged him in his newfound faith.

A few days later, our clinic watchman and his wife were chatting with patients about current events while Mike and I prepared for our daily rounds. All of a sudden I thought I heard comments about the young patient wounded by his father. Both Mike and I pricked up our ears as the rest of the story unfolded.

The father, we learned, had attacked his son, not because he was drunk, but because the son was on his way to *deshoukay* (kill) the doctor...me!... and our OMS field director, Harold Brown! When he intervened, the son grabbed a machete and took a swing at his father, cutting his arm. A sister then hit her brother in the skull with another machete, and the father followed through with that severe gash to his son's forearm.

You can imagine my remorse as I recalled my short-tempered and judgmental response to the one who had possibly saved Harold Brown and myself from death.

Humbly grateful for the father's timely defense as well as his promise to pay for his son's treatment, I apologized to him.

But how was I to feel about Fritz, our pet patient who had suddenly become the villain? Needless to say, now that he has accepted Christ, he readily admits his fault. As his brother in Christ, I rejoice that he has found new life and new purpose to live—as well as apparently miraculous physical healing in a badly injured body.

April 1992   HAITIAN ARMY
By Rachael Picazo

Our evacuation over, we were glad to be back in Haiti. Here at our local church, the young junior pastor gave a simple but powerful message. At the close, the emcee called forward the commandant of the army in Cap-Haitien so the church could get to know him and pray for him.

An enthusiastic Christian, the commandant invited the Haitian Committee for Evangelization to provide teachers and have regular Bible studies with his army contingent. It is not compulsory, but the soldiers are encouraged to attend these services every Thursday. Thus many of the soldiers have accepted Christ, and it is now common to see them in the various churches of the city. One was recently baptized.

The Gideons provide them with New Testaments and Bibles.

1992   GO-YE RADIOS
By Rachael Picazo

Much excitement has attended the distribution of free pocket radios pre-tuned to Radio 4VEH. These are manufactured in Israel under the sponsorship of Galcom International, a Christian manufacturing company whose purpose is to provide durable technical equipment for communicating the Gospel around the world while giving employment to Israelis.

MFMI has ordered 12,000 for Radio 4VEH, and the first 3,000 have reached us. They are attractive blue models called "GO-YE," battery- operated, with ear buds, small enough to fit into a shirt pocket. Even before there was a whisper about the availability of these radios, people began to congregate in hopes of receiving one. After the first day, the station was inundated with hundreds of people.

We decided to distribute 50 radios each day at the radio studios. But there was so much shoving and confusion, we had to hand them out while standing behind locked ironwork gates. Then as the strong tried to push their way forward, many people were trampled and hurt. So now the distribution of the much-sought radios is mostly in the hands of pastors.

The radios we have distributed run on two A-batteries, which are included. But another model coming is solar-powered, with a speaker. Several thousand of these are in customs now.

Mardy gave one of the little radios to one of the officials at the Cap-Haitien airport. The next time he was at the airport, the official told him, "I listen to that little radio from the time 4VEH comes on at 5:00 in the morning. But now my wife is jealous and wants me to give it to her. Can you give me one for my wife so we won't have a fight at our house?"

"Well," Mardy said, "we wouldn't want to cause a family fight!" So he gave him one for his wife.

1994   **SODA BOTTLES OF FUEL**

Haiti continues to suffer under the U.N. embargo. With fuel prices at $10 to $12 per gallon, Radio 4VEH has continued broadcasting the Gospel, although understandably on a restricted schedule. The Haitian people, not wanting to lose the one thing that brightens their day, began showing up at the mission compound carrying small soda cans filled with fuel!

"For the generator, to keep 4VEH on the air," they say with a smile. A soda can filled with fuel?! Talk about the widow's mite! These poor people only have pennies to spend for what food is available. Yet, they give out of their poverty.

Though other ministries have also been restricted, yet the church is alive, growing rapidly, and influencing society. Witchcraft is releasing its hold.

One OMS crusade team of Bible school students reports over 80 conversions in four months.

1994   4VEH RALLY
By Marilyn Shaferly

All of our 4VEH staff were awestruck at the enormous outpouring of affection and enthusiasm from listeners at a 4VEH Rally in St. Louis du Nord, 117 miles by road, northwest of Cap-Haitien. As one person said, an "ocean of listeners" filled the town square. They stood, they sat, and they lay full length in the open area. They crowded every balcony and perched on tops of trucks and buses. Some held parasols to ward off the sun.

From the town, surrounding areas, and distant villages, they poured in, many gathering early in the morning to watch 4VEH technicians set up equipment. All day long they watched and waited for the rally to begin.

Knowing that May is the rainy season, the staff often prayed in preceding days, "Lord, please control the rain."

Sure enough, the sky turned dark, thunder growled ominously, and rain threatened to ruin the valuable electronics equipment as well as rout the ever-increasing crowd.

But, as if on schedule, the sky grew lighter, the misting stopped, and the rally proceeded as planned.

Other potential obstacles had also been lifted in prayer. Transportation presented a major problem. Over inconceivable roads, the trip to St. Louis requires six to seven hours. But God enabled aging vehicles to stand the strain.

All along the route, listeners hailed the 4VEH convoy. A teenager rode her bicycle several kilometers from Gonaives to greet the group at the St. Louis turnoff.

"Pastor William," she shouted, "I want to meet Pastor William. Is he here?"

Pastor William, clutching his recorder, clambered from the Pajero and taped her testimony for his early morning show.

Weeks earlier, the 4VEH planning commission had visited St. Louis and proposed lodging the 4VEH visitors in hotels. "Impossible!" retorted the evangelical leaders.

Besides opening their homes, local believers prepared lavish meals. An aging pastor and wife donated funds to build a platform for the open-air celebration, provided lodging and food, then gave the staff a $60 gift for the station.

Seven staff members, popular personalities as well as behind-the-scenes personnel, were chosen to go. Some 20 others had to stay behind. The well-known Cap-Haitien musical group, "Amen," participated, along with eight other groups from St. Louis. A video of Billy Graham's final "Global Mission" message from Puerto Rico, translated into Creole by 4VEH technician Louis Destiné, climaxed the event.

"Not a fly flew," commented one 4VEHer afterward, "as the crowd listened to the renowned evangelist."

The glorious celebration lasted from 5:00 to 11:30 p.m., unheard of in these days of insecurity and tension. Streets in Haiti now empty soon after dark, but that night no one wanted to leave.

263

"St. Louis must be favored by God to be chosen for this rally," many people declared.

The rally in St. Louis du Nord is the beginning of a new thrust in ministry for Radio 4VEH. The slogan, "Haiti by 2000," coined by the new Radio 4VEH Board of Directors, encompasses a strengthened emphasis on French/Creole ministry to completely cover Haiti with broadcasts. The goal is to offer listeners encouragement and help in turning to God with the heartaches and uncertainties of these difficult days.

To accomplish this, Radio 4VEH equipment is being updated, staff and programming evaluated, and broadcasting converted to a computerized digital operation. And by 4VEH's 50th anniversary, thousands of fix-tuned, solar-powered radios are to be in the hands of Haitians throughout the mountains and valleys to hear 4VEH with its life-changing Gospel of Jesus Christ.

1994   **BOIS CAIMAN**
                          Compiled by Rachael Picazo

1791 At Bois Caiman in Haiti

It was the eve of revolt for the Haitian slaves as they gathered on August 14, 1791, under a huge Caiman Tree (Bois) in northern Haiti for a secret voodoo ceremony. The rituals they brought with them from Africa involved the sacrificing of a pig and the drinking of its warm blood. They were plotting to gain their freedom from the French plantation holders, and they called upon Satan to help them. In payment, they promised to dedicate the country to him for the next two hundred years. It is said that indeed a strange being became visible to them that night in the ceremony. History bears record that the slaves indeed fought fiercely for several years, at last proclaiming their freedom on January 1, 1804.

1991   200 years later at Bois Caiman
There is a huge Caiman Tree about seven miles south of our mission compound, which the Haitians claim was the site of that voodoo ceremony by the slaves the eve of their revolt. It was there a group of the most influential voodoo priests and President Aristide met in 1991 to re-dedicate the country to Satan. However, they were thwarted by heavy rains, wind, and lightning so they had to abandon the place, although we understand he still had a ceremony in the palace.

1994   At Bois Caiman by Marilyn Shaferly
An interesting evidence that God is still in control and will still have the last word happened on August 18 when voodoo priests and Haiti's current de facto president met at Bois Caiman to complete the ceremony of rededicating the country to Satan.
The sacrificial pig had already been killed in the midst of a violent thunderstorm. The lightning, however, kept getting closer and closer, until finally a big ball of it burst so close it scattered the entire group. Valeene Hayes, seven miles away at our mission compound, said it was so loud that she and Brenda Vowles bolted out of their beds.
When the group at Bois Caiman tried to reassemble, there was such confusion and the lightning was still so frightening that they eventually disbanded without ever completing the ceremony. The president went back to Port-au-Prince in the middle of the night.

1997   At Bois Caiman
After 40 days of fasting and prayer, a large group of Haitian Christians converged at Bois Caiman, confessed their nation's sins, repented of their evil deeds, and cleansed the place.

265

1998 At Bois Caiman reported by David and Marilyn Shaferly

There is an increasingly vocal cry throughout the Christian community in Haiti that it is time to break Satan's stranglehold, time for Haiti to be delivered. National calls to prayer and evangelistic crusades are being scheduled constantly.

An evangelistic crusade was scheduled to be held at Bois Caiman, this time dedicating Haiti to God. On Saturday prior to the first service, two local Haitian government officials burned a church brush arbor at Bois Caiman, destroyed 500 cement blocks the people had made for a new church building, and threw them into a community latrine that was being dug.

On Sunday the service was held anyway. On Monday afternoon the three pastors largely responsible for the crusade were arrested, one of them being Pastor Tony Paul. They were charged with treason and held in prison.

But the rest of the team pushed ahead to hold the services. Then two government officials went to arrest the lay pastor who was taking leadership, burned the team's generator, and shot into the crowd, scattering them. So the service was not held that night.

As this news spread, several thousand Christians converged at Bois Caiman in a prayer meeting interceding for the pastors being held in prison.

Later, when the three pastors would have been released, they refused to leave, demanding an official explanation as to why they were arrested. The parties responsible for the harassment were tripping over themselves to find someone else to blame. The Department of Religion did not condone their actions at all, leaving them out on a limb. The government congressman who had been so ferocious against Protestants appeared at one of the crusade services and, with tears, begged forgiveness.

By the time the pastors went free, the whole affair had attracted international attention—the United Nations and the U.S. Embassy. The Haitian Christians were jubilant at what they perceived a major victory, and great impetus was given to the many other evangelistic crusades going on in Haiti that summer.

1994   **U.N. OCCUPATION**
By Rachael Picazo

In the fall of 1994, U.S. Army troops were already enroute to Haiti. Then, at the last moment, former President Jimmy Carter flew into Port-au-Prince and made peaceful negotiations. So the planes were turned around. Later the soldiers did come in, but this time with peaceful intentions.

Marilyn Shaferly in Haiti wrote, Now, *from the vantage point of Sept. 22 (three days into the occupation), we can definitely say that God intervened at the very last moment to save us from wide-spread bloodshed.*

Few people could know about the prayers of the Haitian people prior to this intervention. For the past 14 years, the Christians of our community in Haiti have been meeting every Thursday, under some trees near our compound, to fast and pray all morning until early afternoon. Two or three hundred meet in these local community prayer meetings. We know of another such prayer meeting under the trees in a community about five miles away.

About seven years ago, a group of evangelical pastors formed a Committee of Evangelism in the north of Haiti. They started forming prayer meetings, including Christians from all denominations, which became so well attended they began meeting in the big stadium at Cap-Haitien every Saturday morning. For the past five years, two or three thousand have been meeting while fasting every week. They start gathering in front of the stadium Friday night so they can be sure to have a place inside early Saturday morning. They pray, sing, praise God, and exhort one another until well after noon.

Another prayer meeting was just being started when we left Haiti in 1992. This one met every afternoon at a river about a mile outside the city. People would walk beside the road by the hundreds. About 2,000 met there every afternoon to pray especially for their country.

Pastor Tony Paul, pastor of the big church in Plaine du Nord, reported that his church is praying 40 hours a week specifically for their country.

We know that the amazingly good things that have transpired in Haiti these past few weeks have been in answer to the earnest prayers of the Christians there.

1995   **4VEH IS MY CHURCH**
By Marilyn Shaferly

Wilner Beljour's demeanor was neither imposing nor impressive as he entered the Radio 4VEH studios for his first-ever visit. Obviously one of Haiti's unpretentious country folk, he was somewhat awed by the unfamiliar world of organization and electronics.

Before Wilner left, however, the studio staff realized their unassuming guest was a flesh-and-blood example of how God uses Radio 4VEH to transform lives in troubled, modern-day Haiti. The following live radio interview by Gaudin Charles, 4VEH director, captures Wilner's initial visit to Radio 4VEH:

WILNER: Only the Gospel could have done this for me. I can't imagine a more wonderful welcome until the day Jesus crowns me. I feel like I'm in heaven.

GAUDIN: Brother Wilner, it is a pleasure to have such a faithful listener visit us. I understand you live near Acul du Nord, about ten miles from here. What 4VEH programs do you hear?

WILNER: All of them, every single one, from 5:00 a.m. until 10:00 p.m. I'm such a fanatic that I have one radio at home for my wife and children and load another into my horse's saddlebags to take with me to the fields. Every word that is said on Radio 4VEH, I hear. 4VEH is my church!

GAUDIN: But you do have a church, don't you?

WILNER: Oh yes, I've attended since I was saved in 1971. But the pastor is at the church only once a week, and because of my work, I cannot attend weekday services. With Radio 4VEH, I'm in church every single night.

GAUDIN: How exactly has Radio 4VEH served as your church?

WILNER: 4VEH has built up my faith, Brother Gaudin. Every broadcast means a great deal, yes, a **great deal** to me. Through the broadcasts, I have learned the Bible. I know about Jacob, about Elijah, about Enoch, and how they were taken to heaven. Oh! I feel so rich, so rich! I could die right now, satisfied with the riches Radio 4VEH has brought into my life.

GAUDIN: Brother Wilner, these are encouraging words.

WILNER: Yes, because of Radio 4VEH, I now have two new Bibles. Our pastor had a contest for National Bible Sunday. One prize was for learning four Bible verses each week; the other was for scoring highest in a Bible quiz. Even though I can't read or write, Radio 4VEH helped me to win them.

GAUDIN: What! You can't read or write?

WILNER: No, Brother Gaudin. Everything I know, from Genesis to Revelation, I've learned from Radio 4VEH. I am now the lay preacher in a weekly service, and the people are being instructed because of Radio 4VEH.

GAUDIN: What specific programs have helped you?

269

WILNER: Well, the song request programs make me so happy I don't have time to eat. I'm so busy singing along with them. I also dance along with the songs. Yes, I actually dance.

GAUDIN: What others do you like?

WILNER: Ah, yes. The prayer programs have taught me how to go to my room in secret and my Father will hear and reward me openly.

GAUDIN: As a faithful listener, you know about our program "Who? Why? How?" Do you have a question you'd like to ask?

WILNER: Oh, that is the "People's Dictionary," the program that teaches things you'd never know on this earth otherwise.

Yes, I have a question I've wanted to ask for a long time. Ever since I was a child, I've heard that every human being has a star assigned to him. When Jesus was born, it was a star that led the wise men to Him. When I'm out in the country, the stars tell me when to get up and work in my garden. According to Haitian sayings, when a person dies, his star isn't there any more. Is this true?

GAUDIN: A very good question! I, too, have grown up hearing this. In fact, I've heard that to comment on a falling star is to bring bad luck, because it means someone has died. But, I can tell you from the Bible, when God created the earth, He created the sun, the moon, and the stars. There's no indication of a star for each person. As long as you've been alive, what we call "the morning star" has been there, hasn't it?

If this star represented some person, it should already have fallen, shouldn't it? So, when you ask if every person has his own star, the answer is "No! No! No!"

WILNER: That's why I came to the People's Dictionary. Now I know that the whole idea is nothing but superstition.

GAUDIN: Brother Wilner, what would you like to say to fellow listeners, before we conclude this interview?

270

WILNER: To all the people of Haiti I'd say that if we believed the Gospel, our country wouldn't be like it is right now. When I see all that the Gospel has done for me, the love that has been shown me, I feel like a king. I wish you'd just come to Christ and see what it's like to belong to Him.

If you don't have a radio to hear 4VEH and repent, in the name of Jesus, buy one!

1996   ALL-DAY BROADCASTS

In November 1996, Radio 4VEH returned to all-day transmissions in French and Creole, an increase of five and a half hours per day, after five years of reduced hours following the 1991 Haitian presidential *coup d'etat*. That means 4VEH now broadcasts to Haiti in French and Creole without interruption from 5:00 a.m. to 10:00 p.m. daily.

FM Stereo 95 continues its noon to 11:00 p.m. broadcasts in French and English. It has currently added a block of English programs to its schedule, from 6:00 to 8:30 a.m.

Updated equipment has recently been installed at 4VEH, including a computerized news service (Agence France Presse) and a new digital production studio.

1996   CODO
From the Radio 4VEH Transmitter

Jean-Claude Raphael Ciméus, program director for the French/Creole service of Radio 4VEH since 1993, exclaims, "What an awesome responsibility we have at 4VEH!"

"Codo," as Jean-Claude is known, is responsible for the roster of broadcasts reaching his people throughout northern Haiti, in other parts of the Republic, and in nearby islands. "We must offer a well-rounded program," he says, "of education, culture, and music. But most important of all is the message of Jesus Christ transmitted through preaching, teaching, prayer, and scripture reading."

Joining 4VEH in 1986 as a newscaster and program producer, Codo represented the station at the Caribbean Chapter of the National Religious Broadcasters 1991 annual convention in Puerto Rico. In 1993 he was one of 23 participants from 21 countries in a drug workshop at a seminar on News and Cultural Affairs in Washington, DC.

Born January 6, 1962, in the town of Port Margot in northern Haiti, his mother was an active Christian. His father, who never accepted Christ, died when Codo was eight years old. At the age of 20, he made his own personal decision to follow Christ.

Codo became pastor of the Evangelical Church of Mapou in 1991. Not far from the 4VEH studios, the church has grown from a handful of believers to a membership of over 300. During the same year, he was married to Bunie Docteur, a pastor's daughter, and they now have a 2½-year-old son, Claude.

In these days of upheaval and unrest in Haiti, Christian leaders are often targets of jealousy and intrigue. "My life is in God's hands," affirms Codo. "I have peace, not fear."

1996   *LET THE ROCKS CRY OUT*
                         Radio 4VEH Transmitter

Let the Rocks Cry Out is bringing more people to Christ than perhaps any other single program on 4VEH. Since its beginning in November 1996, scores of conversions have been reported, many of them young adults. According to one listener, when the program is aired, "every radio in Haiti is tuned to 4VEH!"

The hour-long broadcast in Creole on Monday and Wednesday evenings features gripping interviews with people delivered from the bondage of Satanism and voodoo. Jean-Claude "Codo" Ciméus, 4VEH's French/Creole program director and creator of the program, conducts the interviews. "I never dreamed *Kite Roch Yo Pale* (*Let the Rocks Cry Out*) would have this kind of impact," Codo remarks. "This is definitely of the Lord!"

In May, Radio 4VEH aired the powerful testimony of Mr. Ludovic, a former voodoo priest converted eight years ago by the witness of the woman now his wife. Ludovic was well known in Haiti for his satanic activities and murder, even of his own family members. He had appeared often on Port-au-Prince television.

Now he was speaking out for Jesus Christ, telling of God's power that freed him from the bondage of fear and evil under voodooism. Response to his testimony in the French/Creole broadcast was electrifying. Listeners requested tapes of the broadcast and requested that the series be repeated.

In the village of Port-Francais, ten miles south of Cap-Haitien, a voodoo priestess heard Ludovic's astounding testimony of God's transforming power. "If God can save Ludovic, He can save me!" she declared. She did an abrupt spiritual about-face and accepted Jesus Christ as her personal Savior, changing her allegiance from Satan to Jesus. Years earlier, a 4VEH pre-tuned radio had been used by God to plant a church in this remote area.

A voodoo priest in the village of Lory, a few miles from 4VEH studios, was challenged by questions from a group of nonbelievers who had heard Ludovic's testimony. As a result, the priest's Christian grandson came to 4VEH to purchase a tape

273

for his grandfather. "I know he will listen," the young man assured the radio staff.

As tapes of Ludovic's testimony are rebroadcast in the future, God's Spirit can yet transform even others. Believers are praying for God to break Satan's stronghold on the nation of Haiti.

Another Radio 4VEH listener, visiting the station, reported that at least 30 people have found Christ as a direct result of Radio 4VEH in his community of Acul des Pins, a village near the border of the Dominican Republic. Eighteen of those converted have already been baptized and integrated into the church.

The listener, who is responsible for the rural church in Acul des Pins, said that many of these converts have been brought to Christ through the program, *Kite Roch Yo Pale* (*Let the Rocks Cry Out*).

As those interviewed by Codo give their testimonies publicly, perhaps for the first time, they often experience tremendous relief and freedom. Marilyn Shaferly, administrator of 4VEH, observes, "Satan's actions are being exposed for what they are—miserable, enslaving, lying, and destructive. But some are furious at the testimonies aired. They are denouncing the people as liars, sometimes trying to create rumors discrediting the lives of those who have testified.

However, as listeners hear the testimonies, they are encouraged to believe that they, too, can be delivered. There is a new boldness on the part of Christians, both pastors and laymen, to openly speak of the power of Christ to free people spiritually. Others are realizing there is nothing good outside of the Gospel and are making decisions to accept Christ.

Codo Cimeus, 4VEH French program director, produces
the program, "Let the Rocks Cry Out" in 1996

Haitian listing to a new "Go-Ye" radio in 1996

New Studio under construction in 2001

1996   **SOLAR CELLS SAVE SOULS**
By Marilyn Shaferly

Sablée is a quiet Haitian village...**too** quiet, for my ears. I hear the usual village noises—a barking dog, muffled voices, an overloaded donkey plodding down the road. I listen for the sound of radios blaring, specifically Radio 4VEH's gospel music and message, but don't hear it. I poll the villagers to see if they own radios and listen to 4VEH.

"Oh yes, we have radios," they reply. "We would like to hear the programs. We just can't afford batteries."

Then, with 4VEH staff, I visit Acul des Pins. What a difference! The village fairly vibrates with new life. I learn that since January, ten people have been converted because of 4VEH programs. Prior to that, there were 30!

Unlike Sablée, the Gospel has invaded Acul des Pins. Radio 4VEH has fortified the local witness, and young people are responding to Christ in unprecedented numbers.

The staff is committed to duplicating the story of Acul des Pins in places like Sablée. But sending the message into the airwaves is not enough. For people to change, they must hear the Word of God, and we must ensure that people receive it.

Not new to Haiti, the fix-tuned radio is one of the best tools we have to reach homes and hearts. Some 2,000 sets pre-tuned to Radio 4VEH took the Gospel into Haitian villages in the 1960s, and over 40,000 little "Go-Ye" fix-tuned radios saturated the countryside in the early 1990s.

Fix-tuned radios are back and better than ever. In January Galcom International (Hamilton, Ontario, Canada), makers of the previous sets, sent to Haiti 1,000 of a new model of "Go-Ye" radios. This revised version is solar-powered and comes with back-up long-lasting, Nicad-type batteries.

For the first time, 4VEH is selling some of its fix-tuned radios. Enthusiastic listeners at Acul des Pins, among the first to

275

purchase these radios, can be seen carrying the little sets in their hands or tucked into pockets.

The unconverted villagers of Sablée might not care enough about Christian programs to buy radios, but they would gladly accept gifts of little "Go-Ye" sets fix-tuned to 4VEH's French/Creole frequency. They would relish the music, savor the wide variety of programs, and just might discover their lives changed from the inside out.

Note: One thousand pre-tuned radios are now being distributed throughout Haiti. The portable sets with built-in speakers and solar panel (also back-up Nicad batteries) are pre-tuned to Radio 4VEH. The new radios have been improved and are somewhat larger than those distributed a few years ago. Gifts of $30 each to underwrite this ongoing ministry may be designated for 4VEH Pre-tuned Radios, Project # 40124.

1997   LIVING WATER FOR THIRSTY HAITIANS
Action Magazine

Well-driller Don Robertson states emphatically, "Northern Haiti has been so dry lately people are suffering. By supplying them with water wells for their bodies, we also introduced them to Living Water for their souls."

Don's vision is also held by Canadian men and women, many from southern Ontario.

"Haiti has always had a special place in the hearts of Canadians," says Don Giles, former missionary in Haiti. "We hoped that by drilling wells we would also open doors to their hearts."

Sixty Canadians began trekking to the OMS compound near Cap-Haitien in early January, and were still coming in March. Their concentrated effort, capped by a final MFMI team led from the States by Don Robertson of Ashby, Minnesota, was responsible for drilling 43 wells and installing 39 pumps. The teams, who also chlorinated the wells, estimate that each well provides water for 1000 people.

Villagers around Cap-Haitien flocked to the drilling sites to watch the action. Especially excited, the children found a cool bath in running water not only refreshing, but quite a novelty.

Don Robertson emphasizes, "We drill the wells at church schools and always have a local pastor or interpreter present. In that way, the folks learn we're there because Jesus loves them."

"The pumps are a story of their own," remarks Ivadel Giles, Don's wife. "Bill Van Lenthe of Bill Stabling Manufacturing in Arthur, Ontario, went to Haiti with my husband in 1995. His heart was broken, and that year he donated 25 well pumps free of charge. The next year he supplied 100. To put this in perspective, we had been paying $600 for each pump."

1997   ECC TEAMS TAKE GO-YE RADIOS
Radio 4VEH Transmitter, July 1997

Three OMS Every Creature Crusade (ECC) evangelism teams are taking 4VEH's solar-powered, fix-tuned "Go-Ye" radios with them into communities where the teams are planting new churches.

"We realize that if the people hear the programs aired on Radio 4VEH, their hearts will be softened and they may come to Christ. They will also be helped in their daily lives," observes ECC's Haitian coordinator, Daniel Vilvert.

The teams seek to plant churches in areas with relatively little evangelical influence. Other radio stations often do not reach into these areas and, even though 4VEH does, people may not listen. Christian radio may, for the unconverted, be a low priority. The solar-powered, fix-tuned radios, therefore, are a key to opening the door for evangelism.

1997   **A LISTENER**
                        OMS Prayer Sheet

A listener to 4VEH records the programs, studies them, and then gives the message to his people. In the absence of a pastor, he has taken responsibility for a rural church. He never had the opportunity to go to seminary, but he is thankful that 4VEH has enabled him to share the message of God's Word. Thirty have been converted and eighteen baptized as a result of this ministry.

1997   EMMAUS FELLOWSHIP OF CHURCHES

The Emmaus Fellowship of Churches is now registered with the government. These are independent churches started mostly by graduates from the OMS Emmaus Vocational Bible School, who have chosen not to join the Evangelical Church of Haiti. Interest among churches is high, with new inquiries and discussion occurring frequently, presenting the need for a missionary to work in this area of ministry.

A new children's ministry directed by Joetta Lehman saw 1000 children accept Christ during 11 Vacation Bible Schools held in OMS-Haiti churches last summer.

1999   **RADIO TOUCHES HEARTS IN HAITI**
By Marilyn Shaferly (*Action*)

The first weekend of January a young man walked some 20 miles to the station for the specific purpose of having someone pray with him to accept Christ. He had been on the verge of suicide when he heard a meditation program, then a Bible study program on the life of Job. He decided there was hope, after all, and came to seek the program producer who had given the meditation to pray with him. We felt this was God's seal on the ministry of 4VEH for this coming year.

1999   **ALMOST THE LAST CHAPTER**
By Rachael Picazo

I can sympathize with the writer of Hebrews, who arrived in chapter 11 and exclaimed in verse 32: *I do not have time to tell about Gideon, Barak, Samson, Jephthah, David, Samuel and the prophets....*

Here we're almost to the last chapter and I haven't told you about Pastor Amos who was converted while listening to 4VEH as a high school student, a member of a Communist Cell.... nor of our Hospitality Center in Port-au-Prince called Villa Ormiso (Oriental Missionary Society), a lovely place to stay overnight.

Nor have I told you about Cowman Missionary Children's School, started primarily to educate the missionaries' children, but also including Haitians speaking English. Its beautiful facilities are under the direction of Mary Lou Wunker.

I didn't write about the Dental Clinic, with its modern equipment and spacious rooms, a special project of Dr. Virgil

Ullom, and dedicated to the memory of Leon and Lorna Steel, his nephew and niece, children of Valetta Steel Crumley.

There was the agricultural cooperative, a broom-making venture, the Canadians building a lovely church at Petite Anse in memory of MFMer Lyle Martin, the video "Letters of Love," the Haitian Nazarene pastor in Cap-Haitien who declared, "Radio 4VEH is the glue that's holding this country together!"

Somewhere the exciting story of Dr. Hollis Tanksley should be told...

Then there was the building of the Petite Anse wall... There was the Pastors' Conference at Emmaus Bible College March 14-19, 1999, in which Dr. Harold Brown planned for 60 pastors. As it turned out, 214 registered, and many others came without registering. Graduates of the Emmaus Vocational Bible School returned, some having not been on the campus for 15 years. Dr. J. B. Crouse, Dr. Wesley Duewel, and Rev. Randy Spacht from OMS Headquarters spoke to the pastors, and to the thousands listening on their radios as the services were broadcast.

"It has been like a revival!" a listener declared.

Sparked with excitement, and realizing their need for unity in winning Haiti for Christ, churches are steadily applying for affiliation with the Emmaus Fellowship of Churches.

I could go on and on, but I must tell you about.

"OPERATION SATURATION"

In 1999 Men For Missions International announced its bold new plan to reach all of Haiti for Christ through "Operation Saturation." They want to saturate Haiti with hundreds of thousands of small, fix-tuned, solar-powered "Go-Ye" radios to receive the daily ministry of Radio 4VEH, so that every Haitian can hear the Gospel in his or her own language.

In order for Radio 4VEH to blanket Haiti more effectively, the plan includes the construction of a new radio studio building, adequate to house needed staff, and equipped with modern technology.

A ground-breaking ceremony to launch the construction of the new studio building was celebrated on March 21, 1999. The Radio 4VEH staff, board members, listeners, and friends, gathered at the site for the occasion.

In July a group from Alabama dug the first holes and poured the first concrete. A steady stream of Men For Missions teams was slated to continue the work until 4VEH's 50th Anniversary, June 1 - 4, 2000.

In a March 4, 2000, update on the progress of the work, received from Radio 4VEH manager Marilyn Shaferly in Haiti:

Construction of the new radio facilities is progressing beautifully, with back-to-back work teams, sometimes 20 - 24 at a time. We're glad for volunteer hosts to care for them.

The building is up two floors, block walls are nearly finished. We were delayed getting steel for roof trusses. We need to have the second floor covered and lockable to begin building furniture there in mid-April. Two landscapers were here last week to draw up plans.

4VEH's 50th Anniversary plans are also progressing, with many hitches, no money. We are excited, though, about the plans and the prospect of having a great time of reunion and praise as many former missionaries, 4VEH workers, and Emmaus Bible College graduates return June 1-4, 2000.

God realizes our need for celebrations. So He put in Leviticus 25:11:

The 50th year shall be a jubilee for you!

HIGHLIGHTS OF OMS HAITI HISTORY

1950   June 2, 4VEH started broadcasting.

1951   December, lightning burned out transmitter.

1952   July, new 3,000-watt transmitter put 4VEH back on the air.

1953   December, 4VEH in its new studio facilities.

1958   The Oriental Missionary Society (now OMS International) assumed responsiblity for the station from Rev. G. T. Bustin.

1960   First pre-tuned radio placed at Port Francais. Twelve saved in 6 months.

1961   Dedication at Petite Anse: new transmitter buiilding, two new 2500-watt transmitters, 170-ft. tower.

1962   Installation of first 10-kilowatt transmitter.

1965   The first wing of the Bethesda Medical Center ready to be used.

1965   FM transmitter link enables programs to originate at Vaudreuil.

1965   4VEH choir and quartet toured the U.S. for 14 weeks.

1967   Start of simultaneous broadcasts on two separate medium-wave frequencies.

1967   2,000 transistor radio semi-kits arrived from Japan, or assembling and distribution.

1967   Opening of the Emmaus Vocational Bible School.

1968   Dedication of the completed Bethesda Medical Center.

1968   Rebel invasion of Cap-Haitien forced closing of station for 40 days.

1968   Funds for a second 10-Kw transmitter given at OMS Convention in 15 minutes.

1969   Haitian staff now completely responsible for French /Creole programming.

1970   Pre-tuned radio distribution stopped, since tunable radios are available.

1970	"Manne du Matin" Quartet toured the British Isles, France, and U.S.
1971	275' antenna tower erected to replace old 180' tower.
1971	All-day broadcasts in French/Creole for the first time.
1971	Installation of recording studio in OMS Center in Port-au-Prince.
1972	4VEH and Radio Lumiere agreed on cooperation and trans-Haiti network.
1973	Recording studio & office opened in Cap-Haitien.
1973	Engineer Robert A. Jones from Chicago area gave of his professional services to 4VEH.
1973	A separate Dental Clinic building completed.
1974	Installation of directional antenna system for Spanish /English programs.
1975	Installation of directional antenna system for French /Creole broadcasts.
1975	Reduction of power during daytime broadcasts to cut fuel consumption.
1977	Gaudin Charles installed as first Haitian Director of 4VEH.
1978	Installation of repeater mobile equipment .
1979	Test broadcasting on "Skywave" frequency.
1980	Celebration of 30th anniversary. Staff choir performed, "By My Spirit."
1981	The choir of Emmaus Vocational Bible School tours eastern U.S.
1982	Just before Christmas, FM Stereo 95 goes on the air.
1984	The Evangelical Church of Haiti severed relations with OMS.
1990	40th Anniversary celebration at the Vaudreuil Church.
1991	Evacuation of OMS personnel to the States for five months.
1992	Emmaus Vocational Bible School becomes Emmaus Bible College.

1992	New efficient transmitter for French/Creole broadcasts.
1995	A Radio 4VEH Board was formed.
1996	Start of program, "Let the Rocks Cry Out."
1997	Haitian Christians converged at Bois Caiman, repented for their nation.
1999	Ground breaking for the new 4VEH studios.
2000	June 1-4, Jubilee celebration of 4VEH's 50th

PERSONNEL ON THE HAITI FIELD
(* indicates personnel on furlough)

Radio Staff
Rev. G. T. Bustin
Mr. Paul Shirk

1951 Radio Staff
Rev. G. T. Bustin
Mr. Paul Shirk
Mr. Victor & Claudine Chamberlin

1952 Radio Staff
Mr. Victor & Claudine Chamberlin
Mr. Mardy & Rachael Picazo

1953 Radio Staff
Mr. Victor & Claudine Chamberlin
Rev. Mardy & Rachael Picazo

1954 Radio Staff
Mr. Victor & Claudine Chamberlin
Rev. Mardy & Rachael Picazo

1955 Radio Staff
Rev. Richard & Ann Jackson
Rev. Mardy & Rachael Picazo

1956 Radio Staff
Rev. Richard & Ann Jackson
Rev. Mardy & Rachael Picazo
Miss Miriam Stockton

1957 Radio Staff
Mr. Charles & Mary Bustin
Miss Helen Hammer
*Rev. Mardy & Rachael Picazo
Miss Miriam Stockton
Mr. Stewart C. West
Rev. & Mrs. Merlin C. Bidwell
Mr. Aldean Saufley

October, 1958, OMS Personnel
Director: Dr. William Gillam
Mr. and Mrs. Charles Bustin
Rev. and Mrs. M. E. Picazo
Miss Miriam Stockton
Mr. & Mrs. Donald Hamme (aff)
Mr. & Mrs. Kent Ragsdale (aff)

October, 1959, OMS Personnel
Director: Mr. Eldon Turnidge
Mr. & Mrs. Charles Bustin
Rev. & Mrs. Mardy Picazo
Mr. & Mrs. Donald Hamme
Mr. & Mrs. Kent Ragsdale
Miss Miriam Stockton

October, 1960, OMS Personnel
Director: Mr. Eldon Turnidge
*Mr & Mrs. Charles Bustin
Mr. & Mrs. Donald Hamme
Rev. & Mrs. Paul Lund
Rev. & Mrs. M. E. Picazo
Rev. & Mrs. Elry Pontious
Mr. & Mrs. Kent Ragsdale
Mr. Aldean Saufley
* Miss Miriam Stockton
Miss Betty Weigman

October, 1961, OMS Personnel
Director: Mr. Eldon Turnidge
Miss Flora Boyer
Miss Ellen Bressler
Mr. Donald & Glenda Hamme
Rev. Paul & Trudy Lund
Rev. Mardy & Rachael Picazo
Rev. Elry & Lucille Pontious
Mr. Kent & Linda Ragsdale
Mr. John Raisch
Mr. Aldean Saufley
Miss Miriam Stockton
Rev. James & Leone Wallace
    (Language school)

October, 1962, OMS Personnel
Director: Mr. Eldon Turnidge
Miss Flora Boyer
Miss Ellen Bressler
Rev. & Mrs. Paul Lund
* Rev. & Mrs. Mardy Picazo
Mr. & Mrs. Kent Ragsdale
Mr. John Raisch
Mr. Aldean Saufley
Miss Miriam Stockton
Mr. & Mrs. Eldon Turnidge

Oct, 1962, OMS Personnel (cont'd)
Rev. & Mrs. James Wallace

October, 1963, OMS Personnel
Director: Mr. Eldon Turnidge
Miss Flora Boyer
Miss Valeene Hayes
Rev. & Mrs. Paul Lund
Miss Marilyn Murphy
Rev. & Mrs. Mardy Picazo
*Mr & Mrs. Kent Ragsdale
Mr. & Mrs. Aldean Saufley
Miss Miriam Stockton
Mr. & Mrs. Eldon Turnidge
Rev. & Mrs. James Wallace

October, 1964, OMS Personnel
Director: Mr. Eldon Turnidge
*Miss Flora Boyer
Miss Janet Elam
Mr. & Mrs. David Graffenberger
Miss Valeene Hayes
Rev. & Mrs. Hudson Hess
* Rev. & Mrs. Paul Lund
Miss Marilyn Murphy
Mr. & Mrs. Kent Ragsdale
*Mr. & Mrs. Aldean Saufley
Mr. Dale Sloat
Miss Miriam Stockton
Mr. & Mrs. Eldon Turnidge
Mr. & Mrs. Virgil Ullom
Rev. & Mrs. James Wallace

October, 1965, OMS Personnel
Director: Mr. Eldon Turnidge
*Miss Flora Boyer
Miss Janet Elam
Mr. & Mrs. David Graffenberger
Miss Valeene Hayes
Rev. & Mrs. Hudson Hess
* Rev. & Mrs. Paul Lund
Miss Marilyn Murphy
Rev. & Mrs. Mardy Picazo
Mr. & Mrs. Kent Ragsdale
*Mr. & Mrs. Aldean Saufley
Miss Ina Sorensen
Miss Miriam Stockton
Mr. & Mrs. Eldon Turnidge
Mr. & Mrs. Virgil Ullom

* Rev. & Mrs. James Wallace
Miss Marylin Wallar

October, 1966, OMS Personnel
Director: Mr. Eldon Turnidge
Miss Flora Boyer
Miss Shirley Casler
Mr. Philip Chandler
Mr. & Mrs. David Graffenberger
Miss Valeene Hayes
Mr. & Mrs. Oswald Heinrich
Rev. & Mrs. Hudson Hess
Mr. Kenneth Long
Miss Marilyn Murphy
Rev. & Mrs. Mardy Picazo
Mr. & Mrs. Kent Ragsdale
Mr. & Mrs. Aldean Saufley
Miss Ina Sorensen
Miss Miriam Stockton
Mr. & Mrs. Eldon Turnidge
*Mr. & Mrs. Virgil Ullom
Mr. & Mrs. James Wallace

October, 1967, OMS Personnel
Director: Mr. Eldon Turnidge
Mr. and Mrs. Gary Bailey
Mrs. Margaret Bonnette
Miss Flora Boyer
Rev. & Mrs. Harold Brown
Miss Shirley Casler
Miss Lula Mae Fuchs
Mr. & Mrs. David Graffenberger
Mr. & Mrs. Jack Hannay
Miss Valeene Hayes
Mr. & Mrs. Oswald Heinrich
Rev. & Mrs. Hudson Hess
Mr. & Mrs. Cleveland Irvine
Miss Corinne Lowman
Miss Marilyn Murphy
Mr. Leonard Payne
*Rev. & Mrs. Mardy Picazo
Mr. & Mrs. Kent Ragsdale
Mr. & Mrs. Aldean Saufley
Mr. David Shaferly
Miss Ina Sorensen
*Miss Miriam Stockton
Miss Stella Truax
Mr. & Mrs. Eldon Turnidge

286

October, 1968, OMS Personnel
Director: Dr. William A. Gillam
Mr. & Mrs. Gary Bailey
Margaret Bonnette
Miss Flora Boyer
Rev. and Mrs. Harold Brown
Philip Chandler
Miss Esther Close
Miss Lula Mae Fuchs
Mr. Zack Gill
Dr. & Mrs. William A. Gillam
Mr. & Mrs. David Graffenberger
*Miss Valeene Hayes
Mr. & Mrs. Oswald Heinrich
*Rev. & Mrs. Hudson Hess
Mr. & Mrs. Wayne Hodges
Mr. & Mrs. Cleveland Irvine
Miss Corinne Lowman
Mr. & Mrs. Francis Muia
Miss Marilyn Murphy
Rev. & Mrs. Mardy Picazo
*Mr. & Mrs. Kent Ragsdale
Mr. & Mrs. Aldean Saufley
Miss Christina Schwanke
Mr. David Shaferly

October, 1969, OMS Personnel
Direcor: Dr. William A. Gillam
Mr. & Mrs. Gary Bailey
Margaret Bonnette
Miss Flora Boyer
Rev. & Mrs. Harold Brown
Philip Chandler
Miss Esther Close
Miss Lula Mae Fuchs
Mr. Zack Gill
Dr. & Mrs. William A. Gillam
Mr. & Mrs. David Graffenberger
*Miss Valeene Hayes
Mr. & Mrs. Oswald Heinrich
*Rev. & Mrs. Hudson Hess
Mr. & Mrs. Wayne Hodges
Mr. & Mrs. Cleveland Irvine
Miss Corinne Lowman
Mr. & Mrs. Francis Mula
Miss Marilyn Murphy
Rev. & Mrs. Mardy Picazo
*Mr. & Mrs. Kent Ragsdale
Mr. & Mrs. Aldean Saufley

Miss Christina Schwanke
Mr. David Shaferly

October, 1970, OMS Personnel
Director: Rev. Mardy Picazo
Mr. Daniel Blosser
Margaret Bonnette
*Miss Flora Boyer
Mr. Philip Chandler
Miss Esther Close
Mr. Dan Cloud
Mrs. Christine Davenport
Miss Lula Mae Fuchs
Mr. & Mrs. Mark Garringer
Mr. & Mrs. David Graffenberger
*Mr & Mrs. Oswald Heinrich
Rev. & Mrs. Hudson Hess
Mr. & Mrs. Wayne Hodges
Mr. & Mrs. Cleveland Irvine
Miss Corinne Lowman
Mr. & Mrs. Francis Muia
Miss Marilyn Murphy
Rev. & Mrs. Mardy Picazo
Mr. & Mrs. Kent Ragsdale
*Mr. & Mrs. Aldean Saufley
Miss Christina Schwanke
Mr. David Shaferly

October, 1971, OMS Personnel
Director: Rev. Mardy Picazo
Mr. & Mrs. Claude Beachy
Mr. Daniel Blosser
Margaret Bonnette
Dr. & Mrs. Stafford Bourke
Miss Flora Boyer
Miss Lorna Cain
Mr. Philip Chandler
Miss Esther Close
Miss Lula Mae Fuchs
*Mr. & Mrs. David Graffenberger
Mr. & Mrs. Oswald Heinrich
Rev. & Mrs. Hudson Hess
Mr. & Mrs. Wayne Hodges
*Mr. & Mrs. Cleveland Irvine
Miss Corinne Lowman
Mr. & Mrs. Francis Muia
Miss Lynda Arline Myers
Rev. & Mrs. Mardy Picazo
Mr. & Mrs. Kent Ragsdale

Oct, 1971, OMS Personnel (cont'd)
Mr. & Mrs. Aldean Saufley
Miss Christina Schwanke
Mr. & Mrs. David Shaferly

October, 1972, OMS Personnel
Director: David Graffenberger
Mr. & Mrs. Claude Beachy
*Margaret Bonnette
Dr. & Mrs. Stafford Bourke
Miss Flo Boyer
Rev. & Mrs. Harold Brown
*Mr. & Mrs. Philip Chandler
Miss Esther Close
Mr. Wilbert Dunn
Miss Lula Mae Fuchs
Miss Ruth Gamber
Miss Marian Giles
Mr. & Mrs. David Graffenberger
Mr. & Mrs. Oswald Heinrich
Rev. & Mrs. Hudson Hess
Mr. & Mrs. Wayne Hodges
Mr. & Mrs. Cleveland Irvine
Miss Corinne Lowman
Mr. Helmut Markeli
Miss Linda McDonald
Mr. & Mrs. Francis Muia
Miss Lynda Arline Myers
Mr. Daniel Picazo
*Rev. & Mrs. Mardy Picazo
Mr. & Mrs. Kent Ragsdale
Miss Celia Rigby
Mr. & Mrs. Aldean Saufley
Miss Christina Schwanke
Mr. & Mrs. David Shaferly
Mr. & Mrs. Stanley True
Dr. & Mrs. Virgil Ullom

October, 1973, OMS Personnel
Director: Mr.David Graffenberger
Mr. & Mrs. Claude Beachy
Margaret Bonnette
Dr. & Mrs. Stafford Bourke
Miss Flo Boyer
Rev. & Mrs. Harold Brown
Mr. Richard Brown
Mr. & Mrs. Philip Chandler
Mr. Wilbert Dunn
*Miss Lula Mae Fuchs

Miss Ruth Gamber
Miss Marian Giles
Mr. & Mrs. David Graffenberger
Mr. & Mrs. Oswald Heinrich
Rev. & Mrs. Hudson Hess
Mr. & Mrs. Wayne Hodges
Mr. & Mrs. Cleveland Irvine
Miss Ann Johnston
*Miss Corinne Lowman
Mr. Helmut Markeli
*Dr. & Mrs. Francis Muia
Rev. & Mrs. Mardy Picazo
Mr. & Mrs. Kent Ragsdale
Miss Celia Rigby
Mr. & Mrs. Aldean Saufley
Miss Christina Schwanke
*Mr. & Mrs. David Shaferly
Mr. & Mrs. Stanley True
Dr. & Mrs. Virgil Ullom

October, 1974, OMS Personnel
Director: Mr.David Graffenberger
Mr. & Mrs. Lester Babcock
Mr. & Mrs. Claude Beachy
Margaret Bonnette
Dr. & Mrs. Stafford Bourke
Miss Flo Boyer
Rev. & Mrs. Harold Brown
Mr. & Mrs. Richard Brown
Mr. & Mrs. Philip Chandler
Miss Lula Mae Fuchs
Miss Ruth Gamber
Miss Marian Giles
Mr. & Mrs. David Graffenberger
Mr. & Mrs. Oswald Heinrich
*Rev & Mrs. Hudson Hess
*Mr. & Mrs. Wayne Hodges
Mr. & Mrs. Cleveland Irvine
Miss Ann Johnston
Mr. & Mrs. Eugene Lain
    (language school)
Miss Corinne Lowman
Mr. & Mrs. Marvin McClain
Dr. & Mrs. Francis Muia
Miss Elizabeth Nikkel
*Mr. & Mrs. Daniel Picazo
Rev. & Mrs. Mardy Picazo
Mr. & Mrs. Aldean Saufley
*Mr. & Mrs. David Shaferly

Oct, 1974, OMS Personnel (cont'd)
Dr. & Mrs. Virgil Ullom
Mr. & Mrs. Kent VanDervort

October, 1975, OMS Personnel
Director: Mr.David Graffenberger
+Mr. & Mrs. Leslie Babcock
Mr. & Mrs. Claude Beachy
Margaret Bonnette
Dr. & Mrs. Stafford Bourke
*Miss Flo Boyer
Mr. & Mrs. Richard Brown
Miss Lula Mae Fuchs
Miss Ruth Gamber
*Miss Marian Giles
Mr. & Mrs. David Graffenberger
*Mr & Mrs. Oswald Heinrich
Rev. & Mrs. Hudson Hess
Mr. & Mrs. Wayne Hodges
+Mr. & Mrs. Cleveland Irvine
Miss Anne Johnston
Rev. & Mrs. Eugene Lain
Miss Corinne Lowman
Mr. & Mrs. Marvin McClain
Dr. & Mrs. Francis Muia
Miss Elizabeth Nikkel
Mr. & Mrs. Daniel Picazo
Rev. & Mrs. Mardy Picazo
*Mr. & Mrs. Aldean Saufley
Mr. & Mrs. David Shaferly
Dr. & Mrs. Virgil Ullom
Mr. & Mrs. Kent VanDervort

October, 1976, OMS Personnel
Director: Mr.David Graffenberger
Miss Elizabeth Andersen M-1
Mr. Les & Ruth Babcock
Mr. Claude & Edna Beachy
Margaret Bonnette
Miss Robyn Couper
Miss Bonnie Draper M-1
Miss Ruth Gamber
Miss Marian Giles
Mr. Dave & Marilyn Graffenberger
Mr. Os & Kathy Heinrich
Rev. Hudson & Lucy Hess
Mr. Wayne & Edi Hodges
Rev. Eugene & Elaine Lain
Miss Corinne Lowman

Dr. Francis & Iris Muia
Miss Alison Parker
Mr. John & Beth Petersen
Mr. Daniel & Celia Picazo
Rev. Mardy & Rachael Picazo
Mr. Aldean & Ellen Saufley
Mr. Dave & Marilyn Shaferly
Miss Betty Lou Sider M-1
Mr. Art & Betty Tiede
Dr. Virgil & Lea Ullom
Mr. Kent & Jean VanDervort
Mr. Stewart & Edith West

October, 1977, OMS Personnel
Director: Mr.David Graffenberger
Miss Elizabeth Andersen M-1
Mr. Les & Ruth Babcock
Mr. Claude & Edna Beachy
Margaret Bonnette
Miss Robyn Couper
Miss Bonnie Draper M-1
*Miss Ruth Gamber
Miss Marlan Giles
Mr. Dave & Marilyn Graffenberger
Mr. Os & Kathy Heinrich
Rev. Hudson & Lucy Hess
Mr. Wayne & Edi Hodges
Rev. Eugene & Elaine Lain
Miss Corinne Lowman
Dr. Francis & Iris Muia
Miss Alison Parker
Mr. John & Beth Petersen
*Mr Daniel & Celia Picazo
*Rev. Mardy & Rachael Picazo
Mr. Aldean and Ellen Saufley
Mr. Dave & Marilyn Shaferly
Miss Betty Lou Sider M-1
Mr. Art & Betty Tiede
Dr. Virgil & Lea Ullom
Mr. Kent & Jean VanDervort
Mr. Stewart & Edith West

October, 1978, OMS Personnel
Director: Mr.David Graffenberger
Mr. Michael Anderson, M-1
Mr. Leslie & Ruth Babcock
Mr. Claude & Edna Beachy
Margaret Bonnette
Rev. Harold O. & Mary Brown

Oct, 1978, OMS Personnel (cont'd)
Dr. Timothy & Ann Carlson, M-1
Miss Robyn Couper
Miss Ruth Gamber
Miss Marian Giles
Mr. William & Jane Glace
*Mr. David & Marilyn Graffenberger
Mr. Oswald & Kathy Heinrich
Rev. Hudson & Lucy Hess
*Rev. Eugene & Elaine Lain
*Miss Corinne Lowman
*Dr. Francis & Iris Muia
Miss Kathleen Mulhall, M-1
Miss Lynn Patterson
Mr. John & Beth Petersen
*Mr Daniel & Celia Picazo
Rev. Mardy & Rachael Picazo
Mr. Aldean & Dr. Ellen Saufley
Mr. David & Marilyn Shaferly
Miss Betty Lou Sider, M-1
Miss Colleen Taylor
Mr. Arthur & Betty Tiede
Dr. Virgil & Lea Ullom
*Mr. Kent & Jean VanDervort
Miss Loretta Vittoria, M-1
Mr. Stewart & Edith West

October, 1979, OMS Personnel
Director: Rev. Harold O. Brown
Mr. Lyle & Vivian Ang
Mr. Claude & Edna Beachy
Margaret Bonnette
Rev. Harold 0. & Mary Brown
Dr. Timothy & Ann Carlson, M-1
Mr. Marion & Lillian Dunlap
Miss Ruth Gamber
Miss Marian Giles
Mr. William & Jane Glace
Miss Valeene Hayes
Mr. Oswald & Kathy Heinrich
* Rev. Hudson & Lucy Hess
Miss Faith Jones
Rev. Eugene & Elaine Lain
Miss Corinne Lowman
Dr. Francis and Iris Mula
Miss Kathleen Mulhall
Miss Lynn Patterson
Mr. Daniel & Celia Picazo
Rev. Mardy & Rachael Picazo

Mr. Aldean & Dr. Ellen Saufley
Mr. David & Marilyn Shaferly
Miss Betty Lou Sider
Miss Colleen Taylor
Mr. Arthur & Betty Tiede
Dr. Virgil & Lea Ullom
Mr. Kent & Jean VanDervort
Mr. Stewart & Edith West

October, 1980, OMS Personnel
Director: Rev. Harold O. Brown
Mr. Lyle & Vivian Ang
Mr. Claude & Edna Beachy
Margaret Bonnette
Miss Dyann Brodie
Rev. Harold 0. & Mary Brown
Mr. David Clark, M-1
Miss Ruth Gamber
Mr. William & Jane Glace
Mrs. Caroline Hall
Miss Valeene Hayes
Mr. Oswald & Katherine Heinrich
*Rev. Hudson & Lucy Hess
Miss Faith Jones
Rev. Eugene & Elaine Lain
Miss Corinne Lowman
Miss Lynn Patterson
Mr. Daniel & Celia Picazo
*Rev. Mardy & Rachael Picazo
*Mr. Aldean & Dr. Ellen Saufley
Mr. David & Marilyn Shaferly
Miss Betty Lou Sider
Miss Colleen Taylor
*Mr. Arthur & Betty Tiede
Mr. William & Elsie Turpin
Dr. Virgil & Lea Ullom
Mr. Kent & Jean VanDervort
Mr. Stewart & Edith West
Miss Mary Lou Wunker

October, 1981, OMS Personnel
Director: Rev. Harold O. Brown
+Mr. Leslie & Ruth Babcock
*Mr. Claude & Edna Beachy
*Margaret Bonnette
Mr. Clyde & Marian Bowman
Miss Dyann Brodie
Rev. Harold 0. & Mary Brown
Miss Robyn Couper

Oct, 1981, OMS Personnel (cont'd)
Miss Ruth Gamber
+Miss Marian Giles
Mr. William & Jane Glace
Miss Shelia Greer
Miss Valeene Hayes
Rev. Hudson & Lucy Hess
Rev. Eugene & Elaine Lain
Miss Corinne Lowman
Miss Bronwyn Madder
Mr. Daniel & Celia Picazo
Rev. Mardy & Rachael Picazo
Mr. Aldean & Dr. Ellen Saufley
Mr. Stephen & Helen Scholes
Mr. David & Marilyn Shaferly
Mr. Jay & Linda Six
Mr. Arthur & Betty Tiede
Mr. William & Elsie Turpin
Dr. Virgil & Leonora Ullom
Mr. Kent & Jean VanDervort
Miss Mary Lou Wunker

October, 1982, OMS Personnel
Director: Claude Beachy
+Mr. Leslie & Ruth Babcock
Mr. Claude & Edna Beachy
*Margaret Bonnette
Mr. Clyde & Marian Bowman
*Rev. Harold O. & Mary Brown
Miss Robyn Couper
Miss Valeene Hayes
Rev. Hudson & Lucy Hess
Rev. Eugene & Elaine Lain
*Rev. Mardy & Rachael Picazo
Mr. Aldean & Dr. Ellen Saufley
Mr. David & Marilyn Shaferly
Mr. Jay & Linda Six
Mr. Arthur & Betty Tiede
Mr. William & Elsie Turpin
Mr. Kent & Jean VanDervort
Miss Mary Lou Wunker

October, 1983, OMS Personnel
Director: Rev. Harold O. Brown
Mr. Claude & Edna Beachy
Margaret Bonnette
Mr. Clyde & Marian Bowman
*Rev. Harold O. & Mary Brown
Miss Robyn Couper

*Miss Valeene Hayes
Rev. Hudson & Lucy Hess
*Rev. Eugene & Elaine Lain
Miss Sally Overton
Rev. Mardy & Rachael Picazo
Mr. Aldean & Dr. Ellen Saufley
Mr. Stephen & Jean Scholes
Mr. David & Marilyn Shaferly
Mr. Jay & Linda Six
Mr. Arthur & Betty Tiede
Mr. William & Elsie Turpin
Miss Mary Lou Wunker
Miss Debra Zacharias

October, 1984, OMS Personnel
Director: Rev. Harold O. Brown
Mr. Les & Ruth Babcock
Mr. Claude & Edna Beachy
Margaret Bonnette
Mr. Clyde & Marian Bowman
Rev. Harold O. & Mary Brown
Miss Robyn Couper
Dr. Harry & Anne Davis
Mr. William & Myrna Durr
+Miss Ruth Gamber
Dr. Vernon & Lois Hall
Miss Valeene Hayes
*Rev. Hudson & Lucy Hess
Rev. Eugene & Elaine Lain
Miss Sally Overton
Mr. Daniel & Celia Picazo
Rev. Mardy & Rachael Picazo
Mr. Aldean & Dr. Ellen Saufley
Mr. Stephen & Jean Scholes
Mr. David & Marilyn Shaferly
Mr. Art & Betty Tiede
Miss Mary Lou Wunker
Miss Debbi Zacharias

October, 1985, OMS Personnel
Director: Rev. Harold O. Brown
Mr. Les & Ruth Babcock
Mr. Claude & Edna Beachy
Margaret Bonnette
Mr. Clyde & Marian Bowman
Rev. Harold O. & Mary Brown
Dr. Harry & Anne Davis
Mr. Doug & Polly Fowler
Miss Ruth Gamber

Oct, 1985, OMS Personnel (cont'd)
Miss Valeene Hayes
Rev. Eugene & Elaine Lain
Rev. Mardy & Rachael Picazo
Mr. Aldean & Dr. Ellen Saufley
Mr. Stephen & Jean Scholes
Mr. David & Marilyn Shaferly
Miss Mary Lou Wunker
Miss Debbi Zacharias

October, 1986, OMS Personnel
Director: Rev. Harold O. Brown
Margaret Bonnette
*Mr. Clyde & Marian Bowman
Rev. Harold 0. & Mary Brown
*Dr. Harry & Anne Davis
Dr. Vernon & Lois Hall
Miss Valeene Hayes
Rev. Mardy & Rachael Picazo
Mr. Aldean & Dr. Ellen Saufley
*Mr. Stephen & Jean Scholes
*Mr. David & Marilyn Shaferly
Miss Mary Lou Wunker

October, 1987, OMS Personnel
Director: Rev. Brown (Shaferly)
Mr. Clyde & Marian Bowman
*Rev. Harold 0. & Mary Brown
Dr. Vernon & Lois Hall
Miss Valeene Hayes
*Rev. Mardy & Rachael Picazo
Mr. Aldean & Dr. Ellen Saufley
*Mr. Stephen & Jean Scholes
Mr. David & Marilyn Shaferly
Miss Mary Lou Wunker

October, 1988, OMS Personnel
Director: Rev. Harold O. Brown
Mr. Clyde & Marian Bowman
Rev. Harold 0. & Mary Brown
Dr. Harry & Anne Davis
Dr. Vernon & Lois Hall
Miss Valeene Hayes
Rev. Mardy & Rachael Picazo
Mr. Gerald Rempel
Mr. Aldean & Dr. Ellen Saufley
Mr. Stephen & Jean Scholes
Mr. David & Marilyn Shaferly
Miss Mary Lou Wunker

October, 1989, OMS Personnel
Director: Rev. Harold O. Brown
Mr. Clyde & Marian Bowman
Rev. Harold 0. & Mary Brown
Dr. Harry & Anne Davis
Melva Eichel
*Dr. Vernon & Lois Hall
Miss Valeene Hayes
Rev. Mardy & Rachael Picazo
Mr. Aldean & Dr. Ellen Saufley
Mr. Stephen & Jean Scholes
Mr. David & Marilyn Shaferly
Mr. Michael & Dawn VanDervort
Miss Mary Lou Wunker

October, 1990, OMS Personnel
Director: Rev. Harold O. Brown
Mr. Clyde & Marian Bowman
Rev. Harold 0. & Mary Brown
Dr. Harry & Anne Davis
Melva Eichel
Mr. Donald & Ivadel Giles
Miss Valeene Hayes
Mr. Craig & Brenda Hess Osterhus
Mr. Daniel & Celia Picazo (Affil.)
Rev. Mardy & Rachael Picazo
*Mr. Aldean & Dr. Ellen Saufley
Mr. David & Marilyn Shaferly
Mr. Michael & Dawn VanDervort
Miss Mary Lou Wunker

October, 1991, OMS Personnel
Director: Rev. Harold O. Brown
Rev. Harold 0. & Mary Brown
Dr. Vernon & Lois Hall
*Miss Valeene Hayes
Dr. Eugene & Elaine Lain
Mr. Craig & Brenda Hess Osterhus
Mr. Daniel & Celia Picazo (Affil.)
Rev. Mardy & Rachael Picazo
*Mr. Aldean & Dr. Ellen Saufley
Mr. David & Marilyn Shaferly
Mr. Kent & Jean VanDervort
Mr. Michael & Dawn VanDervort
Miss Mary Lou Wunker

October, 1992, OMS Personnel
Director: Rev. Harold O. Brown
Rev. Harold 0. & Mary Brown

Oct, 1992, OMS Personnel (cont'd)
Mrs. Dorothy Frederickson
Dr. Vernon & Lois Hall
Miss Valeene Hayes
Rev. Hudson & Lucy Hess
Dr. Eugene & Elaine Lain
Michael & Heather Nicholson
Mr. Craig & Brenda Osterhus
Mr. Daniel & Celia Picazo (Affil.)
Mr. Aldean & Dr. Ellen Saufley
Mr. David & Marilyn Shaferly
Phyllis Stanley
Mr. Michael & Dawn VanDervort
Miss Mary Lou Wunker

October, 1993, OMS Personnel
Director: Dr. Francis Muia
Dorothy Frederickson
Dr. Vernon & Lois Hall
Miss Valeene Hayes
Rev. Hudson & Lucy Hess
Mr. Michael & Heather Nicholson
Mr. Daniel & Celia Picazo (Affil.)
Mr. Aldean & Dr. Ellen Saufley
*Mr. David & Marilyn Shaferly
*Mr. Michael & Dawn VanDervort
Miss Mary Lou Wunker

October, 1994, OMS Personnel
Director: Mr. David Shaferly
Dr. Vernon & Lois Hall
Miss Valeene Hayes
Rev. Hudson & Lucy Hess
Dr. Aldean and Dr. Ellen Saufley
Mr. David & Marilyn Shaferly
*Mr. Michael & Dawn VanDervort
Miss Mary Lou Wunker

October, 1995, OMS Personnel
Director: Mr. David Shaferly
Dr. Vernon & Lois Hall
Miss Joetta Lehman
Dr. Aldean and Dr. Ellen Saufley
Mr. David & Marilyn Shaferly
Mr. Michael & Dawn VanDervort
Mr. Gordon & Doreen Wallace
Mr. Carl & Heidi Walton
Miss Mary Lou Wunker

October, 1996, OMS Personnel
Director: Mr. David Shaferly
Mr. Michael Haines
Dr. Vernon & Lois Hall
Miss Valeene Hayes
Miss Joetta Lehman
Rev. Paul & Trudy Lund
Mr. Michael & Heather Nicholson
Mr. Brian & Holly O'Malley
*Dr. Aldean & Dr. Ellen Saufley
Mr. David & Marilyn Shaferly
Mr. Michael & Dawn VanDervort
Mr. Gordon & Doreen Wallace
Mr. Carl & Heidi Walton
Miss Mary Lou Wunker

October, 1997, OMS Personnel
Director: Mr. David Shaferly
Miss Esther Cann
Miss Valeene Hayes
Miss Joetta Lehman
Mr. Charles & June Oliver
Dr. Aldean and Dr. Ellen Saufley
Mr. David & Marilyn Shaferly
*Mr. Gordon & Doreen Wallace
Mr. Carl & Heidi Walton
Peggy Warren
Miss Mary Lou Wunker

October, 1998, OMS Personnel
Director: Mr. David Shaferly
Mrs. Rachel Buller
Mr. Jason Camplbell
Miss Joetta Lehman
Dr. Aldean and Dr. Ellen Saufley
*Mr. David & Marilyn Shaferly
Mr. Gordon & Doreen Wallace
Miss Mary Lou Wunker

October, 1999, OMS Personnel
Director: Mr. David Shaferly
Mr. Brett & Angie Bundy
*Miss Joetta Lehman
Mr. Jerry & Carrie Maurer
Dr. Aldean & Dr. Ellen Saufley
Mr. David & Marilyn Shaferly
Julie Sherk
Dr. Hollis Tanksley
Jill Tusant

Oct, 1999, OMS Personnel (cont'd)
Mr. Gordon & Doreen Wallace
Miss Mary Lou Wunker

March, 2000, OMS Personnel
Director: Mr. David Shaferly
Mr. Brett & Angie Bundy
Mr. Jason Campbell
Miss Joetta Lehman

Mr. Jerry & Carrie Maurer
Dr. Aldean & Dr. Ellen Saufley
Mr. David & Marilyn Shaferly
Julie Sherk
Dr. Hollis Tanksley
Jill Tusant
Mr. Gordon & Doreen Wallace
Miss Mary Lou Wunker

PLEASE NOTE: If you find a mistake in a date or information, please let me know so it can be corrected for the next printing. Rachael O. Picazo, E-mail: mepicazo@juno.com
7935 US 60 East, Morehead, KY 40351   Ph. (606) 784-6444
Thank you!

OMS INTERNATIONAL

OMS International (formerly The Oriental Missionary Society) is an independent, non-denominational mission founded in 1901 by Charles Cowman, Ernest Kilbourne, and Juji Nakada. Charles' wife, Lettie, is well known as the author of the best-selling devotional, *Streams in the Desert*.

OMS began work in Japan. Later, fields were opened in Korea, China, India, Taiwan, Hong Kong, and Indonesia. Today the mission ministers in 18 countries in Asia, Latin America, The Caribbean, Europe, and Africa. OMS-related churches number more than 5,000 with a combined membership in excess of one million.

OMS ministry includes (1) aggressive evangelism, led by Every Creature Crusade teams, (2) planting indigenous churches, (3) training nationals in Bible colleges and seminaries, and (4) joining them in partnership to reach the world.

For more information about OMS International please write to:
U.S. World Headquarters:
P.O. Box A, Greenwood, IN 46142-6599
Australia: P.O. Box 897, Ringwood, VIC 3134
United Kingdom:
1 Sandileigh Avenue, Didsbury, Manchester M20 3LN
Canada:
2289 Fairview Street, Unit 105, Burlington, ON L7R 2E3
New Zealand: P.O. Box 962, Hamilton
South Africa: P.O. Box 640, Roodepoort TVL 1725

BOOK ROOM
Order from OMS Bookroom, Box A, Greenwood, IN 46142.
For single books include $1.50 for postage and handling.
USA prices listed.
Phone : 317-881-6751, or e-mail pwinfrey@omsinternational.org